14th Joint ACL-ISO Workshop on Interoperable Semantic Annotation 2018 (ISA-14)

Santa Fe, New Mexico, USA
25 August 2018

ISBN: 978-1-5108-6912-7

Proceedings 14th Joint ACL - ISO Workshop on Interoperable Semantic Annotation (isa-14)

August 25, 2018

at COLING 2018
Santa Fé, New Mexico, USA

Harry Bunt, editor

Proceedings of the 14th Joint ACL - ISO Workshop on Interoperable Semantic Annotation (**isa-14**)

Workshop at COLING
Santa F'é, New Mexico, USA, August 25, 2018

TiCC, Tilburg center for Cognition and Communication
Tilburg University, The Netherlands

Workshop Program

08.45 -- 09:00 Registration
09:00 – 09:05 Opening by the Program Committee Chair

09:05 -- 09:35 Ramesh Manuvirakurike, Jacqueline Brixey, Trung Bui, Walter Chang, Ron Artstein and Kalliroi Georgila: *DialEdit: Annotations for spoken conversational image editing*
09:35 -- 10:05 Jun Araki, Lamana Mulaffer, Arun Pandian, Yukari Yamakawa, Kemal Oflazer and Teruko Mitamura: *Interoperable Annotation of Events and Event Relations across Domains*
10:05 – 10:35 Harry Bunt, Volha Petukhova, Emer Gilmartin, Simon Keizer, Catherine Pelachaud, Laurent Prévot and Mariët Theune: *Downward Compatible Revision of Dialogue Annotation*

10:35 – 11:00 Coffee break

11:00 -- 11:30 Kiyong Lee, James Pustejovsky and Harry Bunt: *The Revision of ISO-Space, Focused on the Movement Link*
11:30 -- 12:10 Short paper presentations:
>   11:30 -- 11:40 Emer Gilmartin and Carl Vogel: *Chat, Chunk, and Topic in Casual Conversations*
>   11:40 – 11:50 Mark-Matthias Zymla: *Annotation of the Syntax/Semantics Interface as a Bridge between Deep Linguistic Parsing and TimeML*
>   11:50 – 12:00 Ramesh Manuvirakurike, Sumanth Bharawadj and Kalliroi Georgila: *An Annotation Scheme for Weight Management Chat using the Theoretical Model of Health Behavior Change*
>   12:00 – 12:10 Tianyong Hao, Haotai Wang, Xinyu Cao and Kiyong Lee: *Annotating Measurable Quantitative Information for an ISO Standard*

12:10 – 12:30 poster visits

12:30 – 14:00 Lunch break

14:00 -- 14:30 David Woods and Tim Fernando: *Feedback Improving String Processing for Temporal Relations*
14:30 -- 15:00 Rashmi Prasad, Bonnie Webber, Alan Lee and Aravind Joshi: *Discourse Annotation in the PDTB-3: The Next Generation*
15:00 -- 15:30 Deepthi Karkada, Ramesh Manuvirakurike and Kalliroi Georgila: *Towards end-of trip instructions in a taxi ride scenario*

15:30 -- 16:00 Closing and tea break

Workshop Organizers/Organizing Committee

Harry Bunt   Tilburg University
Nancy Ide   Vassar College, Poughkeepsie, NY
Kiyong Lee   Korea University, Seoul
James Pustejovsky   Brandeis University, Waltham, MA
Laurent Romary   INRIA/Humboldt Universität Berlin

Workshop Programme Committee

Jan Alexandersson   DFKI, Saarbrücken
Ron Artstein   University of Southern California
Harry Bunt   Tilburg University
Nicoletta Calzolari   ILC-CNR, Pisa
Jae-Woong Choe   University of Korea, Seoul
Robin Cooper   University of Gothenburg
Thierry Declerck   DFKI, Saarbrücken
Liesbeth Degand   Université Catholique de Louvain
David DeVault   University of Southern California
Jens Edlund   KTH, Stockholms University
Alex Chengyu Fang   City University Hong Kong
Robert Gaizauskas   University of Sheffield
Jan Hajic   Charles University, Prague
Koiti Hasida   Tokyo University
Elisabetta Jezek   Università degli Studi di Pavia
Simon Keizer   Vrije Universiteit Brussel
Kiyong Lee   University of Korea, Seoul
Adam Meyers   New York University
Philippe Muller   IRIT, Université Paul Sabatier, Toulouse
Milvina Nissim   Groningen University
Patrizia Paggio   L-Università tà Malta
Silvia Pareti   Google Inc.
Volha Petukhova   Universität des Saarlandes, Saarbrücken
Massimo Poesio   Queen Mary University, London
Rashmi Prasad   University of Wisconsin, Milwaukee
Laurent Prévot   Aix-Marseille University
Laurent Romary   INRIA/Humboldt Universität Berlin
Merel Scholman   Universität des Saarlandes, Saarbrücken
Manfred Stede   Universität Potsdam
Matthew Stone   Rutgers, the State University of New Jersey
Thorsten Trippel   University of Bielefeld
Carl Vogel   Trinity College Dublin
Piek Vossen   Vrije Universiteit Amsterdam
Annie Zaenen   Stanford University
Heike Zinsmeister   Universität Hamburg
Sandrine Zufferey   Université de Berne

Table of Contents

DialEdit: Annotations for Spoken Conversational Image Editing

Ramesh Manuvinakurike[2*]**, Jacqueline Brixey**[2*]**, Trung Bui**[1]**,
Walter Chang**[1]**, Ron Artstein**[2]**, Kallirroi Georgila**[2]
[1]Adobe Research
[2]Institute for Creative Technologies, University of Southern California
`[manuvinakurike,brixey,artstein,kgeorgila]@ict.usc.edu`
`[bui,wachang]@adobe.com`

Abstract

We present a spoken dialogue corpus and annotation scheme for conversational image editing, where people edit an image interactively through spoken language instructions. Our corpus contains spoken conversations between two human participants: users requesting changes to images and experts performing these modifications in real time. Our annotation scheme consists of 26 dialogue act labels covering instructions, requests, and feedback, together with actions and entities for the content of the edit requests. The corpus supports research and development in areas such as incremental intent recognition, visual reference resolution, image-grounded dialogue modeling, dialogue state tracking, and user modeling.

1 Introduction

Photographs have emerged as a means for sharing information, effective storytelling, preserving memories, and brand marketing among many other applications. The advent of photo-centric social media platforms such as Instagram, Snapchat, etc. along with easy access to high quality photo-taking devices has only made photographs a more powerful medium.

Photographs are often edited with the intention of improving their quality (e.g., fixing the lighting), for use in a narrative (e.g., for an ad campaign), for alteration (e.g., removing objects from the image), for preservation of memories (by restoring old photographs), and for other reasons. Social media platforms support popular and extensively used editing methods called presets (or filters). Such presets can also be found in cameras on many current smartphones, and can be applied to photographs almost instantaneously. However, image editing is far from choosing the right filter or preset values. Photo editing is a complex task often involving diligently and skillfully executed steps that require expertise.

Seeking professional help for editing photographs is common, and can be seen in popular forums such as Reddit Photoshop Request (https://www.reddit.com/r/PhotoshopRequest/) and Zhopped (http://zhopped.com/), where users post their photographs and request help from professionals. The professionals then either volunteer for free or do the job for a fee. The process typically starts with users publicly posting their request and the photograph they desire to be edited. These requests are formulated in an abstract manner using natural language (Ex: "I love this photo from our trip to Rome. Can someone please remove my ex from this photo? I am the one on the right."), rather than intricate multi-step instructions (Ex: "Free select the person on the left, replace the region with the building on the bottom left using replacement tools, fix the blotch by the healing tool..."). The professionals download these photographs, edit them, and post them back. They have knowledge about the image editing tool used, skills, time, and artistic creativity to perform the changes. If the users are not happy with the results, they post their modification requests, and then the professionals incorporate these changes and post the updated photographs. While these forums are popular, such methods have a few drawbacks. Because the expert editors edit the photographs without the requester being able to see the changes being performed in real time, (i) the users are not able to provide real-time feedback; (ii) it is hard for the users to provide requests for all needed modifications; and (iii) the professional editors cannot ask for minor clarifications while editing the photographs. These drawbacks often result in modifications that do not match the users'

---

 * Work done while at Adobe Research.

expectations. The alternative solution of the users performing the edits themselves is difficult and time consuming as the image editing tools have a steep learning curve.

Our ultimate goal is to develop a conversational agent that can understand the user requests, perform the edits, guide the user by providing suggestions, and respond in real time. In this paper we present a novel corpus that captures the conversation between the user who wants to edit a photograph and the expert human wizard who performs the edits (playing the role of a future dialogue system). We introduce a novel annotation scheme for this task, and discuss challenging sub-tasks in this domain. Conversational image editing combines spoken language, dialogue, and computer vision, and our real-world domain extends the literature on domains that are at the intersection of language and computer vision. We will publicly release our corpus in the near future.

2 Related Work

Conversation in the context of visual information has been studied for a long time. Clark and Wilkes-Gibbs (1986) studied reference resolution of simple figures called tangrams. Kennington and Schlangen (2015) and Manuvinakurike et al. (2016) performed incremental understanding and incremental reference resolution respectively in a domain of geometric shape descriptions, while Schlangen et al. (2016) resolved references to objects in real-world example images. Much work has been done in the context of gamified scenarios where the interlocutors interact and resolve references to real-world objects (Kazemzadeh et al., 2014; Paetzel et al., 2014; Manuvinakurike and DeVault, 2015). Also, such gamified scenarios have served as platforms for developing/learning incremental dialogue policies regarding whether the system should respond immediately or wait for more information (Paetzel et al., 2015; Manuvinakurike et al., 2017). Referential domains in the context of dialogue have also been studied using virtual reality technologies and spatial constraints (Stoia et al., 2008; Das et al., 2018) as well as robots (Whitney et al., 2016; Skantze, 2017).

A more recent direction of research involving dialogue and vision has been in the context of answering factual questions on images (Das et al., 2017; Antol et al., 2015) using the MSCOCO data set (Lin et al., 2014). The task may also involve a gamified scenario with the interlocutors playing a yes-no question-answer game as in de Vries et al. (2017). In these works the focus is less on the dialogue aspects and more on the factual aspects of the images, i.e., if an object is present or what a certain component of the image is. Mostafazadeh et al. (2017) extended this line of work with conversations grounded on images. Furthermore, Huang et al. (2016) built a data set of images with corresponding descriptions in sequence, for the task of visual storytelling.

Other gamified real-world scenarios involve object arrangement (DeVault and Stone, 2009), puzzle completion (Iida et al., 2010; Takenobu et al., 2012), map navigation (Anderson et al., 1991; Lemon et al., 2001; Johnston et al., 2002), furniture-buying scenarios (Di Eugenio et al., 2000), and treasure-hunt tasks in a virtual environment (Byron and Fosler-Lussier, 2006). A multi-modal interface for image editing combining speech and direct manipulation was developed by (Laput et al., 2013). With this interface a user can for example select a person's hat in an image and say "this is a hat". Then the system learns to associate the tag "hat" with the selected region of the image. Finally, Manuvinakurike et al. (2018a) recently introduced a corpus containing one-shot image editing instructions.

3 Data

The task of image editing is challenging for the following reasons: (i) The user needs to understand whether changes applied to a given image fit the target narrative or not. (ii) Image editing is a time consuming task. The user typically experiments with various features often undoing, redoing, altering in increments, or even completely removing previously performed edits before settling on the final image edit. (iii) The users may know at an abstract level what changes they want to perform, but be unaware of the image editing steps or parameters that would produce the desired outcome. (iv) Image editing tools are complicated due to the availability of innumerable options, and can have a steep learning curve often requiring months of training.

Our task is particularly well suited for spoken dialogue research. Besides understanding the user utterances and mapping them to commands supported by the tool, the task also involves a high degree of interactivity that requires real-time understanding and execution of the user requests. For instance, in a dialogue setting and in order to increase the saturation value, the user can utter "more, more, more" until the desired target value has been set. An annotation scheme should support such incremental changes as well as requests for new changes, updates of ongoing changes (including undoing and redoing), comparing the current version of the image with previous versions, and question-answer exchanges between the user and the wizard (including suggestions, clarifications, and feedback).

3.1 Data Collection

We collected spoken dialogues between users (who request image edits) and wizards (who perform the edits); a total of 28 users and 2 wizards participated in the collection. Prior to data collection, our wizards (the first two authors) were trained in executing a range of image edits.

We tested several image editing tools and found that very simple tools that did not support a high degree of functionality resulted in extremely restrictive dialogues lacking variety. Conversely, tools with rich functionality, such as Adobe Photoshop or GNU GIMP, resulted in user image edit requests that required hours to complete. Such interactions yielded creative image edit requests but did not yield timely dialogue phenomena. The tool ultimately used for image editing in this study was Adobe Lightroom. This tool produced diverse and highly interactive dialogues for image editing. The tool is popular among photographers and supports a wide variety of functionality. Users were able to make creative requests with few restrictions, and these requests could often be executed rapidly.

3.2 Experiment Setup

The recruited users were given images (digital photographs) sampled from the Visual Genome data set (Krishna et al., 2017) which in turn were sampled from the MSCOCO data set (Lin et al., 2014). The photos selected from the sampled image data sets were based on observations of 200 random request submissions from Zhopped and Reddit Photoshop forums. The forum submissions were often about eight high-level categories of images: animals, city scenes, food, nature/landscapes, indoor scenes, people, sports, and vehicles. Thus we selected images from the MSCOCO data set that fit into at least one of these eight categories.

Users were given one photograph from each category in an experiment session. They were given time to think about the changes they wanted to perform before the dialogue session, and were informed about the tool that was going to be used and the fact that it did not support complex functionality. If they were unsure of what functionality was supported they were instructed to ask the wizard. Users were asked to perform as many edits as they desired per image. Participants were encouraged (but not required) to participate for 40 minutes, and communicated via remote voice call. Users did not have the freedom to perform the edits themselves. Any edits they wished to be performed on the image had to be conveyed to the wizard through voice. The wizard responded to the requests in a natural human-like manner. The screen share feature was enabled on the wizard's screen so that the user could see in real time the wizard's edits on the image. While users were not explicitly told that the wizard was human, this was obvious due to the naturalness of the conversation.

The interaction typically started with the user describing a given image to the wizard. The wizard was not aware of the images provided to the user. The wizard chose the image from the available images based on the user description; following user confirmation, the image was then loaded for editing. The image editing session generally began with the user describing desired changes to the image in natural language. The wizard interpreted the request provided by the user and performed these edits on the image. The interaction continued until the user was satisfied with the final outcome. Figure 1 shows an example of an interaction between the user and the wizard.

3.3 Annotation Scheme

We designed a set of 26 dialogue act types, for the ultimate goal of building a conversational agent. Some of the dialogue acts were motivated by Bunt et al. (2012), while others are specific to the domain

Figure 1: Sample interaction between the user and the wizard.

Dialogue Act	Description
Image Edit Request (IER)	user requests changes to the image (IER-N, IER-U, IER-R, IER-C)
Comment (COM)	user comments on the image or edits (COM-L, COM-D, COM-I)
Request Recommendation (RQR)	user requests recommendation from the wizard on editing ideas
Question Feature (QF)	user asks question on the functionality of the editing tool
Question Image Attribute (QIA)	user asks question about the image
Request Feedback (RF)	user requests feedback about the image edits
Image Location (IL)	user & wizard locate the image at the beginning
Action Directive (AD)	user asks wizard to act on the application, e.g., "click the button"
Finish (FIN)	user wants to end the editing session
Suggestions (S)	wizard suggests ideas for editing the image
Request IER (RQIER)	wizard requests user to provide IER
Confirm Edit (CE)	wizard confirms the edit being performed
Feature Preference (FP)	wizard requests which tool option to use for achieving the user edits
Narrate (N)	wizard gives narration of the steps being performed
Elucidate (E)	these are wizard responses to QF & QIA
No Support (NS)	wizard informs user that the edit is not supported by the tool
Respond Yes/No (RSY/RSN)	yes/no response
Acknowledge (ACK)	acknowledgment
Discourse Marker (DM)	discourse marker
Other (O)	all other cases

Table 1: Dialogue act types.

of conversational image editing. Dialogue acts apply to segmented utterances, with each segment annotated with one dialogue act. Note that an utterance is defined as a portion of speech preceded and/or followed by a silence interval greater than 300 msec. Most of the dialogue act types are summarized in Table 1; below we elaborate on three specific classes: image edit requests (IER), comments (COM), and suggestions (S).

Image Edit Requests (IER): Image edit requests are grouped into four categories. New requests (IER-N) are edits that the users desire to see in the image, which are different from previous requests. Update requests (IER-U) are refinements to a previous request (users often request updates until the target is achieved). Revert requests (IER-R) occur when users want to undo the changes done to the image until a certain point. Compare requests (IER-C) occur when users want to compare the current version of the image to a previous version (before the most recent changes took place). The image edit requests IER-N and IER-U are labeled further with action and entity labels, which specify the nature of the edit request (the use of actions and entities is inspired by the intents and entities of Williams et al. (2015)). These labels serve as an intermediary language to map a user's utterance to executable commands that can be carried out in an image editing program. Actions are a predefined list of 18 functions common to most

Segments	Dialogue Act	Action	Attribute	Loc/Obj	Mod/Val
uh	O	-	-	-	-
make the tree brighter	IER-N	Adjust	brightness	tree	-
like a 100	IER-U	Adjust	brightness	tree	100
nope too much	COM-D	-	-	-	-
perfect	COM-L	-	-	-	-
let's work on sharpness	IER-N	Adjust	sharpness	-	-

Table 2: Example annotations of dialogue acts, actions, and entities.

Dialogue Act	% Words	% Utterance Segments	Dialogue Act	% Words	% Utterance Segments
IER-N	19.4	9.2	FIN	1.5	1.0
IER-U	16.3	12.5	S	4.7	4.0
IER-R	1.0	0.8	RQIER	2.1	2.6
IER-C	0.5	0.3	CE	1.6	1.9
COM-L	4.9	6.0	FP	0.1	0.1
COM-D	1.8	1.5	N	3.1	4.2
COM-I	2.5	1.5	E	1.3	0.7
RQR	0.7	0.0	NS	1.0	0.6
QF	1.1	0.6	RSY	2.3	6.8
QIA	0.3	0.2	RSN	0.9	1.2
RF	0.0	0.0	ACK	6.4	17.6
IL	3.0	1.5	DM	2.3	6.5
AD	4.8	3.9	O	16.4	14.8

Table 3: Percentages of words and of utterance segments for each dialogue act type; "0.0" values are close to 0.

image editing programs, such as cropping. Each IER contains at most one action. The entities provide additional information without which the action cannot be applied to the given image. The entities are made up of attributes (saturation, contrast, etc.), region/object (location where the image edit action is to be applied), value (modifiers or cardinal values accompanying the action-attribute). Table 2 shows example annotations.

Comments (COM): Three types of user comments are annotated: (i) Like comments (COM-L) where users show a positive attitude towards the edits that are being performed ("that looks interesting", "that's cool"). (ii) Dislike comments (COM-D) are the opposite of like comments ("I don't like that", "I don't think it's what I want"). (iii) Image comments (COM-I) are neutral user comments such as comments on the image ("it looks like a painting now", "her hair looks pretty striking").

Suggestions (S): Suggestions were the recommendations issued by the wizards to the users recommending the image editing actions. Suggestions also included the utterances that were issued with the goal of helping the user achieve the final image edits desired.

Table 3 shows the prevalence of our 26 dialogue acts in the corpus (percentage of words and of utterance segments in the corpus per dialogue act).

3.4 Data Preparation

The conversations were recorded using the OBS software which is a free open-source program for streaming video and audio. Then the audio data were extracted from the videos. Transcription was done on small audio chunks which was more convenient and faster than transcribing long clips. The

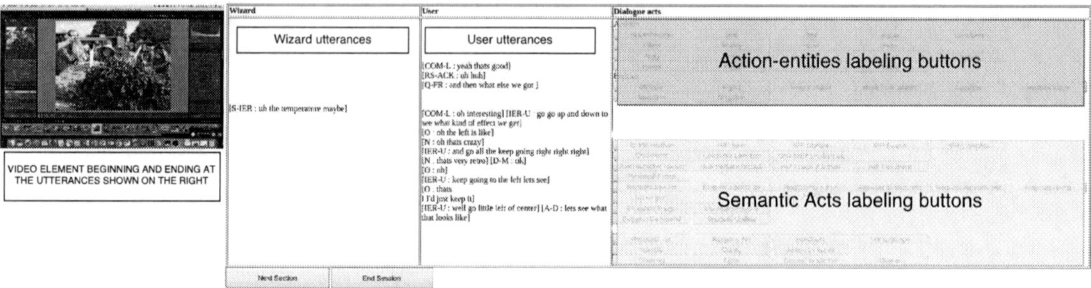

Figure 2: Web annotation tool used to annotate the dialogue. The figure shows the wizard and the user utterance aligned with time. The video element is shown to the left. The annotation is performed by highlighting the text and clicking the buttons corresponding to the dialogue act.

small audio clips were obtained by splitting the audio at the silence points using the webRTC Voice Activity Detection (https://pypi.python.org/pypi/webrtcvad). Transcriptions were performed using the Amazon MTurk platform. The transcribed audio data were then validated and annotated with dialogue acts, actions, and entities using a custom-built web annotation tool (Figure 2). The annotations were performed by two expert annotators who were well versed with the annotation scheme. Figure 2 shows the tool that was built for annotating the dataset. The tool was web-based, with the annotators being able to see the video, audio interaction and the transcriptions shown in small chunks (typically around 45 seconds) which were to be annotated by selecting the text and the corresponding dialogue act. In order to calculate the validity of the annotation scheme we calculated inter-rater reliability for dialogue act labeling by having two expert annotators annotate a single dialogue session; kappa was 0.81. In total 28 users contributed to 129 dialogues with 8890 user utterances, 4795 wizard utterances, and 858 minutes of speech. The total number of tokens in the user and wizard utterances is 59653 and 26284 respectively. Also, there are 2299 unique user tokens, 1310 unique wizard tokens, and 2650 total unique tokens.

4　Discussion

The transitions between dialogue acts for the user acts were analyzed (for this analysis we ignore the label "Other-O"). We found that the most common transition was from IER-U to IER-U. This is particularly interesting as it shows that users provide a series of updates before attaining the final image edits. This transition was more common than IER-N to IER-U, which is the second most frequently found transition. Users were found to like the image edits after IER-Us, and after issuing a COM-L (like edit) comment they usually move on to the next IER. We also found that when users disliked the edits (COM-D) they did not entirely cancel the edits but continued updating (IER-U) their requests until the final image version fit their needs. Transitions from IER-N to IER-N were also common; users could issue a complete new image edit request IER-N and then move on to another new image edit request IER-N.

The corpus can support research on the following (but not limited to) challenging sub-tasks:

Object detection: Understanding to which objects or regions the user refers in the image edit requests needs object identification. This is an actively researched topic in the computer vision research community.

Dialogue act labeling: Human speech is spontaneous, ungrammatical, and filled with disfluencies, among many other characteristics. Understanding the user intentions through dialogue act labeling on spontaneous human speech is a challenging problem. Our corpus has similar challenges as the Switchboard data set (Godfrey et al., 1992), however, in our case the dialogue takes place in a situated domain involving a visual environment. Our corpus has recently been used for incremental dialogue act identification (Manuvinakurike et al., 2018b).

State tracking: Dialogue state tracking means accurately tracking the user goals during a dialogue. In our work, state tracking refers to tracking the users' goals as they are making edits to an image.

Dialogue management: Designing a dialogue policy for this task is challenging due to the instantaneous and rapid nature of the interaction. A good dialogue policy should support incrementality. For example, users would often say "more, more, more" until the desired value of saturation was obtained. Thus the dialogue system should be able to process the user's utterance and perform the corresponding actions, as soon as the user's speech becomes available (Manuvinakurike et al., 2018b). Incrementality in dialogue is analogous to input autocomplete or typeahead used in search engines which accelerates the user's interaction by predicting the full query intention as a user is typing. Furthermore, the dialogue manager should be capable of generating the right utterances so that the interaction results in the desired image.

Nature of interactions: The task is very interactive. The users provide feedback and issue image edit updates in real time, which means that the user's input needs to be tracked in real time. The like (COM-L) and dislike (COM-D) user comments can be useful for tracking the likelihood that the user will keep the edits. The wizards are usually not static performers but also need to track the changes occurring in the image, and play an important role in helping the users achieve their goal. The wizards issue suggestions to the users when they need help with editing the images and issue clarifications about the tool and features supported by it (e.g., "User: Can we fade the picture? Wizard: We can try the clarity tool.").

5 Conclusion

We presented a novel spoken dialogue corpus on "conversational image editing". We described our data collection process and novel dialogue act labeling scheme. Our annotation scheme consists of 26 dialogue act labels covering instructions, requests, and feedback. The corpus supports research and development in areas such as incremental intent recognition (Manuvinakurike et al., 2018b), dialogue modeling, and dialogue state tracking. Furthermore, the data set is constructed using richly annotated images, which makes it an ideal platform for studying reference resolution in images, question answering, image-grounded dialogue modeling, tracking user likeness of images, and user modeling (providing suggestions to users depending on their preferences and knowledge of the tool). The corpus will be publicly released in the near future.

Acknowledgments

Apart from his internship at Adobe, the first author was also supported by a generous gift of Adobe Systems Incorporated to USC/ICT. The second author thanks the National GEM Consortium for fellowship funding and internship placement at Adobe. The last two authors were supported by the U.S. Army; statements and opinions expressed do not necessarily reflect the position or policy of the U.S. Government, and no official endorsement should be inferred.

References

Anne H. Anderson, Miles Bader, Ellen Gurman Bard, Elizabeth Boyle, Gwyneth Doherty, Simon Garrod, Stephen Isard, Jacqueline Kowtko, Jan McAllister, Jim Miller, et al. 1991. The HCRC map task corpus. *Language and Speech*, 34(4):351–366.

Stanislaw Antol, Aishwarya Agrawal, Jiasen Lu, Margaret Mitchell, Dhruv Batra, C. Lawrence Zitnick, and Devi Parikh. 2015. VQA: Visual Question Answering. In *Proceedings of ICCV*, pages 2425–2433, Santiago, Chile.

Harry Bunt, Jan Alexandersson, Jae-Woong Choe, Alex Chengyu Fang, Koiti Hasida, Volha Petukhova, Andrei Popescu-Belis, and David R. Traum. 2012. ISO 24617-2: A semantically-based standard for dialogue annotation. In *Proceedings of LREC*, pages 430–437, Istanbul, Turkey.

Donna K. Byron and Eric Fosler-Lussier. 2006. The OSU Quake 2004 corpus of two-party situated problem-solving dialogs. In *Proceedings of LREC*, pages 395–400, Genoa, Italy.

Herbert H. Clark and Deanna Wilkes-Gibbs. 1986. Referring as a collaborative process. *Cognition*, 22(1):1–39.

Abhishek Das, Satwik Kottur, Khushi Gupta, Avi Singh, Deshraj Yadav, José M. F. Moura, Devi Parikh, and Dhruv Batra. 2017. Visual dialog. In *Proceedings of CVPR*, pages 326–335, Honolulu, Hawaii, USA.

Abhishek Das, Samyak Datta, Georgia Gkioxari, Stefan Lee, Devi Parikh, and Dhruv Batra. 2018. Embodied question answering. In *Proceedings of CVPR*, Salt Lake City, Utah, USA.

Harm de Vries, Florian Strub, Sarath Chandar, Olivier Pietquin, Hugo Larochelle, and Aaron Courville. 2017. GuessWhat?! visual object discovery through multi-modal dialogue. In *Proceedings of CVPR*, pages 5503–5512, Honolulu, Hawaii, USA.

David DeVault and Matthew Stone. 2009. Learning to interpret utterances using dialogue history. In *Proceedings of EACL*, pages 184–192, Athens, Greece.

Barbara Di Eugenio, Pamela W. Jordan, Richmond H. Thomason, and Johanna D. Moore. 2000. The agreement process: An empirical investigation of human–human computer-mediated collaborative dialogs. *International Journal of Human-Computer Studies*, 53(6):1017–1076.

John J. Godfrey, Edward C. Holliman, and Jane McDaniel. 1992. SWITCHBOARD: Telephone speech corpus for research and development. In *Proceedings of ICASSP*, pages 517–520, San Francisco, California, USA.

Ting-Hao (Kenneth) Huang, Francis Ferraro, Nasrin Mostafazadeh, Ishan Misra, Aishwarya Agrawal, Jacob Devlin, Ross Girshick, Xiaodong He, Pushmeet Kohli, Dhruv Batra, C. Lawrence Zitnick, Devi Parikh, Lucy Vanderwende, Michel Galley, and Margaret Mitchell. 2016. Visual storytelling. In *Proceedings of NAACL–HLT*, pages 1233–1239, San Diego, California, USA.

Ryu Iida, Shumpei Kobayashi, and Takenobu Tokunaga. 2010. Incorporating extra-linguistic information into reference resolution in collaborative task dialogue. In *Proceedings of ACL*, pages 1259–1267, Uppsala, Sweden.

Michael Johnston, Srinivas Bangalore, Gunaranjan Vasireddy, Amanda Stent, Patrick Ehlen, Marilyn Walker, Steve Whittaker, and Preetam Maloor. 2002. MATCH: An architecture for multimodal dialogue systems. In *Proceedings of ACL*, pages 376–383, Philadelphia, Pennsylvania, USA.

Sahar Kazemzadeh, Vicente Ordonez, Mark Matten, and Tamara Berg. 2014. ReferItGame: Referring to objects in photographs of natural scenes. In *Proceedings of EMNLP*, pages 787–798, Doha, Qatar.

Casey Kennington and David Schlangen. 2015. Simple learning and compositional application of perceptually grounded word meanings for incremental reference resolution. In *Proceedings of ACL*, pages 292–301, Beijing, China.

Ranjay Krishna, Yuke Zhu, Oliver Groth, Justin Johnson, Kenji Hata, Joshua Kravitz, Stephanie Chen, Yannis Kalantidis, Li-Jia Li, David A Shamma, et al. 2017. Visual Genome: Connecting language and vision using crowdsourced dense image annotations. *International Journal of Computer Vision*, 123(1):32–73.

Gierad P Laput, Mira Dontcheva, Gregg Wilensky, Walter Chang, Aseem Agarwala, Jason Linder, and Eytan Adar. 2013. PixelTone: A multimodal interface for image editing. In *Proceedings of the SIGCHI Conference on Human Factors in Computing Systems*, pages 2185–2194, Paris, France.

Oliver Lemon, Anne Bracy, Alexander Gruenstein, and Stanley Peters. 2001. Information states in a multi-modal dialogue system for human-robot conversation. In *Proceedings of the 5th Workshop on Formal Semantics and Pragmatics of Dialogue (Bi-Dialog)*, pages 57–67.

Tsung-Yi Lin, Michael Maire, Serge Belongie, James Hays, Pietro Perona, Deva Ramanan, Piotr Dollár, and C. Lawrence Zitnick. 2014. Microsoft COCO: Common objects in context. In *Proceedings of the European Conference on Computer Vision*, pages 740–755, Zurich, Switzerland.

Ramesh Manuvinakurike and David DeVault. 2015. Pair me up: A web framework for crowd-sourced spoken dialogue collection. In Gary Geunbae Lee, Hong Kook Kim, Minwoo Jeong, and Ji-Hwan Kim, editors, *Natural Language Dialog Systems and Intelligent Assistants*, chapter 18, pages 189–201. Springer.

Ramesh Manuvinakurike, Casey Kennington, David DeVault, and David Schlangen. 2016. Real-time understanding of complex discriminative scene descriptions. In *Proceedings of SIGDIAL*, pages 232–241, Los Angeles, California, USA.

Ramesh Manuvinakurike, David DeVault, and Kallirroi Georgila. 2017. Using reinforcement learning to model incrementality in a fast-paced dialogue game. In *Proceedings of SIGDIAL*, pages 331–341, Saarbrücken, Germany.

Ramesh Manuvinakurike, Jacqueline Brixey, Trung Bui, Walter Chang, Kim Doo Soon, Ron Artstein, and Kallirroi Georgila. 2018a. Edit me: A corpus and a framework for understanding natural language image editing. In *Proceedings of LREC*, pages 4322–4326, Miyazaki, Japan.

Ramesh Manuvinakurike, Trung Bui, Walter Chang, and Kallirroi Georgila. 2018b. Conversational image editing: Incremental intent identification in a new dialogue task. In *Proceedings of SIGDIAL*, pages 284–295, Melbourne, Australia.

Nasrin Mostafazadeh, Chris Brockett, Bill Dolan, Michel Galley, Jianfeng Gao, Georgios Spithourakis, and Lucy Vanderwende. 2017. Image-grounded conversations: Multimodal context for natural question and response generation. In *Proceedings of IJCNLP*, pages 462–472, Taipei, Taiwan.

Maike Paetzel, David Nicolas Racca, and David DeVault. 2014. A multimodal corpus of rapid dialogue games. In *Proceedings of LREC*, pages 4189–4195, Reykjavik, Iceland.

Maike Paetzel, Ramesh Manuvinakurike, and David DeVault. 2015. So, which one is it? The effect of alternative incremental architectures in a high-performance game-playing agent. In *Proceedings of SIGDIAL*, pages 77–86, Prague, Czech Republic.

David Schlangen, Sina Zarrieß, and Casey Kennington. 2016. Resolving references to objects in photographs using the words-as-classifiers model. In *Proceedings of ACL*, pages 1213–1223, Berlin, Germany.

Gabriel Skantze. 2017. Predicting and regulating participation equality in human-robot conversations: Effects of age and gender. In *Proceedings of HRI*, pages 196–204, Vienna, Austria.

Laura Stoia, Darla Magdalene Shockley, Donna K. Byron, and Eric Fosler-Lussier. 2008. SCARE: A situated corpus with annotated referring expressions. In *Proceedings of LREC*, pages 650–653, Marrakech, Morocco.

Tokunaga Takenobu, Iida Ryu, Terai Asuka, and Kuriyama Naoko. 2012. The REX corpora: A collection of multimodal corpora of referring expressions in collaborative problem solving dialogues. In *Proceedings of LREC*, pages 422–429, Istanbul, Turkey.

David Whitney, Miles Eldon, John Oberlin, and Stefanie Tellex. 2016. Interpreting multimodal referring expressions in real time. In *Proceedings of ICRA*, pages 3331–3338, Stockholm, Sweden.

Jason D. Williams, Eslam Kamal, Mokhtar Ashour, Hani Amr, Jessica Miller, and Geoffrey Zweig. 2015. Fast and easy language understanding for dialog systems with Microsoft Language Understanding Intelligent Service (LUIS). In *Proceedings of SIGDIAL*, pages 159–161, Prague, Czech Republic.

Interoperable Annotation of Events and Event Relations across Domains

Jun Araki[*], **Lamana Mulaffer**[†], **Arun Pandian**[†],
Yukari Yamakawa[*], **Kemal Oflazer**[†] **and Teruko Mitamura**[*]
[*]Carnegie Mellon University, Pittsburgh, PA 15213, USA
[†]Carnegie Mellon University in Qatar, PO Box 24866, Doha, Qatar
junaraki@cs.cmu.edu, fmulaffe@andrew.cmu.edu, apandian@andrew.cmu.edu,
yukariy@andrew.cmu.edu, ko@cs.cmu.edu, teruko@andrew.cmu.edu

Abstract

This paper presents methodologies for interoperable annotation of events and event relations across different domains, based on notions proposed in prior work. In addition to the interoperability, our annotation scheme supports a wide coverage of events and event relations. We employ the methodologies to annotate events and event relations on Simple Wikipedia articles in 10 different domains. Our analysis demonstrates that the methodologies can allow us to annotate events and event relations in a principled manner against the wide variety of domains. Despite our relatively wide and flexible annotation of events, we achieve high inter-annotator agreement on event annotation. As for event relations, we obtain reasonable inter-annotator agreement. We also provide an analysis of issues on annotation of events and event relations that could lead to annotators' disagreement.

1 Introduction

Events are a key semantic component integral to information extraction and natural language understanding. They are a ubiquitous linguistic phenomenon, appearing in numerous domains, and compose rich discourse structures via various relations between events, forming a coherent story over multiple sentences. However, these properties of events have received relatively little attention in the literature. From the perspective of information extraction, much previous work on events pays attention to domain-specific clause-level argument structure (e.g., attackers kill victims, plaintiffs sue defendants, etc), putting less emphasis on what semantically constitutes events. The formalization focusing on domain-specific clause-level argument structure often involves its own definition of events based on instantiation of event ontology for a particular domain, aimed at automatic extraction of closed-domain events, as illustrated in ACE (Doddington et al., 2004), TAC KBP (Mitamura et al., 2017), PASBio (Wattarujeekrit et al., 2004), and BioNLP (Kim et al., 2009). For clarification, we use the term 'domain' to refer to a specific genre of text, such as biology, finance, and so forth. The closed-domain formalization might be of practical use in some domain-specific scenarios. However, it designs event definitions and annotation schemes arbitrarily within the respective domains. For example, ACE considers resulting states (resultatives)[1] as events, but others might exclude them or include a broader notion of states as events. Therefore, it is questionable whether a collection of the existing heterogenous annotation schemes for closed-domain events adequately contribute to interoperable and consistent annotation of events across domains.

On the other hand, prior work on open-domain events have some limitations with respect to coverage of events and their relations. Lexical databases such as WordNet (Miller et al., 1990), FrameNet (Baker et al., 1998) and PropBank (Palmer et al., 2005) can be viewed as a superset of event lexicon, and their subtaxonomies seem to provide an extensional definition of events. However, these databases have a narrow coverage of events because they generally do not cover current terminology and proper nouns due to their dictionary nature. For instance, none of WordNet, FrameNet and PropBank cover the proper noun 'Hurricane Katrina'. In addition, they do not provide any principles or guidelines about how to annotate events in text by themselves due to their different focus. TimeML (Pustejovsky et al., 2003) focuses on temporal aspects of events and does not deal with multi-word and generic events. ISO-TimeML (ISO,

---

[1]One example of resulative events in ACE is "They have been married for 3 years."

2012) provides a wider coverage of events than TimeML, but still has a focus on temporal relations. Event annotation in OntoNotes (Weischedel et al., 2011) is restricted to a small number of event nouns. Also importantly, some of the work mentioned above involves theoretical formalization of some relations between events (e.g., temporal relations), but none of the work provides annotation of a variety of event relations such as event coreference, subevents and causality. Richer Event Description (RED) (Palmer et al., 2016) defines events and their relations in a general manner, but its annotation was performed only in the clinical domain (O'Gorman et al., 2016).

In this work, we present our methodologies for annotating events and relations between events in unrestricted domains. The goal of our annotation project is to provide human-annotated data to build a generation generation application to enhance reading comprehension for English as second language (ESL) students, as a continuous effort of (Araki et al., 2016). Using the notion of eventualities (Bach, 1986) and event nuggets (Mitamura et al., 2015), our event annotation scheme defines events and annotates event spans of text while not assigning any specific event types to them. In that sense, our event annotation is span-oriented, as compared to the traditional argument-oriented annotation of events. As for relations between events, we choose to annotate five relations from the perspective of the goal: event coreference, subevent, causality, event sequence ('after' relations), and simultaneity. To our knowledge, this is the first work that performs human annotation of events and the five relations in unrestricted domains. We believe that this work contributes not only to the goal of the annotation project but also to an important step toward interoperable annotation of events and their relations across domains. The five event relations cover various semantic and temporal aspects of events, deeply connected with common-sense and domain-specific knowledge. Thus, we assume that a mixture of the five relations forms meaningful event structures as semantic backbones to facilitate natural language understanding and sophisticated document-level reasoning. Such event structures are valuable for generating high-level questions for reading comprehension, such as the one that requires learners to infer answers over multiple sentences (Araki et al., 2016).

Our contribution is twofold. First, we annotate a wide coverage of events, comprising verbs, nouns, adjectives, and phrases which are continuous or discontinuous (see Section 3). Despite this relatively wide and flexible annotation of events on text in 10 different domains, we show that our annotation achieved high inter-annotator agreement. Second, unlike previous methodologies which generally focus on deal only with event coreference such as ECB+ (Cybulska and Vossen, 2014), we present methodologies to annotate five event relations in unrestricted domains (see Section 4).

2 Data and Annotation Procedures

In this section, we describe our data and annotation procedures. Our annotation target is not restricted in any specific domains. Thus, ideally speaking, our annotation should include all kinds of events in a domain-agnostic manner. However, annotating all kinds of events manually in unrestricted domains would be unrealistic due to annotation cost. Therefore, in order to make the corpus creation manageable while retaining the domain diversity, we select 100 articles in Simple English Wikipedia[2], comprising 10 from each of 10 different domains.[3] The domains are: architecture, chemistry, disasters, diseases, economics, education, geology, history, politics, and transportation. We choose Simple Wikipedia because our annotators are not necessarily experts in these domains, and the simplified sentences could facilitate our annotation of events and event relations against text from the wide variety of domains. We refer to the corpus as **SW100**.

Our annotation is done by two annotators and a more experienced annotator whom we call the adjudicator. We first write our annotation guidelines to guide how to annotate events and event relations. We then set up an initial learning period in which the three annotators learn how to annotate events through answering their questions. We use BRAT (Stenetorp et al., 2012) as an annotation tool. We take a two-stage approach: (1) annotating and finalizing events and (2) annotating and finalizing event relations. Finalization is the adjudicator's process of comparing annotations, resolving annotation differences, and

---

[2] https://simple.wikipedia.org

[3] For more detailed corpus statistics, see Section 3.3 for events and Section 4.3 for event relations.

producing a single set of annotations. More detailed steps are as follows:

1. Three annotators identify event spans, following the annotation guidelines.
2. We compute inter-annotator agreement on event annotation.
3. The adjudicator finalizes event annotation.
4. Three annotators identify event relations on top of the finalized events, following the annotation guidelines.
5. We compute inter-annotator agreement on event relation annotation.
6. The adjudicator finalizes event relation annotation.

3 Annotation of Events

This section describes our definition of events and principles for annotation of events.

3.1 Definition of Events: Eventualities

As with TimeML (Pustejovsky et al., 2003) and ISO-TimeML (ISO, 2012), our definition of events uses *eventualities* (Bach, 1986), which are a broader notion of events, including states, processes, and events. This definition is inclusive in the sense that it includes states in addition to events and processes. We define the three classes on the basis of durativity and telicity (Moens and Steedman, 1988; Pulman, 1997):

- **states**: notions that remain unchanged until their change or are brought as a result of an event, e.g., He **owns** a car. Tom was **happy** when he received a present;
- **processes**: notions that involve a change of state without an explicit goal or completion, e.g., it was **raining** yesterday;
- **events**[4]: notions that involve a change of state with an explicit goal or completion, e.g., **walked** to Boston, **buy** a book.

We recognize that annotating states is generally more difficult than annotating processes and actions because states are often confused with attributes which are not eventive and thus should not be annotated. For example, let us consider the following examples:

(1) Mary was **talkative** at the **party**.
(2) Mary is a *talkative* person.

In (1), 'talkative' is eventive because it implies that Mary talked a lot at the party, whereas 'talkative' in (2) is not because it just indicates Mary's personal attribute. Note that we introduce the notion of eventualities in order to clarify the semantic boundary between eventive and non-eventive, not because we are interested in classifying events into the three classes of actions, processes, and states.

3.2 Annotation of Events: Event Nuggets

We also define what textual units are annotated as events. For this purpose, we use the notion of *event nugget* (Mitamura et al., 2015). An event nugget is defined as a semantically meaningful unit that expresses an event. It can be either a single word (verb, noun, or adjective) or a phrase which is continuous or discontinuous, depending on how we interpret the semantic meaningfulness of an event that the event nugget refers to. We give several examples below, where we use boldface to highlight event nuggets and underlines to show units of multi-word ones.

(3) The gunman **shot** the teller in the bank.
(4) The gunmen **opened fire** at the teller in the bank.
(5) I **cried** when my grandpa **kicked the bucket**.
(6) Susan **turned** the TV **on**.
(7) She **responded** his email **dismissively**.

---

[4]These notions were named 'transitions' in ISO-TimeML.

In (3), 'shot' is the only verb representing an event, and we annotate 'shot' as a single-word event nugget. On the other hand, in (4) we annotate 'open fire' as a single multi-word event nugget because the phrase 'open fire' indicates more complete meaning than either 'opened' or 'fire.' Similarly, in (6) we annotate 'turned ... on' as a single discontinuous multi-word event nugget, excluding 'the TV'. As a result, we can consider the phrase semantically meaningful and annotate it as a single event nugget. In (7), we annotate 'dismissively' as a part of an event nugget because it implies the action of her dismissing.

3.3 Corpus Analysis of Events

We show statistics of event annotations in SW100 in Table 1. Multi-word event nuggets amount to 955. 24% of the 955 are discontinuous, and most (97%) of the discontinuous multi-word event nuggets are verb phrases. 'Others' in Table 1(b) include pronouns, demonstrative determiners, and numbers.[5]

Domain	# (%)	Domain	# (%)
Architecture	475 (8.8)	Education	653 (12.1)
Chemistry	576 (10.7)	Geology	483 (8.9)
Disaster	510 (9.4)	History	486 (9.0)
Disease	618 (11.4)	Politics	534 (10.0)
Economics	479 (8.9)	Transportation	583 (10.8)

(a) Event nuggets with respect to domains.

	Single-word	Multi-word	All
Verb	2799 (51.9)	560 (10.4)	3359 (62.2)
Noun	1273 (23.6)	382 (7.1)	1655 (30.6)
Adjective	192 (3.6)	2 (0.0)	194 (3.6)
Others	178 (3.3)	11 (0.2)	189 (3.5)
All	4442 (82.3)	955 (17.7)	5397 (100.0)

(b) Event nuggets with respect to syntactic types.

Table 1: Statistics of events in SW100. Percentages (%), shown in parentheses, indicate ratios to the total number of event nuggets (i.e., 5397).

3.4 Inter-annotator Agreement on Event Annotation

Event annotation involves annotation of text spans. Thus, we measure inter-annotator agreement using the pairwise F1 score under two conditions: strict match and partial match. The former checks whether two annotations have exactly the same span. The latter checks whether there is an overlap between annotations, with the restriction that each annotation can only be matched to one annotation by the other annotator. Regarding the adjudicator's annotation as gold standard, we compute a pairwise F1 score between the adjudicator and one of the other two annotators, and another pairwise F1 score between the adjudicator and the other annotator. We then take the average of the F1 scores as our inter-annotator agreement. As a result, the inter-annotator agreement was 80.2% (strict match) and 90.2% (partial match).

3.5 Issues on Annotation of Events

The main challenge of event annotation is ambiguities on eventiveness. No matter how well eventiveness is defined, there is a lot of discretion required from the subjective viewpoint of the annotator to resolve ambiguous cases. For instance, let us consider the following sentences:

(8) These were issues of interest like the welfare state.
(9) Force equals mass times acceleration.

It is not entirely clear whether 'issues' in (8) should be annotated as an event nugget as it may constitute a set of events as well as a set of non-events. 'Force' in (9) is associated with its physical sense, but still determining whether it is eventive is difficult. Therefore, we conjecture that deciding eventiveness is not a clear binary classification problem, and there exists a continuum between eventive and non-eventive in the space of event semantics.

Another type of ambiguities arises from semantic meaningfulness of event spans in the definition of event nuggets. When we annotate multi-word event nuggets, it can be unclear which set of words constitute a semantically meaningful unit. For example, let us consider the following sentence:

(10) Bricks are used in masonry construction.

---

[5]Examples of the pronouns and demonstrative determiners are 'it' and 'this event', respectively, referring to previously mentioned events. An example of the numbers is 'one', which also refers a previously mentioned event.

One interpretation is that 'masonry construction' in (10) can be seen as a semantically meaningful unit. In contrast, another plausible interpretation is that only 'construction' is a semantically meaningful unit while 'masonry' is considered a mere specifier. Other challenges include knowing idiomatic expressions to annotate event nuggets. Because such expressions are often cultural, it could be an challenge to arrive at an consensus on idiomatically expressed events such as 'kicked the bucket'.

4 Annotation of Event Relations

In this section, we define event relations that we annotate and describe our principles of annotation of event relations.

4.1 Definition and Annotation Principles of Event Relations

As mentioned in Section 1, we define and annotate 5 event relations: event coreference, subevent, causality, event sequence, and simultaneity.

Event coreference. We define event coreference as a linguistic phenomenon that two event nuggets refer to the same event. For two event nuggets to corefer, they should be semantically identical, have the same participants (e.g., agent, patient) or attribute (e.g., location, time), and have the same polarity. For instance, 'Great Fire of London' and 'fire' are coreferential in (11).

(11) The **Great Fire of London** happened in 1666. The **fire** lasted for three days.

When considering event identity for event coreference, we use the notion of *event hopper* from Rich ERE (Song et al., 2015), which is a more inclusive, less strict notion than the event coreference defined in ACE.

Subevent. Following (Hovy et al., 2013), we define subevent relations as follows. Event A is a subevent of event B if B represents a stereotypical sequence of events, or a script (Schank and Abelson, 1977), and A is a part of that script. For example, 'affected', 'flooded' and 'broke' are three subevents of 'Hurricane Katrina' in (12). We refer to 'Hurricane Katrina' as a parent (event) of the three subevents.

(12) On August 29, 2005, New Orleans was **affected** by **Hurricane Katrina** which **flooded** most of the city when city levees **broke**.

Causality. We define causality to be a cause-and-effect relation, in which we can explain the causation between two event nuggets X and Y, saying "X causes Y". One example of causality is "The **tsunami** was caused by the **earthquake**." Causality also adds another distinctive characteristic to annotation. Causality inherently entails an event sequence. For example, if we say "The **tsunami** was caused by the **earthquake**", it means that the tsunami happened after the earthquake. To distinguish causality from event sequences and other relations such as preconditions (Palmer et al., 2016), we perform causality tests, largely based on (Dunietz et al., 2017):

1. The "why" test: After reading the sentence, can an annotator answer "why" questions about the potential effect argument? If not, it is not causal.
2. The temporal order test: Is the cause asserted to precede the effect? If not, it is not causal.
3. The counterfactuality test: Would the effect have been just as probable to occur or not occur had the cause not happened? If so, it is not causal.
4. The ontological asymmetry test: Could you just as easily claim the cause and effect are reversed? If so, it is not causal.
5. The linguistic test: Can the sentence be rephrased as It is because (of) X that Y or X causes Y? If so, it is likely to be causal.
6. The granularity test: Does X have the same event granularity as Y? If not, it is not causal. We define event granularity to be the scale of an event indicating how large the event is (e.g., events 'lunch' and 'dinner' have the same granularity, but 'ordering' is a finer-grained event than dinner. We add a constraint that two events with causality must have the same event granularity.

Event sequence. We define event sequence ('after' links) as follows. If event A is after event B, A happens after B happens under stereotypicality within a script or over multiple scripts. Note that we do not consider an event sequence relation just by the chronological order to avoid trivial (nonsensical) sequence relationships. We give an example from a restaurant script:

(13) We **went**(E1) to **dinner**(E2) at a famous restaurant. We **ordered**(E3) steak and **ate**(E4) it. We then __got a call__(E5). After the **call**(E6), we **paid**(E7) and **left**(E8) the restaurant.

In this example, we annotate event sequence relations as follows: E1 $\xrightarrow{\text{after}}$ E3 $\xrightarrow{\text{after}}$ E4 $\xrightarrow{\text{after}}$ E7 $\xrightarrow{\text{after}}$ E8. Note that we do not annotate 'after' links between E4 and E5 and between E6 and E7, even an explicit discourse marker 'After' at the beginning of the third sentence. This is because we do not see stereotypicality of the restaurant script in the sequence of E4, E5 and E6. The merit of our script-based approach for event sequences is that we can still sequence events utilizing the streotypicality of a script when temporal information is not explicitly provided in texts. In addition, it also allows us to frame texts in a story-like structure because of the scripts that we identify in the course of annotation, which is suitable to the goal of our annotation project described in Section 1.

Simultaneity. We define simultaneity as a relation that two event nuggets occur at the same time. We add a 'simultaneous' link between events when you realize that those events take place at the same time. The conjunctions such as 'when' and 'while' are clear markers for simultaneity. We give some examples:

(14) My boss was **talking** over the phone when I __stopped by__ his office.
(15) **Right-click** on the mouse button while __holding down__ the Shift key.

When annotating simultaneity, we make sure that two events connected with a simultaneous link have the same event granularity. This is helpful to differentiate simultaneity from subevent relations. Below are two examples:

(16) He __kept quiet__ during the **meeting**.
(17) He **testified** in the **trial**.

In (16), 'kept quiet' and 'meeting' happened at the same time, but we do not annotate a simultaneity relation between them because they do not have the same granularity. Similarly, we do not annotate a simultaneity relation between 'testified' and 'trial' in (17).

Unlike event sequence, we do not consider the notion of scripts in the case of simultaneity. Considering scripts in annotating simultaneity seems rather restrictive. From the goal of the annotation project, we conjecture that we can annotate many useful simultaneity relations by not considering scripts.

4.2 Facilitating Annotation of Event Relations

As described in Section 2, we use the BRAT tool to annotate events and event relations. However, our initial analysis reveals that although the original version[6] of BRAT supports annotation of relations within a single sentence well, it hinders annotation of relations spanning multiple sentences significantly due to its sentence-oriented visualization. In particular, if one annotates many relations over multiple sentences, a stack of the corresponding horizontal arrows make a working screen too vertically long for human annotators to perform annotation. Therefore, we modified BRAT so that events in different sentences can be directly connected by straight arrows without expanding the screen too much. This modification improves BRAT's visualization and facilitates our event relation annotation greatly. Figure 1 illustrates the improved visualization with some examples of our annotation of events and event relations.

4.3 Corpus Analysis of Event Relations

Table 2 shows statistics of the corpus. As for event coreference, we count the number of event coreference clusters instead of the number of event coreference relations. An event coreference cluster means a cluster grouping two or more coreferential events. For the other four event relations, we adopt the notion of link propagation by Mitamura et al. (2017) and only count relations between event coreference clusters, which avoids counting semantically equivalent (redundant) relations. For instance, if we have

---

[6]This is the latest version v1.3, available at `http://brat.nlplab.org/`.

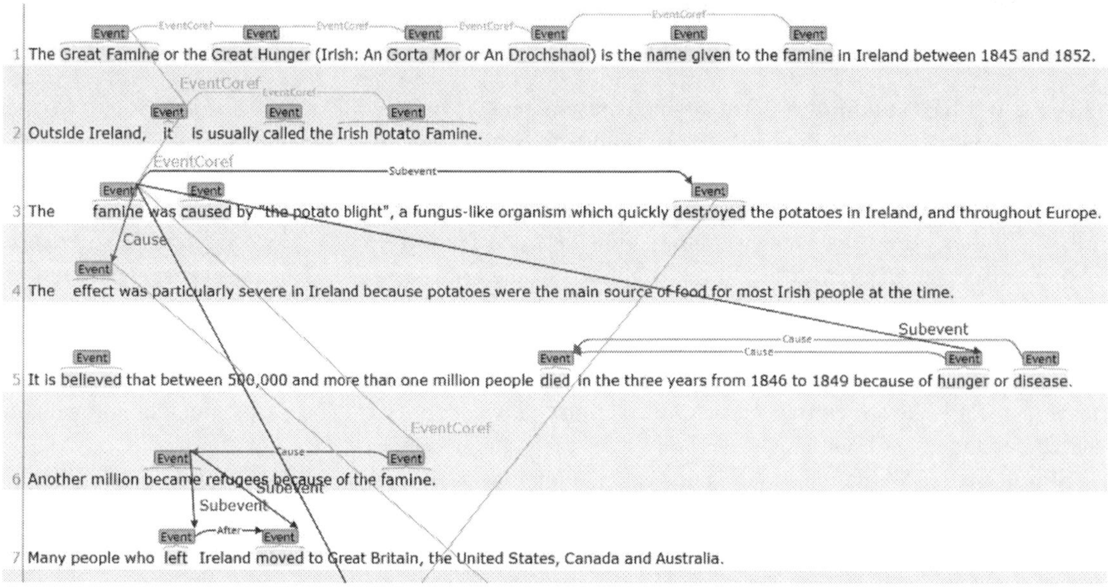

Figure 1: Some examples of our annotation of events and event relations. Our modified version of BRAT facilitates human annotation of event relations adequately, supporting relations spanning multiple sentences along with relations within a single sentence in compact visualization.

event coreference between E1 and E2 and two subevent relations from E1 to E3 and from E2 to E3, we count one event coreference cluster [E1,E2] and one (cluster-level) subevent relation [E1,E2] $\xrightarrow{\text{subevent}}$ [E3]. Overall, subevents are most frequently annotated among the four event relations, and the number of subevent relations is 6.5 times larger than that of simultaneity relations. It is also interesting to see that causality relations appear more frequently in the disease, geology and disaster domains than others. We observed that scientific domains such as diseases and geology generally tend to have more cause-and-effect relationships, but also often require domain-specific knowledge to distinguish between causality and preconditions, as seen in chemical reactions. We also found that the history domain has the largest number of event sequences and the second largest number of subevent relations, indicating that script-based structures tend to appear more frequently in that domain.

	Arch	Chem	Disa	Dise	Eco	Edu	Geo	Hist	Poli	Tran	Total
# Event coreference clusters	32	61	49	67	51	61	52	42	46	51	512
# Subevent relations	74	81	98	94	48	101	91	119	147	93	946
# Causality relations	31	63	71	105	37	28	87	68	36	60	586
# Event sequence relations	48	38	63	30	73	62	58	117	66	88	643
# Simultaneity relations	8	11	21	10	15	17	8	21	24	11	146

Table 2: Statistics of event coreference clusters and cluster-level event relations in SW100. For brevity, we use a prefix with 3 or 4 characters to refer to each domain.

4.4   Inter-annotator Agreement on Annotation of Event Relations

One way to compute inter-annotator agreement on event coreference is to use evaluation metrics developed by prior work, such as MUC (Vilain et al., 1995), B^3 (Bagga and Baldwin, 1998), $CEAF_e$ (Luo, 2005), and BLANC (Recasens and Hovy, 2011). However, these metrics are appropriate specifically for (event) coreference and cannot be consistently applied to other event relations such as subevents. Instead, a single consistent metric is ideal for comparing inter-annotator agreement. Since we have three annotators, we use Fleiss' Kappa (Fleiss, 1971) to compute inter-annotator agreement on the five event relations annotated by the three annotators. Specifically, we consider all pairwise relations between events and propagate event relations via event coreference, following (Mitamura et al., 2017). Table 3 shows the result. According to the interpretation of Fleiss' Kappa by Landis and Koch (1977), the inter-annotator agreement on event coreference is substantial agreement, those on subevent and causality relations are fair agreement, and those on after and simultaneity relations are slight agreement.

Relation	κ
Event coreference	0.645
Subevent	0.223
Causality	0.298
Event sequence	0.139
Simultaneity	0.108

Table 3: Inter-annotator agreement (Fleiss' Kappa) on event relations.

4.5 Issues on Annotation of Event Relations

As compared to the high inter-annotator agreement on events described in Section 3.4, our inter-annotator agreement on event relations (especially on the four relations of subevent, causality, event sequence, and simultaneity) is quite low, as shown in Table 3. This low inter-annotator agreement reflects many difficulties that the annotators faced in their event relation annotation. This section describes the difficulties in detail.

Event annotation error. Missing event nuggets or event nuggets with incorrect spans can end up with false annotation of event relations. Note that we do not make any changes to annotated event nuggets during the process of annotating event relations, since we first finalized event nugget annotation before annotating event relations, as described in Section 2. One example is:

(18) Chronic Obstructive Pulmonary Disease (COPD) can **make** breathing gradually **difficult**. **Breathing difficulties** caused by COPD can be compounded by ...

The first event nugget in (18) is 'make ... difficult'. If 'make breathing ... difficult' were annotated instead, it would be coreferent with 'Breathing difficulties'. However, if event nuggets are annotated as shown above, event coreference should not probably be annotated even if it does exist.

Event granularity. When we annotate a subevent relation between event X and Y, we need to figure out a difference in event granularity between X and Y along with a certain script. However, it is sometimes difficult to discern whether X and Y are expressed at different levels in event hierarchy. For example, let us consider the following sentence:

(19) When Mount St. Helens **erupted** in 1980, it **released** 1000 times less material.

The first event 'erupted' can be seen as a parent event of 'released' under the eruption script. Another interpretation is that the two events have the same granularity and there is a causality relation: 'erupted' $\xrightarrow{\text{cause}}$ 'released'. We often need to examine surrounding contexts deeply to resolve the ambiguity.

Script identification. The identification of scripts and their underlying subevents depends largely on common-sense knowledge and intuition of annotators. Thus, it is not easy to arrive at an consensus for subevent relations and event sequences. One example is:

(20) He **sought treatment** for his **cancer**, after which he **got better**.

Some annotators might decide that this sentence constitutes a sickness script which corresponds to the typical life cycle of falling sick and recovering from it. However, this kind of decision can also be subjective, depending on annotators' common-sense knowledge, and others might not admit stereotypicality in the set of events.

Domain-specific knowledge. Annotation of causality and subevent relations can require annotators to have extensive background knowledge. This difficulty can break annotators' agreement easily. We give two examples:

(21) The **start** of the **<u>Cultural Revolution</u> followed** the **failure** of the **<u>Great Leap Forward</u>**. Mao **tried** to **remove** capitalists from the Communist Party of China.

(22) The 1973 **<u>oil crisis</u> started** on October 17, 1973, when the members of Organization of Arab Petroleum Exporting Countries (OAPEC) **said**, because of the **<u>Yom Kippur War</u>**, that they would no longer **ship** petroleum to nations that had **supported** Israel in its **conflict** with Syria and Egypt.

In (21), whether event 'tried (to remove capitalists)' is a subevent of 'Cultural Revolution' is heavily subjective to annotators' knowledge about the Cultural Revolution. The sentence in (22) has seven events, and the correct annotation of event relations among them requires comprehensive understanding of the 1973 oil crisis and the Yom Kippur War at least, which can cause annotators' disagreement.

Causality vs. Event sequence. Since causality connotes an event sequence by its nature, we employ causality tests to differentiate causality from event sequences, as described in Section 4.1. Even with the causality tests, there are still some ambiguous cases:

(23) Igneous rock can **melt** into magma, **erode** into sediment, or be **pressed** tightly together to **<u>become metamorphic</u>**.

Some annotators may see causality between 'pressed' and 'become metamorphic' whereas others may find it to be an event sequence.

Simultaneity vs. Event sequence. It turns out that our definition and annotation principles on simultaneity described in Section 4.1 are not completely informative with respect to how to deal with the duration of events. For example, it is not entirely clear whether we should annotate simultaneity when two events overlap in time to a large extent but not fully. As a result, this issue confuses annotators when they annotate simultaneity or event sequences. We give two examples:

(24) When 1,500 missiles were **shipped**, three hostages were **released**.

(25) A person can **<u>have dyslexia</u>** even if he or she is very smart or **educated**.

In one interpretation of (24), 'released' happened at the same time as 'shipped'. Another possible interpretation is that 'released' happened after 'shipped'. We observe similar ambiguity in (25).

5   Conclusion and Future Work

We have presented our methodologies for annotating events and five types of event relations: event coreference, subevents, causality, event sequence, and simultaneity. To our knowledge, this is the first work that performs human annotation of events and five event relations of event coreference, subevent, causality, event sequence and simultaneity in a domain-agnostic manner. Using 100 articles in Simple Wikipedia from 10 different domains, we have demonstrated that the methodologies can allow us to annotate a wider coverage of events and event relations than prior work in a principled manner against the wide variety of domains. In addition, we have achieved high inter-annotator agreement on event annotation. Given lower inter-annotator agreement on event relation annotation, we have provided an analysis of issues on annotation of event relations.

There are a number of avenues for future work. The main piece of future work is to improve inter-annotator agreement on event relations by refining the annotation principles and guidelines. It is necessary to develop a more sophisticated annotation scheme for differentiating between subevent relations, causality, event sequences, and simultaneity. As for more temporarily-oriented relations, such as event sequences and simultaneity, we need to introduce a consistent principle for annotators to comprehend the duration of events more precisely, such as interval temporal logic (Allen, 1983). Besides the five event relations that we dealt with in this work, there exist many other event relations such as memberships (Hovy et al., 2013) and bridging (Palmer et al., 2016). Providing more comprehensive annotation guidelines including these event relations would also lead to an improvement on inter-annotator agreement. With respect to event annotation, one could define event spans more adequately than the 'semantically meaning unit' in the event nugget definition, thereby reducing annotators' subjective discretion and improving inter-annotator agreement.

Acknowledgements

This publication was partly made possible by grant NPRP-08-1337-1-243 from the Qatar National Research Fund (a member of the Qatar Foundation). The statements made herein are solely the responsibility of the authors.

References

James F. Allen. 1983. Maintaining knowledge about temporal intervals. *Communications of the ACM*, 26(11):832–843.

Jun Araki, Dheeraj Rajagopal, Sreecharan Sankaranarayanan, Susan Holm, Yukari Yamakawa, and Teruko Mitamura. 2016. Generating questions and multiple-choice answers using semantic analysis of texts. In *Proceedings of COLING*, pages 1125–1136.

Emmon Bach. 1986. The algebra of events. *Linguistics and Philosophy*, 9:5–16.

Amit Bagga and Breck Baldwin. 1998. Algorithms for scoring coreference chains. In *Proceedings of LREC Workshop on Linguistics Coreference*, pages 563–566.

Collin F. Baker, Charles J. Fillmore, and John B. Lowe. 1998. The Berkeley FrameNet project. In *Proceedings of COLING*, pages 86–90.

Agata Cybulska and Piek Vossen. 2014. Using a sledgehammer to crack a nut? Lexical diversity and event coreference resolution. In *Proceedings of LREC*, pages 4545–4552.

George Doddington, Alexis Mitchell, Mark Przybocki, Lance Ramshaw, Stephanie Strassel, and Ralph Weischedel. 2004. The automatic content extraction (ACE) program tasks, data, and evaluation. In *Proceedings of LREC*, pages 837–840.

Jesse Dunietz, Lori Levin, and Jaime Carbonell. 2017. The BECauSE corpus 2.0: Annotating causality and overlapping relations. In *Proceedings of the 11th Linguistic Annotation Workshop*, pages 95–104.

Joseph L. Fleiss. 1971. Measuring nominal scale agreement among many raters. *Psychological Bulletin*, 76(5):378–382.

Eduard Hovy, Teruko Mitamura, Felisa Verdejo, Jun Araki, and Andrew Philpot. 2013. Events are not simple: Identity, non-identity, and quasi-identity. In *Proceedings of NAACL-HLT Workshop on Events: Definition, Detection, Coreference, and Representation*, pages 21–28.

ISO. 2012. ISO 24617-1 language resource management – semantic annotation framework – part 1: Time and events. In *International Standardization Organization*.

Jin-Dong Kim, Tomoko Ohta, Sampo Pyysalo, Yoshinobu Kano, and Jun'ichi Tsujii. 2009. Overview of BioNLP'09 shared task on event extraction. In *Proceedings of BioNLP-ST Workshop*, pages 1–9.

J. Richard Landis and Gary G. Koch. 1977. The measurement of observer agreement for categorical data. *Biometrics*, 33(1):159–174.

Xiaoqiang Luo. 2005. On coreference resolution performance metrics. In *Proceedings of HLT/EMNLP*, pages 25–32.

George A. Miller, Richard Beckwith, Christiane Fellbaum, Derek Gross, and Katherine Miller. 1990. Introduction to WordNet: An on-line lexical database. *International Journal of Lexicography*, 3(4):235–244.

Teruko Mitamura, Yukari Yamakawa, Susan Holm, Zhiyi Song, Ann Bies, Seth Kulick, and Stephanie Strassel. 2015. Event nugget annotation: Processes and issues. In *Proceedings of NAACL-HLT Workshop on Events: Definition, Detection, Coreference, and Representation*, pages 66–76.

Teruko Mitamura, Zhengzhong Liu, and Eduard Hovy. 2017. Events detection, coreference and sequencing: What's next? Overview of the TAC KBP 2017 Event track. In *Proceedings of Text Analysis Conference*.

Marc Moens and Mark Steedman. 1988. Temporal ontology and temporal reference. *Computational Linguistics*, 14(2):15–28.

Tim O'Gorman, Kristin Wright-Bettner, and Martha Palmer. 2016. Richer Event Description: Integrating event coreference with temporal, causal and bridging annotation. In *Proceedings of the 2nd Workshop on Computing News Storylines*, pages 47–56.

Martha Palmer, Daniel Gildea, and Paul Kingsbury. 2005. The Proposition Bank: An annotated corpus of semantic roles. *Computational Linguistics*, 31(1):71–105.

Martha Palmer, Will Styler, Kevin Crooks, and Tim O'Gorman, 2016. *Richer Event Description (RED) Annotation Guidelines*. University of Colorado at Boulder. Version 1.7, `https://github.com/timjogorman/ RicherEventDescription/blob/master/guidelines.md`.

Stephen G. Pulman. 1997. Aspectual shift as type coercion. *Transactions of the Philological Society*, 95(2):279–317.

James Pustejovsky, José M. Castaño, Robert Ingria, Roser Sauri, Robert J. Gaizauskas, Andrea Setzer, and Graham Katz. 2003. TimeML: Robust specification of event and temporal expressions in text. In *Fifth International Workshop on Computational Semantics (IWCS-5)*, pages 28–34.

Marta Recasens and Eduard Hovy. 2011. BLANC: Implementing the Rand index for coreference evaluation. *Natural Language Engineering*, 17(4):485–510.

Roger C. Schank and Robert P. Abelson. 1977. *Scripts, Plans, Goals, and Understanding: An Inquiry into Human Knowledge Structures*. Lawrence Erlbaum Associates.

Zhiyi Song, Ann Bies, Stephanie Strassel, Tom Riese, Justin Mott, Joe Ellis, Jonathan Wright, Seth Kulick, Neville Ryant, and Xiaoyi Ma. 2015. From Light to Rich ERE: Annotation of entities, relations, and events. In *Proceedings of NAACL-HLT Workshop on Events: Definition, Detection, Coreference, and Representation*, pages 89–98.

Pontus Stenetorp, Sampo Pyysalo, Goran Topić, Tomoko Ohta, Sophia Ananiadou, and Jun'ichi Tsujii. 2012. BRAT: A Web-based tool for NLP-assisted text annotation. In *Proceedings of EACL: Demonstrations Session*, pages 102–107.

Marc Vilain, John Burger, John Aberdeen, Dennis Connolly, and Lynette Hirschman. 1995. A model-theoretic coreference scoring scheme. In *Proceedings of MUC-6*, pages 45–52.

Tuangthong Wattarujeekrit, Parantu K. Shah, and Nigel Collier. 2004. PASBio: predicate-argument structures for event extraction in molecular biology. *BMC Bioinformatics*, 5:155.

Ralph Weischedel, Eduard Hovy, Mitchell Marcus, Martha Palmer, Robert Belvin, Sameer Pradhan, Lance Ramshaw, and Nianwen Xue. 2011. OntoNotes: A large training corpus for enhanced processing. In *Handbook of Natural Language Processing and Machine Translation: DARPA Global Autonomous Language Exploitation*, pages 54–63. Springer-Verlag New York.

Downward Compatible Revision of Dialogue Annotation

Harry Bunt[1]**, Emer Gilmartin**[2]**, Simon Keizer, Catherine Pelachaud,**
Volha Petukhova, Laurent Prévot and Mariët Theune
[1]Tilburg University, harry.bunt@uvt.nl
[2]Trinity College Dublin, egil@tdc.ei
[3]Vrije Universiteit Brussel, keizer.simon@gmail.com
[4]Université Paris VIII, catherine.pelachaud@upmc.fr
[5]Saarland University, v.v.petukhova@gmail.com
[6]Aix-Marseille Université, laurent.prevot@lpl-aix.fr
[7]University of Twente, Enschede, m.theune@utwente.nl

Abstract

This paper discusses some aspects of revising the ISO standard for dialogue act annotation (ISO 24617-2). The revision is aimed at making annotations using the ISO scheme more accurate and at providing more powerful tools for building natural language based dialogue systems, without invalidating the annotated resources that have been built, with the current version of the standard. In support of the revision of the standard, an analysis is provided of the downward compatibility of a revised annotation scheme with the original scheme at the levels of abstract syntax, concrete syntax, and semantics of annotations.

1 Introduction

ISO standards are examined every five years for the need to be brought up to date or to be improved. The ISO standard for dialogue act annotation, ISO 24617-2,[1], was published in September 2012 and is thus up for revision, if deemed necessary,[2]

When a revised annotation scheme is used to annotate corpus data, the resulting annotations will be in some respects differ from those according to the original version. An important issue concerning the usefulness of a revision is the compatibility between annotations according to the two versions. In particular, it is desirable that old annotations are still valid in the revised version, and do not require to be re-annotated (or converted). In other words, the revised standard should preferably be *downward compatible* with the original version. Downward compatibility is a well-known design property of computer hardware and software, and can be applied also to annotation schemes. This is discussed in Section 3, where the compatibility of annotation schemes is analysed and related to the properties of extensibility, optionality, and restrictability.

First, Section 2 briefly summarizes the ISO 24617-2 standard. Section 3 introduces the notion of *downward compatibility* for the revision of an annotation scheme, and relates it to different forms of optionality. Section 4 discusses some inaccuracies, and outlines possible solutions to be implemented in its second edition. Section 5 briefly considers four different use cases of the standard, and what kind of extensions would be relevant for which use case. Section 6 discusses some inconvenient limitations of the current version, and corresponding extensions that respect the requirement of downward compatibility. Section 7 ends the paper with conclusions and perspectives for revising the standard.

2 The ISO 24617-2 Standard

The ISO 24617-2 annotation standard consists of two main components: (a) a comprehensive, domain-independent set of concepts that may be used in dialogue act annotation, meticulously defined in the form of ISO data categories, and (b) the markup language DiAML (Dialogue Act Markup Language). In its stock of annotation concepts, in particular its taxonomy of communicative functions, ISO 24617-2 builds on previously designed annotation schemes such as DIT^{++}, DAMSL, MRDA, HCRC Map

---

[1]ISO 24617-2, Language Resources Management, Semantic Annotation Framework, part 2: Dialogue acts.

[2]This issue was discussed at the ISO-13 workshop in September 2017, where it was felt to be desirable to improve and extend the existing standard in some respects. The present paper is partly based on recommendations for revising the standard that were reached at a two-day workshop in April 2018.

Task, Verbmobil, SWBD-DAMSL, and DIT.[3] The ISO 24617-2 scheme supports semantically richer annotations than most of its predecessors in including the following aspects:

Dimension: The ISO scheme supports multidimensional annotation, i.e. the assignment of multiple communicative functions to dialogue segments; following DIT^{++}, an explicitly defined notion of 'dimension' is used that corresponds to a certain category of semantic content. Nine orthogonal dimensions are defined: (1) *Task:* dialogue acts that move forward the task or activity which motivates the dialogue; (2-3) *Feedback*, divided into *Auto-* and *Allo-Feedback*: acts providing or eliciting information about the processing of previous utterances by the current speaker or by the current addressee, respectively; (4) *Turn Management:* activities for obtaining, keeping, releasing, or assigning the right to speak; (5) *Time Management:* acts for managing the use of time in the interaction; (6) *Discourse Structuring:* dialogue acts dealing with topic management or otherwise structuring the dialogue; (7-8) *Own-* and *Partner Communication Management:* actions by the speaker to edit his current contribution or a contribution of another speaker; (9) *Social Obligations Management:* dialogue acts for dealing with social conventions such as greeting, apologizing, and thanking.

Qualifiers for expressing that a dialogue act is performed conditionally, with uncertainty, or with a particular sentiment.

Dependence relations for semantic dependences between dialogue acts, e.g. question-answer (functional dependence), or for relating a feedback act to the utterance(s) that the act reacts to (feedback dependence).

Rhetorical relations , for example for indicating that the performance of one dialogue act explains that of another dialogue act.

The ISO schema defines 56 communicative functions, which are listed in Appendix A. Some of these are specific for a particular dimension; for instance *Turn Take* is specific for Turn Management; *Stalling* for Time Management, and *Self-Correction* for Own Communication Management. Other functions can be applied in any dimension; for example, *You misunderstood me* is an *Inform* in the Allo-Feedback dimension. All types of question, statement, and answer can be used in any dimension, and the same is true for commissive and directive functions, such as *Offer, Suggest,* and *Request.* Such functions are called *general-purpose* functions; the former *dimension-specific* functions.

ISO 24617-2 annotations assume that a dialogue act has seven components: a sender, a set of one or more addressees, zero or more other participants, a dimension, a communicative function, possibly one or more functional or feedback dependence relations (depending on the type of dialogue act), possibly one or more qualifiers, and possibly one or more rhetorical relations to other dialogue acts.

The DiAML markup language was designed in accordance with the ISO Linguistic Annotation Framework (LAF)[4] and the ISO Principles of Semantic Annotation (ISO 24617-6).[5] LAF distinguishes between *annotations* and *representations*: 'annotation' refers to the linguistic information that is added to segments of language data, independent of format; 'representation' refers to the rendering of annotations in a particular format.

Following the ISO Principles, this distinction is implemented in the DiAML definition by distinguishing an *abstract syntax* that specifies a class of *annotation structures* as set-theoretical

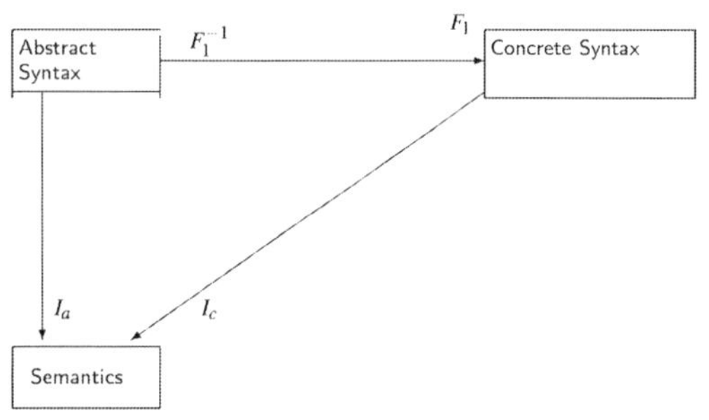

Figure 1: Abstract and concrete syntax, and semantics

---

[3] See Bunt (2007); Allen & Core (1997); Dhillon et al. (2004); Anderson et al. (1991); Alexandersson et al. (1998); Jurafsky et al. (1997); and Bunt (1994; 2000), respectively.

[4] ISO 24612:2010; see also Ide & Romary (2004).

[5] ISO 24617-6; see also Bunt (2015).

constructs, like pairs and triples of concepts, and a *concrete syntax* that specifies a rendering of these annotation structures in a particular format. A representation format is defined called DiAML-XML, which uses abbreviated XML-expressions. The annotations have a semantics which is defined for the abstract syntax (see Fig. 1), thus allowing alternative representation formats to share the same semantics.

According to ISO 24617-2, dialogue acts are expressed by 'functional segments', defined as *minimal stretches of communicative behaviour that have a communicative function and a semantic content*, 'minimal' in the sense of excluding material that does not contribute to the expression of the dialogue act. Functional segments may be discontinuous, may overlap, and may contain parts contributed by different speakers.

Example (1) shows a DiAML-XML annotation representation. It illustrates among other things the annotation of relations between dialogue acts: a rhetorical relation (Elaboration) between the dialogue acts in utterances 1 and 3, a functional dependence relation between the question in 2 and the answer in 3, and a feedback dependence relation between the dialogue acts in utterances 3 and 4.

(1)
1. G: go south and you'll pass some cliffs on your right
2. F: uhm... straight south?
3. G: yes, passing some adobe huts on your left
4. F: oh okay

Functional segments:

fs1 = o south and you'll pass some cliffs on your right

fs2 = uhm...

fs3 = straight south?

fs4 = yes

fs5 = passing some adobe huts on your left

fs6 = oh okay

```
<diaml xmlns="http://www.iso.org/diaml">
<dialogueAct xml:id="da1" target="#fs1" sender="#g" addressee='#f'
    dimension="task" communicativeFunction="instruct"/>
<dialogueAct xml:id="da2" target="#fs2" sender="#f" addressee="#g"
    dimension="turnManagement" communicativeFunction="turnTake"/>
<dialogueAct xml:id="da3" target="#fs2" sender="#f" addressee="#g"
    dimension="timeManagement" communicativeFunction="stalling"/>
<dialogueAct xml:id="da4" target="#fs3" sender="#f" addressee="#g"
    dimension="autoFeedback" communicativeFunction="question"/>
<dialogueAct xml:id="da5" target="#fs4" sender="#g" addressee="#f"
    dimension="alloFeedback" communicativeFunction="answer"
    functionalDependence="#da4"/>
<dialogueAct xml:id="da6" target="#fs5" sender="#g" addressee="#f"
    dimension="task" communicativeFunction="inform"/>
<rhetoricalLink dact="#da6" rhetoAnteceden="#da1" rhetoRel="elaboration"
<dialogueAct xml:id="da7" target="#fs6" sender="#f" addressee="#g"
    dimension="autoFeedback" communicativeFunction="autoPositive"
    feedbackDependence="#da1 #da6"/>
</diaml>
```

3 Formal Properties of Schema Revision

3.1 Compatibility, Optionality, Extensibility, and Restrictibility

Designing a revised version of the ISO 24617-2 standard in a downward compatible way is greatly facilitated by the *extensibility* of the original version, which means that it allows its stock of concepts to be extended with additional concepts. ISO 24617-2 is extensible in four respects:

- **Dimensions**: Due to the orthogonality of the set of dimensions, additional dimensions may be introduced as long as they are orthogonal to the already existing dimensions and to each other.

- **Communicative functions**: The taxonomy of communicative functions defined in the standard expresses the semantic relations between functions: dominance relations express different degrees of specialization; and sister relations express mutually exclusivity of functions. Communicative functions may be added to the taxonomy as long as they respect these relations.

- **Qualifiers**: Like dimensions, due to the orthogonality of the qualifier attributes and their values.

- **Rhetorical relations**: The ISO standard does not specify a particular set of relations, but allows any such set to be plugged in.

The extensibility of ISO 24617-2 is in turn facilitated by the *optionality* of some of its components. Following the ISO Principles of semantic annotation, three types of optionality can be distinguished:

Type I (semantic optionality): a component that a certain type of annotation structure may contain, but does not have to. If it does contain that component then this provides extra information, compared to the case where it does not. Example: the specification of a set of 'other participants' for a dialogue act.

Type II (syntactic optionality): a component may be but does not need to be specified in annotation representations, since it has a default value in the abstract syntax, which is assumed in the encoded annotation structure if it is not specified. Example: the polarity in the annotation of an event by means of an <event> element in ISO-TimeML.

Type III (uninterpreted optionality): a component may be specified in annotation representations but does not encode anything in the abstract syntax, and thus has no semantic interpretation (but the component may be useful for an annotation process or for other purposes). Example: the indication of the part of speech of an event description by means of an <event> element in ISO-TimeML.

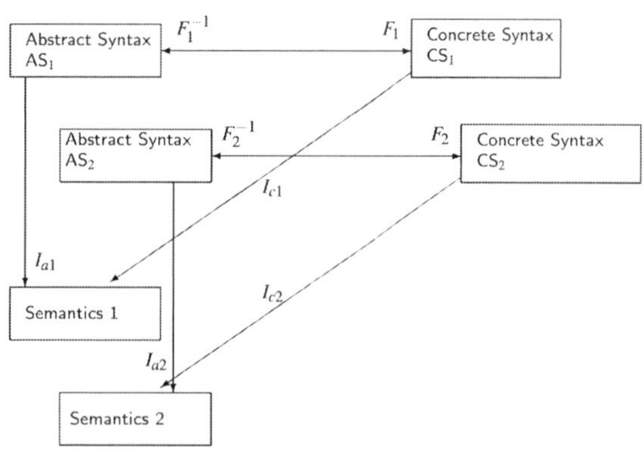

Figure 2: Optionality in abstract and concrete syntax, and semantics

These distinctions can be made precise in terms of the abstract and concrete syntax of annotations and their semantics, as shown in Figure 2, where two versions of an annotation scheme are considered, with abstract syntax specifications AS$_1$ and AS$_2$, two semantic specifications by means of the interpretation functions I_{a1} and I_{a2}, and two concrete syntax specifications CS$_1$ and CS$_2$. The encoding and decoding functions F_1, F_1^{-1}, F_2, and F_2^{-1} relate the structures generated by the two abstract and concrete syntax specifications, respectively, and define the semantics of concrete representations by means of the composite functions $I_{c1} = I_{a1} \circ F_1^{-1}$ and $I_{c2} = I_a \circ F_2^{-1}$.

Let α be an annotation structure generated by AS_1, with encoding $F_1(\alpha) = \beta$. Let δ_a be an optional addition to α according to the abstract syntax AS$_2$, forming the annotation structure designated by $\alpha + \delta_a$, and let δ_c be the corresponding element in the concrete syntax CS$_2$, forming an annotation representation designated by $\beta + \delta_c$.

Semantic optionality (Type I) can now be defined formally as the case where δ_c represents additional semantic information:

$$(2)\quad F^{-1}(\beta + \delta_c) = \alpha + \delta_a$$
$$I_c(\beta + \delta_c) = I_a(F^{-1}(\beta + \delta_c)) = I_a(\alpha + \delta_a)$$

Syntactic optionality (Type II) is the case that an optional addition δ_c in a representation $\beta + \delta_c$ (such as polarity="positive") indicates that the abstract annotation structure $\alpha[\delta_a]$ that it encodes, includes its default value δ_{ad}:

(3) $F^{-1}(\beta + \delta_c) = \alpha[\delta_{ad}]$
$\quad I_c(\beta + \delta_c) = I_a(F^{-1}(\beta)) = I_a(\alpha[\delta_{ad}])$

Finally, uninterpreted optionality (Type III) is the case where the representation with the optional element encodes the same semantic information as the structure without the optional element, not requiring a default value in the abstract annotation structure:

(4) $F^{-1}(\beta + \delta_c) = F^{-1}(\beta)$
$\quad I_c(\beta + \delta_c) = I_a(F^{-1}(\beta + \delta_c)) = I_a(F^{-1}(\beta)) = I_a(\alpha)$

The following elements of ISO 24617-2 are optional in one of these three senses:

- **Qualifiers:** The qualifier attributes *Certainty* and *Conditionality* have default values ('certain' and 'unconditional', respectively), hence they form a Type II optionality. The attribute *Sentiment* has no values defined; in this respect the annotation scheme is extensible: any set of values may be used. If this set contains a default value; then the specification of that value is an optionality of Type II; for all other values it is of Type I, since the semantics is defined (in terms of predicates used in information state updates, see Bunt, 2014).

- **Rhetorical relations:** If specified, these add semantic information about relations between dialogue acts or their semantic content. There is no 'default' rhetorical relation, hence this is a Type I optionality.

ISO 24617-2 currently has no cases of Type III optionality, but its revision is expected to have some.

Annotation schemes are usually considered only at the level of concrete syntax, and have no abstract syntax or semantics. Notions such as extensibility are thus typically considered only at that level, in terms of adding attributes and/or values to XML elements. In the 3-layer architecture of DiAML, extensibility must be considered at all three levels; extending the representations defined by the concrete syntax is only semantically significant if the corresponding extensions are introduced in the abstract syntax, and their semantic interpretation is defined. Since this is technically nontrivial, user-defined extensions are typically Type III optional, and are disregarded by software that interprets the annotations.

The converse of extensibilty is the *'restrictability'* of an annotation scheme: the possibility to not use the entire stock of concepts offered by the scheme, but only a subset. ISO 24617-2 is restrictable in its set of dimensions and its set of communiative functions; as the official description of the standard in the ISO 24617-2:2012 document stipulates:

- *"A dimension and the corresponding set of dimension-specific communicative functions may be left out; by virtue of the orthogonality of the set of core dimensions, this has no influence on the remaining dimensions."*

- *"Communicative functions may be left out for which there is a less specific function in the taxonomy"*

In order to ensure that desirable extensions of ISO 24617-2 are well-defined at all three levels, it seems attractive to define such extensions in ISO 24617-2 Edition 2 while insisting on its restrictability, thus supporting the use of additional dimensions and communicative functions with a well-defined semantics without making their use obligatory.

3.2 Constraints on Revisions

Figure 3 shows the three levels of an Edition 1 annotation scheme and a revised version, Edition 2 with the functions A_{12}, S_{12}, and C_{12} which describe the revision at each level, i.e. if α_1 is an Edition 1 annotation structure, then $A_{12}(\alpha_1)$ is the revised annotation structure, and similarly at the other levels.

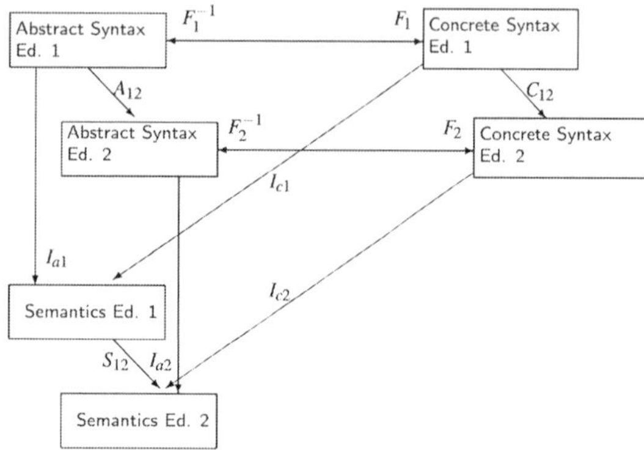

Figure 3: Annotation schema revision in abstract and concrete syntax, and semantics

Note that the revised representation of an Edition 1 annotation structure α_1 can be computed in two ways: (1) by applying the Edition 2 encoding function F_2 to the revised annotation structure $A_{12}(\alpha_1)$, and (2) by applying the representation revision function C_{12} to the Edition 1 representation $F_1(\alpha_1)$. The result should in both cases of course be the same:

$$(5)\quad F_2(A_{12}(\alpha_1)) = C_{12}(F_1(\alpha_1)).$$

Since this is true for any Edition 1 annotation structure α_1, a requirement on consistent revision is that the function compositions $F_2 \circ A_{12}$ and $C_{12} \circ F_1$ are identical:

$$(6)\quad F_2 \circ A_{12} = C_{12} \circ F_1.$$

Similarly, two ways of computing the Edition 2 meaning of an Edition 1 annotation structure are: (1) computing its Edition 1 meaning $I_{a1}(\alpha_1)$ according to Edition 1 and applying the semantic revision function S_{12}, and (2) determining the revised annotation structure $A_{12}(\alpha_1)$ and computing its Edition 2 meaning by applying the interpretation function I_{a2}. Again, the result should in both cases be the same:

$$(7)\quad S_{12}(I_{a1}(\alpha_1)) = I_{a2}(A_{12}(\alpha_1))$$

Since this is true for any Edition 1 annotation structure α_1, a second consistency requirement on annotation schema revision is:

$$(8)\quad S_{12} \circ I_{a1} = I_{a2} \circ A_{12}$$

3.3 Downward Compatible Revision

Whether an annotation according to the original standard ('Edition 1') is valid according to its revised version ('Edition 2'), should be considered at all three levels of the definitions: abstract syntax, concrete syntax, and semantics. An Edition 1 annotation structure α_1 is valid according to Edition 2 if and only if (1) it belongs to the set of annotation structures defined by the Edition 2 abstract syntax and (2) it has the same meaning as in Edition 1. In other words, for Edition 2 to be downward compatible with Edition 1 the functions A_{12} and S_{12} are the identity function, and the interpretation functions I_{a1} and I_{a2} assign the same meanings to Edition 1 annotation structures and their Edition 2 versions, respectively (thus respecting constraint (8)). The Edition 2 set of annotation structures is thus a superset of the Edition 1 set of annotation structures, whose meanings are not changed. (Additional, in particular 'richer' meanings, are assigned to the Edition 2 annotation structures that are not also Edition 1 annotation structures.)

The Edition 2 annotation representations are defined by the Edition 2 concrete syntax, and in order to be downward compatible also at the level of concrete representations, this representation is preferably the same as the Edition 1 representation, but there is room for variation here: according to constraint (6) with A_{12} being the identity function, the representation conversion function C_{12} and the Edition 2 encoding function F_2 may be defined in such a way that, applied to an annotation structure that is also an Edition 1 annotation structure:

$$(9)\quad F_2(\alpha) = (C_{12} \circ F_1)(\alpha)$$

(For those Edition 2 annotation structures that are not also Edition 1 annotation structures there are no consistency constraints on the definition of the encoding function F_2.) The effect of this is that, while the revision leaves the annotation structures of the Edition 1 abstract syntax unchanged, a conversion procedure implementing the function C_{12} may change their representations into a new form to become Edition 2 representations.

Note that, if a revision of an annotation scheme consists of extensions, optional elements, and/or refinements (more fine-grained annotations, or annotations with greater accuracy), then the revised version may indeed be downward compatible in the sense described here; if, by contrast, the revision includes corrections of errors in the earlier version, then the revised edition is not entirely downward compatible. The revisions of ISO 24617-2 recommended in this paper can all be viewed as extensions, including new optional elements, and refinements, leading to a downward compatible Edition 2.

4 Accuracy of Annotations

4.1 Dependence Relations

4.1.1 Dependence Relations for Feedback

ISO 24617-2 defines a feedback act as a *"dialogue act which provides or elicits information about the sender's or the addressee's processing of something that was uttered in the dialogue"*. A feedback act is thus a dialogue act in either the auto-feedback or the allo-feedback dimension. Moreover, it defines the feedback dependence relation as the *"relation between a feedback act and the stretch of communicative behaviour whose processing the act provides or elicits information about"*. The feedback dependence relation serves to identify this "something that was uttered in the dialogue". This is illustrated in (10), where the segment "The first train to the airport on Sunday" in S's utterance repeats material from C's question, which can be interpreted as a positive auto-feedback act by which S indicates to have understood which train C wants to know the departure time of.

(10) C: Do you know what time the first train to the airport leaves on Sunday?
      S: The first train to the airport on Sunday is at 6:15.

The annotation of S's utterance thus considers this segment as a functional segment, with the communicative function *autoPositive*, and with a feedback dependence relation to what C said. However, ISO 24617-2 does not consider segments other than *functional* segments, so rather than a dependence relation to the corresponding (discontinuous) segment in C's utterance, the feedback dependence relation uses the smallest functional segment that includes the repeated material - in this case C's entire utterance. This is rather inaccurate. It is therefore recommended that ISO 24617-2 Edition 2 should include the possibility to refer to non-functional segments, whose relevance comes from the fact that they are referred to by feedback acts – "reference segments".

4.1.2 Dependence Relations for Own and Partner Communication Management

Reference segments are also needed for the accurate annotation of Own Communication Management acts and Partner Communication Management acts. For example, the accurate annotation of a self-correction (in the OCM dimension) or a partner correction (in the PCM dimension) requires the specification of the dialogue segment that is corrected, which may very well be a single word or morpheme.

4.1.3 Types of Dependence Relations

ISO 24617-2 defines the functional dependence relation as the *"relation between a given dialogue act and a preceding dialogue act on which the semantic content of the given dialogue act depends due to its communicative function."* Examples of such dialogue acts are the inherently responsive acts such as answers, (dis-)confirmations, (dis-)agreements, corrections and the acceptance or rejection of requests, offers, and suggestions.

Auto- and allo-feedback acts, which in a different sense are also responsive, come in two varieties: those whose communicative function is specific for these dimensions (*AutoPositive, AutoNegative, AlloPositive, AlloNegative, FeedbackElicitation*) and those whose communicative function is a general purpose function, such as *Question* (for clarification), *CheckQuestion*, or *Confirm*. The two varieties aare illustrated by the examples in 11):

(11) a. G: the turn left just above the adobe huts
        F: okay [AutoPositive]

b. C: Best before nine on Monday, or else on Tuesday
   S: Monday before nine you said? [Auto-Feedback, CheckQuestion]
   C: That's right. [Allo-Feedback, Confirm]

The specification in ISO 24617-2 could be understood as saying that for the latter type of feedback act, if it has a responsive communicative function, like the *Confirm* act in (11b), then it should be annotated as having both a functional and a feedback dependence relation. This was not intended, however. In such cases the functional dependence relation, required for interpreting the responsive act, identifies the material that the feedback is about, so the use of both would be redundant. The same applies to dialogue acts in the OCM and PCM dimensions with a responsive communicative function. It is therefore recommended that the assignment of functional and feedback dependence relations should be specified more accurately than in ISO 24617-2 Edition 1, as follows:

1. For all dialogue acts in the Auto-Feedback, Allo-Feedback, OCM or PCM dimension:

   (a) if the communicative function is a responsive one, then assign a *functional* dependence relation to the dialogue act that is responded to;

   (b) if the communicative function is a general-purpose function but not a responsive one, or is dimension-specific for Auto-Feedback, Allo-Feedback, OCM or PCM, then assign a *feedback* dependence relation to the material that is reacted to.

2. In all other cases do not assign a dependence relation.

Note that, according to this specification, a feedback dependence relation is assigned to a feedback question like the CheckQuestion in (11b).

4.2   Rhetorical Relations

The dialogue acts that make up a dialogue are often rhetorically related. ISO 24617-2 supports the marking up of rhetorical relations (also know as *discourse relations*) as an optional addition to dialogue act annotation, but does not specify any particular set of relations to be used; it only specifies *how* a rhetorical relation may be marked up as relating two dialogue acts. The experience in dialogue act annotation is that rhetorical relations tend to be very important for a good understanding of the interaction. Users of the ISO scheme have often added these annotations, using a variant of the set of relations defined in ISO standard 24617-8, a.k.a. 'DR-Core'. This is a set of 18 'core' relations that are shared by many annotation schemes. It has been used in most of the dialogues in the DialogBank. Two problems were noted when annotating discourse relations in ISO 24617-2.

First, many rhetorical relations have two arguments that play different roles, for example, a Cause relation has a "Reason" and a "Result" argument. DiAML currently has no provision for indicating the roles in a rhetorical relation between dialogue acts. The DR-Core annotation scheme does have attributes and values for this purpose, so the annotation of rhetorical relations in dialogue could be made more accurate by importing some of the elements from DR-Core into DiAML.

Second, rhetorical relations may occur either between two dialogue acts, or between their semantic contents, or between one dialogue act and the semantic content of another. This phenomenon is known in the literature as the 'semantic-pragmatic' distinction. Example (12) illustrates this.

(12) a. *'Semantic Cause':*
     A: Have you seen Pete today?
        B: He didn't come in. He has the flu.

     b. *'Pragmatic Cause':*
     A: Have you seen Pete today?
        B: He didn't come in. He sent me a message saying that he has the flu.

This distinction can only be made in DiAML if it is extended with the possibility to say something about the semantic content of a dialogue act. This is taken up in Section 6.4.

5 Use cases

The concepts and mechanisms defined in ISO 24617-2 can be used in at least four different situations:

U1 manual annotation of corpus data;

U2 automatic annotation of corpus data;

U3 online recognition of dialogue acts by interactive systems;

U4 dialogue management and dialogue act generation by a dialogue system.

These different use cases present different desiderata and requirements, in particular concerning the granularity of the available communicative functions. Concerning use cases U1 and U2, a trained manual annotator may bring richer background and context information to bear in the annotation process than an automatic system, and may therefore benefit from the availability of fine-grained, context-dependent communicative functions. Manual annotators with little training or experience may, on the other hand, benefit more from the use of more coarse-grained functions in order to produce consistent results.

Concerning use cases U3 and U4, for example, Malchanau et al. (2017) have shown the usefulness of DiAML as an interface language between the modules of a multimodal dialogue system, and Keizer et al. (2011) have shown the use of the DIT^{++} taxonomy of communicative functions, which underlies the ISO standard, in a multidimensional Dialogue Manager. In both cases issues of granularity of the communicative functions arise, in particular in the generation of feedback acts, where the Dialogue Manager typically has detailed information about the level of processing that it would be appropriate to provide feedback about. The DIT^{++} taxonomy of communicative functions distinguishes between feedback acts at five different levels of processing: (1) attention; (2) perception; (3) understanding; (4) evaluation; and (5) execution. For use cases U3 and U4 such a fine-grained set of feedback functions would be useful.

Given the restrictability that would be required from the second edition in order to be downward compatible, it follows that it is recommended to add more fine-grained concepts to the standard, and to provide use-case dependent guidelines for how to optimally make use of the concepts that the standard makes available.

6 ISO 24617-2 Extensions

6.1 Dimensions

Users of ISO 24617-2 have mentioned two dimensions that they missed, namely Task Management, known from DAMSL, and Contact Management, known from DIT^{++}. Task Management acts discuss or explain a certain task or activity that is pursued through the dialogue (as opposed to performing that task/activity). They occur for example in TV debates and in interactive games (see e.g. Petukhova et al., 2014).

Contact Management acts serve to establish and manage contact and attention. Casual conversations are known to contain a rich variety of greetings and leavetaking acts (Gilmartin et al., 2017), which often have such a function (see also the next subsection).

Since one of the attractive features of the ISO scheme is that its dimensions are 'orthogonal', Task Management and Contact Management can be added as optional additions without interfering with the existing 9-dimensional system, keeping the extended system downward compatible with the existing system, and are available in a given use case when needed.

6.2 Communicative Functions

The taxonomy of communicative functions in ISO 24617-2 makes it possible to add fine-grained communicative functions without making existing annotations incompatible with the standard. Experience in applying the ISO standard has given rise to the desire to have more fine-grained communicative functions for Social Obligations Management, Discourse Structuring, and Auto- and Allo-Feedback.

ISO 24617-2 was intended to be domain-independent, applicable to a wide range of tasks and domains, and consequently does not have domain-specific communicative functions. This has been felt as a limitation when using the concepts of the standard for online dialogue act recognition or generation. It is recommended that the documentation of the standard discusses (informatively) two ways of defining domain-specific communicative functions: (a) as a way of specifying the semantic content of a general-purpose function (as illustrated by communicative functions for negotiation in the MIB corpus (Petukhova et al., 2016) ; and (b) as a dimension-specific communicative function for the Task domain, in which case the information-state update semantics of dialogue acts with that communicative function has to be defined.

Note that there can be no objection to the introduction of some examples of task-specific communicative functions in view of the restrictability of the standard in the use of the communicative functions that it defines.

6.3 Qualifiers

The available qualifiers for optional representation of certainty (default: certain) and conditionality (default: unconditional) seem adequate for their intended purpose. For emotion and sentiment the DiAML concrete syntax has the optional attribute 'sentiment', for which the standard does not specify any set of possible values, let alone a semantics, which makes the use of sentiment qualifiers Type III optional. For specifications of possible sets of emotion and sentiment values, and for more sophisticated annotation of the affective aspects of dialogue behaviour, it is recommended to look to EmotionML.

EmotionML, the W3C standard for annotating emotion (Baggio et al., 2014), does not prescribe the use of any particular set of emotion values, but supports the articulate annotation of emotions using alternative sets of values. Moreover, EmotionML is explicitly aimed at supporting the integration of emotion descriptions with other annotations. It would be attractive to extend the possibility to annotate emotion and sentiment (especially in multimodal dialogue) in DiAML by allowing EmotionML expressions in the concrete syntax of DiAML as optional elements of Type III that represent emotions with reference to dialogue acts.

6.4 Semantic Content

In dialogue act theory, a dialogue act is formally defined as a 8-tuple of which one of the elements is a semantic content (see Bunt, 2014). ISO 24617-2 focuses on the functional meaning of dialogue acts, and therefore annotates dialogue acts in DiAML (in the abstract syntax) as 7-tuples (see Section 2), leaving out the semantic content. For use in dialogue annotation (use cases U1 and U2) and for online recognition of dialogue acts (use case U3) this seems appropriate, but in online use in the dialogue management of a dialogue system (use case U4), there is a need to be able to specify information about the semantic content of dialogue acts. It is therefore recommended to explore the possibilities of extending DiAML with semantic content information. This has for example been done in the Virtual Negotiation Coach (Petukhova et al., 2017), where semantic content is specified by a set of attribute-value pairs that represent the state of a negotiation.

It may be noted that the semantics of dialogue act annotations is defined in a way that expects the specification of a semantic content as the argument of an update function, defined by the 7-tuples used in DiAML, namely as a mechanism for updating the dialogue participants' information states with that content. From a semantic point of view, it is thus fairly straightforward to extend DiAML with the semantic content of dialogue acts. Moreover, when DiAML is used in a dialogue system, the way in which semantic content is specified can be customized for the system's application domain.

The marking up of semantic content would mean in the concrete syntax the introduction of a <semanticContent> element which can be used e.g. for the improved annotation of rhetorical relations as follows (annotating B's utterance in example (12a)) :

```
(13)    <dialogueAct xml:id="da2" target="#s2" sender="#b" addressee="#a"
            dimension="task" communicativeFunction="answer"
            functionalDependence="#da1">
        <dialogueAct xml:id="da3" target="#s3" sender="#b" addressee="#a"
            dimension="task" communicativeFunction="inform" >
        <event xml:id="e3" target="#s3" type="ill" />
        <semanticContent dialogAct="#da3" content="#e3"/>
        <DRLink rel="cause" reason="#e3" result="#da2" />
```

The <event> element introduced in (13) for specifying information about the semantic content of a dialogue act could be the same as, or a simplified version of, the element with the same name that is used in the ISO standards for time and events (ISO 24617-2, see also Pustejovsky et al., 2010), for annotating semantic roles (ISO 24617-4, see also Bunt & Palmer, 2013), and for spatial information (ISO 24617-7, see also Pustejovsky et al., 2013), and that has also been proposed for the annotation of modality (Lapina & Petukhova, 2017) and quantification (Bunt et al., 2017). This suggests that the introduction of <semanticContent> and <event> elements, with their underlying abstract syntax and semantics, may open the possibility to specify quite detailed information about the semantic content of dialogue acts.

7 Conclusions and Perspectives

In this paper we have considered the requirements for a revision of the ISO standard for dialogue act annotation. One of the requirements is that, where possible, a second edition should be downward compatible with the original (current) version of the standard. The notion of compatibility between annotation schemes was analysed and related to the properties of extensibility, restrictability, and optionality.

Applying the ISO 24617-2 scheme in various use cases, such as the creation of the DBOX corpus (Petukhova et al., 2014) and the ADELE corpus (Gilmartin et al., 2017), and the design of the Virtual Debate Coach (Malchanau et al., 2017) show that it would be convenient to add Task Management and Contact Management to the ISO dimensions, as well as certain communicative functions for more fine-grained annotation of feedback, social obligations management, and discourse structuring.

Limitations of ISO 24617-2 were brought to light by the development of ISO standard 24617-6 for discourse relation annotation, of which rhetorical relations between dialogue acts or their semantic contents are a special case. The possibility was discussed to import elements from DR-Core into the annotation scheme for dialogue acts and to optionally add provisions for indicating the semantic content of a dialogue act. Doing so could be a step towards a more general merging of elements from annotation schemes for different semantic information, such as time and events, spatial information, semantic roles and quantification.

Acknowledgement

Thanks are due to the participants in a two-day meeting in April 2018 where ideas for a possible revision of ISO 24617-2 was discussed, including (besides the authors of this paper) also Pierre Albert, Shammur Chowdhury, Andrei Malchanau, and Kars Wijnhoven.

References

Allen, J. and M. Core (1997) DAMSL: Dialogue Act Markup in Several Layers. Technical Report, Multiparty Discourse Group.

Alexandersson, J., B. Buschbek-Wolf, T. Fujinami, E. Maier, N. Reithinger, B. Schmitz, and M. Siegel 1998 Dialogue acts in Verbmobil-2. Second edition. *Report 226.* DFKI Saarbrücken.

Andersson, A., M. Bader, E. Bard, E. Boyle, G. Doherty, S. Garrod, S. Isard, J. Kowtko, J. McAllister, Miller, F. Sotillo, H. Thompson, and R. Weinert (1991) The HCRC Map Task Corpus. *Language and Speech* 34, 351-366.

Baggio, P. , Pelachaud, C., Peter, C. and Zovato, E. (2014) Emotion Markup Language (EmotionML) 1.0. W3C Recommendation, 22 May 2014, edited by F. Burkhardt and M. Schröder. http://www.w3.org/TR/emotionml/

Bunt, H. (1994) Context and dialogue control. *Think Quarterly 3(1)*, 19-31.

Bunt, H. (2000) Dialogue pragmatics and context specification. In Harry Bunt and William Black (eds.) *Abduction, Belief, and Context in Dialogue. Studies in Computational Pragmatics.* Benjamins, Amsterdam, pp. 81-150.

Bunt H. (2009) The DIT^{++} taxonomy for functional dialogue markup. In: D. Heylen, C. Pelachaud, and D. Traum (eds) *Proceedings of EDAML/AAMAS Workshop "Towards a Standard Markup Language for Embodied Dialogue Acts"*, Budapest, pp. 13–24. Available (with updates) at http://dit.uvt.nl

Bunt, H. (2010) A methodology for designing semantic annotation languages exploiting syntactic-semantic iso-morphisms. In A.Fang, N. Ide, and J. Webster (eds.) *Proceedings of ICGL 2010, Second International Conference on Global Interoperability for Language Resources*, Hong Kong, pp. 29-45.

Bunt, H. (2011) The Semantics of Dialogue Acts. In *Proceedings 9th International Conference on Computational Semantics (IWCS 2011)*, Oxford, pp. 1-14.

Bunt, H. (2014) A Context-change Semantics for Dialogue Acts. In Harry Bunt, Johan Bos and Stephen Pulman (eds) *Computing Meaning, Vol. 4*, Berlin: Springer, pp. 177-201.

Bunt, H. (2015) On the principles of semantic annotation. In *Proceedings 11th Joint ACL-ISO Workshop on Interoperable Semantic Annotation (ISA-11)*, London, pp. 1-13.

Bunt, H. (2016) The DialogBank. In *Proceedings 10th International Conference on Language Resources and Evaluation (LREC 2016)*, Portoroz, Slovenia,

Bunt, H. (2017) Towards Interoperable Annotation of Quantification. In *Proceedings 13th Joint ACL-ISO Workshop on Interoperable Semantic Annotation (ISA-13)*, Montpellier.

Bunt, H. and M. Palmer (2013) Conceptual and Representational Choices in Defining an ISO Standard for Semantic Role Annotation. In *Proceedings 9th Joint ACL-ISO Workshop on Interoperable Semantic Annotation (ISA-9)*, Potsdam, pp. 45-54.

Bunt, H. and R. Prasad (2016) ISO DR-Core (ISO 24617-8): Core concepts for the annotation of discourse relations. In *Proceedings 12th Joint ACL-ISO Workshop on Interoperable Semantic Annotation (ISA-12)*, Portoroz, Slovenia, pp. 45-54.

Bunt, H., Alexandersson, J., Carletta, J., Choe, J.-W., Fang, A., Hasida, K., Lee, K., Petukhova, V., Popescu-Belis, A., Romary, L., Soria, C. and Traum, D. (2010) Towards an ISO standard for dialogue act annotation. In *Proceedings 8th International Conference on Language Resources and Evaluation (LREC 2010)*, Malta, pp. 2548-2558.

Bunt, H, J. Alexandersson, J.-W. Choe, A.Fang, K. Hasida, K. Lee, V. Petukhova, A. Popescu-Belis, L. Romary, and D. Traum (2012) A semantically-based standard for dialogue annotation. In: *Proc. 8th Intern. Conference on Language Resources and Evaluation (LREC 2012)*, Istanbul. ELRA, Paris.

Bunt, H., V. Petukhova, D. Traum, J. Alexandersson (2016) Dialogue Act Annotation with the ISO 24617-2 Standard. In: D. Dahl (ed.) *Multimodal Interaction with W3C Standards*, Springer, Berlin, pp. 109-135.

Carletta, J., A. Isard, S. Isard, J.Kowtko and G. Doherty-Sneddon (1996) HCRC dialogue structure coding manual. *Technical Report HCRC/TR-82*, University of Edinburgh.

Dhillon, R., S. Bhagat, H. Carvey, and E. Shriberg (2004) Meeting recorder project: dialogue labelling guide, ICSI Technical Report TR-04-002.

Gilmartin, E., B. Spillane, M. O'Reilly, C. Saam, K. Su, B.R. Cowan, K. Levacher, A.Calvo Devesa, L. Cerrato, N. Campbell, and V. Wade (2017) Annotation of Greeting, Introduction, and Leavetaking in Text Dialogues. In *Proc. ISA-13*, Montpellier.

Ide, N. and L. Romary (2004) International Standard for a Linguistic Annotation Framework. *Natural Language Engineering* 10: 221-225.

ISO 24610 (2006) *Language Resource Management: Feature structures.* International Standard. International Organisation for Standardisation ISO, Geneva.

ISO 12620 (2009) *Terminology and other language and content resources – Specification of data cateories and management of a Data Category Registry for language resoures.* International Standard. International Organisation for Standardisation ISO, Geneva.

ISO 24612 (2010) *ISO 24612: Language resource management: Linguistic annotation framework (LAF).* International Organisation for Standardisation ISO, Geneva.

ISO 24617-1 (2012) *ISO 24617-1: Language resource management – Semantic annotation framework – Part 1: Time and events.* International Organisation for Standardisation ISO, Geneva.

ISO 24617-2 (2012) *ISO 24617-2: Language resource management – Semantic annotation framework – Part 2: Dialogue acts.* International Organisation for Standardisation ISO, Geneva.

ISO 24617-4 (2014) *ISO 24617-4: Language resource management – Semantic annotation framework – Part 4: Semantic roles.* International Organisation for Standardisation ISO, Geneva.

ISO 24617-6 (2016) *ISO 24617-6: Language resource management – Semantic annotation framework – Part 6: Principles of semantic annotation.* International Standard. International Organisation for Standardisation ISO, Geneva.

ISO 24617-7 (2015) *ISO 24617-7: Language resource management – Semantic annotation framework – Part 7: Spatial information (ISOspace).* International Organisation for Standardisation ISO, Geneva.

Jurafsky, D., E. Schriberg, and D. Biasca (1997) *Switchboard SWBD-DAMSL Shallow-Discourse-Function Annotation: Coders Manual*, Draft 13. University of Colorado, Boulder.

Keizer, S., H.Bunt and V. Petukhova (2011) Multidimensional Dialogue Management. In A. van den Bosch and G. Bouma (eds.) *Interactive Multi-modal Question Answering*, Springer, Berlin, pp. 57-86.

Lapina, V. and V. Petukhova (2017) Classification of Modal Meaning in Negotiation Dialogues. In *Proceedings 13th Joint ACL-ISO Workshop on Interoperable Semantic Annotation (ISA-13)*, Montpellier.

Malchanau, A., V. Petukhova, and H. Bunt (2017) 'Virtual Debate Coach design: Assessing multimodal argumentation performance.' In *Proceedings International Conference om Multimodal Interaction ICMI 2017.*

Petukhova, V., C. A. Stevens, H. de Weerd, N. Taatgen, F. Cnossen, A. Malchanau (2016) Modelling Multi-issue Bargaining Dialogues: Data Collection, Annotation Design and Corpus. *LREC 2016.*

Petukhova, V. and A. Malchanau and H. Bunt (2014) Interoperability of Dialogue Corpora through ISO 24617-2-based Querying. In *Proceedings 9th International Conference on Language Resources and Evaluation (LREC 2014*, Reykjavik, pp. 4407-4414.

Petukhova, V., Gropp, M., Klakow, D., Eigner, G., Topf, M., Srb, S., Moticek, P., Potard, B., Dines, J., Deroo, O., Egeler, R., Meinz, U., Liersch, S., Schmidt, A. (2014) The DBOX Corpus Collection of Spoken Human-Human and Human-Machine Dialogues. In *Proceedings 9th International Conference on Language Resources and Evaluation (LREC 2014*, Reykjavik.

Petukhova, V. and L. Prévot, and H. Bunt (2011) Discourse Relations in Dialogue. In: *Proceedings 6th Joint ACL-ISO Workshop on Interoperable Semantic Annotation (ISA-6)*, Oxfor, pp. 80-92.

Pustejovsky, J., J. Moszkowicz,, and M. Verhagen (2013) A linguistically grounded annotation language for spatial information. *Traitement Automatique des Langues* 53: 87-113.

Pustejovsky, J., K. Lee, H. Bunt, and L. Romary (2010) ISO-TimeML: An International Standard for Semantic Annotation. In: *Proceedings Seventh International Conference on Language Resources and Evaluation (LREC 2010)*, Malta. ELRA, Paris, pp. 394–397.

Wijnhoven, K. (2016) Annotation Representations and the Construction of the DialogBank. MA Thesis, Tilburg University.

Appendix A Dimensions and Communicative Functions in ISO 24617-2:2012

The table below lists the 56 communicative functions defined in ISO 24617-2.

Table 1: ISO 24617-2 communicative functions

General-Purpose Communicative Functions	Dimension-Specific Communicative Functions	
	Function	Dimension
Inform	AutoPositive	Auto-Feedback
- Agreement	AutoNegative	
- Disagreement	AlloPositive	Allo-Feedback
- - Correction	AlloNegative	
- Answer	FeedbackElicitation	
- - Confirm	Stalling	Time Management
- - Disconfirm	Pausing	
Question	Turn Take	Turn Management
- Set-Question	Turn Grab	
- Propositional Question	Turn Accept	
- - Check-Question	Turn Keep	
- Choice-Question	Turn Give	
Request	Turn Release	
- Instruct	Self-Error	Own Communication Man.
- - Address Offer	- Retraction	
- - - Accept Offer	- - Self-Correction	
- - - Decline Offer	Completion	Partner Communication Man.
Suggest	Correct Misspeaking	
Address Suggest	Interaction Structuring	Discourse Structuring
- Accept Suggest	- Opening	
- Decline Suggest	Init-Greeting	Social Obligations Man.
Offer	Return Greeting	
- Promise	Init-Self-Introduction	
Address Suggest	Return Self-Introduction	
- Accept Suggest	Apology	
- Decline Suggest	Accept Apology	
	Thanking	
	Accept Thanking	
	Init-Goodbye	
	Return Goodbye	

The Revision of ISO-Space, Focused on the Movement Link

Kiyong Lee
Korea University
Seoul, Korea
`ikiyong@gmail.com`

James Pustejovsky
Brandeis University
Waltham, MA, U.S.A.
`jamesp@cs.brandeis.edu`

Harry Bunt
Tilburg University
Tilburg, the Netherlands
`harry.bunt@uvt.nl`

Abstract

Focusing on the revision of the movement link in the annotation scheme, tagged <moveLink>, this paper presents a systematic way of converting the first official edition of ISO-Space to its second edition with revisions required at the specification levels, both abstract and concrete. Even after the loss of its status as an ISO standard, the first edition is still expected to be compatible with the second edition at least at the level of semantics.

1 Introduction

The annotation scheme for static and dynamic spatial information, commonly called *ISO-Space*[1], was officially published as part of the first edition of ISO 24617-7:2014 (E) standard. Before the publication of this standard, there were some preliminary working versions such as the ones proposed by Pustejovsky et al. (2010) and Pustejovsky and Yocum (2013) that had treated event-paths as part of the basic entity types for the spatial annotation scheme. Following these preliminary proposals, the first official edition of ISO-Space (ISO, 2014b), henceforth to be referred to by ISO-Space (2014), also listed event-paths as a basic entity type, but failed to implement them in constructing annotation structures overall.

As Lee (2016) pointed out, this failure made the annotation structures, specified in abstract set-theoretic terms by the first edition of ISO-Space, non-isomorphic to the corresponding structures represented in a concrete markup format. This is a serious mismatch in an annotation scheme between its so-called *abstract syntax* and each of its representation formats, called *concrete syntaxes*, based on the abstract syntax.[2] Pustejovsky and Lee (2017) and Lee (2018) continued to show that the annotation of the movement link, tagged <moveLink>, mostly overlapped the task of semantic role annotation, specified in ISO (2014a). Furthermore, the movement link in the first edition failed to conform to the general triplet link structure $<\eta, E, \rho>$, first formulated by Bunt et al. (2016) and then specified as required by another ISO standard 24617-6 Principles of semantic annotation (ISO, 2016). The conformance of the movement link to this triplet structure is basically required to be made interoperable with other parts of the ISO 24617 standard on semantic annotation frameworks such as ISO-TimeML (ISO, 2012), which treats event-based temporal annotation.

Much work has already been done in applying ISO-Space (2014) as an ISO standard to the semantic annotation of raw corpora or the construction of semantic systems. It is thus necessary to make the first edition of ISO-Space compatible with its second edition so that earlier applications still remain valid and can easily be updated according to the second edition if needs arise. This paper aims at showing how the first official edition of ISO-Space (ISO, 2014b) can be made compatible with the revised edition,[3] by:

---

[1] See Pustejovsky (2017) for an overview of ISO-Space.

[2] According to Bunt (2010) and Bunt (2011), a semantic annotation scheme consists of an abstract syntax, a set of concrete syntaxes, and a semantics. The abstract syntax defines well-formed annotation structures in set-theoretic terms, while a concrete syntax based on it provides a format for representing annotation structures. The annotation structures defined by the abstract syntax can be represented in different formats which are semantically equivalent, since the semantics specifies the interpretation of the abstract annotation structures.

[3] Following Bunt et al. (2018), this paper focuses on the compatibility of the original version with a new version in order to save various applications based on the original. The revisions in the new version are required for various independent reasons. The compatibility of a revised version with its original is thus not considered as a necessity, but rather as something desirable.

relating old annotation structures into new ones in a systematic way (sections 4.2 and 4.3) and turning the semantic interpretations of old annotations into those based on event-paths as in the new annotations (section 4.4).

2 Specification of <moveLink> in ISO-Space (2014)

ISO-Space (2014) has no event-paths implemented in its concrete syntaxes. As a result, the movement link, tagged <moveLink> in XML, carries many of the path-related features.[4]

(1) List A.12 Attributes for the <moveLink> tag

```
attributes = identifier, [trigger], [source], [goal], [midPoint], [mover],
[ground], [goalReached], [pathID], [motionSignalID], [comment];
identifier = mvl, decimal digit, decimal digit;
   {*The identifier is tagged "xml:id" for XML documents,
   otherwise "id".  Examples are:  mvl3, mvl20*}
trigger = IDREF; {*ID of a <motion> that triggered the link*}
source = IDREF; {*ID of a location/entity/event tag at the
   beginning of the event-path *}
goal = IDREF; {*ID of a location/entity/event tag at the end of the event-path*}
midPoint = IDREFS;
   {*ID(s) of event-path midpoint location/entity/event tags*}
mover = IDREF; {*ID of the location/entity/event tag whose location changes*}
ground = IDREF;
   {*ID of a location/entity/event tag that the @mover participant's motion
   is relative to *}
goalReached = "yes" | "no" | "uncertain";
pathID = IDREF;
   {*ID of a <path> tag that is identical to the event-path of the
   @trigger <motion>*}
motionSignalID = IDREFS;
   {*ID(s) of <motionSignal> tag(s) that contributes path or manner information
   that the @trigger <motion> carries *}
comment = CDATA;
```

The following example shows how the 2014 specification of <moveLink> operates:

(2) a. Markables Tagged:

> John$_{se1}$ flew$_{m1}$ to$_{ms1}$ Miyazaki$_{pl1}$ through$_{ms2}$ Narita$_{pl2}$ and Haneda$_{pl3}$.

b. Annotated:

```
<moveLink xml:id="mvl1" trigger="#m1" goal="#pl1" midPoint="#pl2,#pl3"
mover="#se1" goalReached="yes" motionSignalID="#ms1,#ms2"/>
```

This specification fails to represent what entities are being related by <moveLink>.

3 Revised Specifications

3.1 Metamodel and Basic Assumptions

Figure 1 presents the metamodel or general structure of revised ISO-Space.

Here we focus on the movement link, tagged <moveLink>, only. It is triggered by a motion and then relates a spatial entity to an event-path. This spatial entity is a mover or object which is triggered by a motion to traverse its trajectory, called *event-path*. A case referred to by "An overcrowded bus plunged

---

[4]See ISO 24617-7:2014, List A.12.

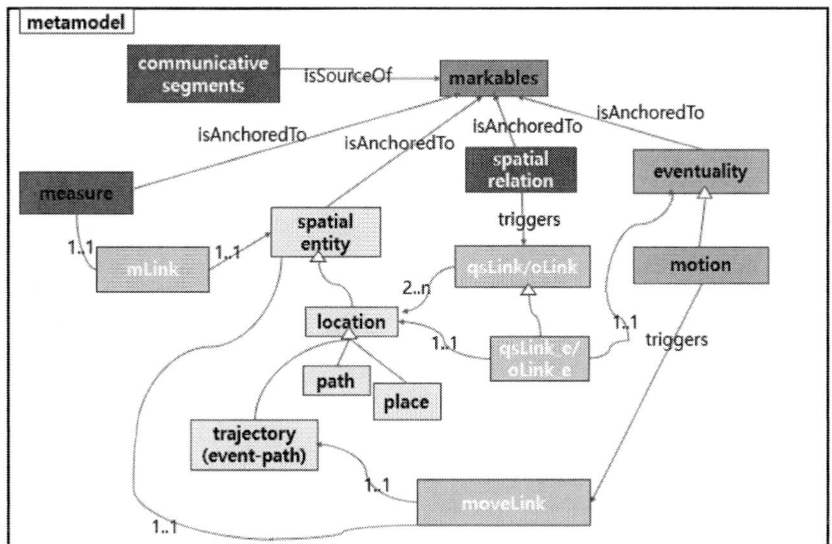

Figure 1: Metamodel of Revised ISO-Space

off a mountain road into a gorge in northern India" is an example, where the bus is treated as a *spatial entity* and a trajectory from the mountain road down to a gorge is an *event-path*.[5]

There are some basic assumptions according to which the movement link, `<moveLink>`, is reformulated in revised ISO-Space:

(3) a. **Axiom**: Every motion-event triggers a trajectory or route, called *event-path*, that a mover traverses: $\forall e[motion(e) \rightarrow \exists\{r, x\}[eventPath(r) \wedge triggers(e, r) \wedge mover(x, e) \wedge traverses(x, r)]]$[6]

  b. **Definition**: An event-path is a finite directed series of locations.

  c. **Implementation**: An event-path is represented as a *non-consuming tag*, which is anchored to an empty string of text segments, but uniquely identifiable.

In the revised edition of ISO-Space, the `<moveLink>` is treated as a path-delimiting relation that conveys information about a moving about, traversing a trajectory or event-path. As a genuine but directed finite path, the event-path is understood to have a *start* and an *end* with denumerably many *mid* locations between them. Locations may include points, intervals, paths or (two-dimensional) areas. For a case like an event expressed by "A truck sped off Massachusetts Turnpike", the truck's speeding off is understood to have started on Massachusetts Turnpike or some point on that highway (path). Hence, terms such as *begin point* or *endpoint* are replaced by more general terms like *start* or *end*, respectively. These locations delimiting event-paths may not be explicitly mentioned, but they must exist, each being uniquely defined.

3.2 Serialization in a Concrete Syntax

In an XML-based concrete syntax, the two elements `<eventPath>` and `<moveLink>` are implemented each with a list of attribute-value specifications. These may be represented in extended BNF (ISO/IEC, 1996), which is found expressively more powerful than DTD (data-type declaration), as follows:

(4) Attribute-Value Specification for `<eventPath>`

```
attributes = identifier, target, trigger, start, mids, end,
```

---

[5]ISO-Space includes among spatial entities those objects that are not genuinely spatial, but are involved in a spatial relation or in a motion.

[6]Rather than the variable p, which is reserved for propositions, the variable r is chosen to represents event-paths, which may also be called *routes*.

```
        [spatialRelator], [comment];
    {*The attributes in brackets [ ] are opitonal; others are required.*}
  identifier = ep, positive integer;
  target = EMPTY;
  trigger = IDREF; {*ID of a motion*}
  start = IDREF | EMPTY;
    {*ID of a location or EMPTY. A location may include a path or area.*}
  mids = IDREFS | IDREF | EMPTY; {*IDs of locations, ID of a path, or EMPTY*}
  end = IDREF | EMPTY; {*ID of a location or EMPTY*}
  spatialRelator = IDREFS; {*IDs of <spatialRelation>s that delimit an event-path
    with its @start, @end or @mids*}
  comment = CDATA;
```

Each instance of a motion-event triggers an event-path and each event-path is uniquely associated with a motion-event. Such a motion-event is represented by the attribute @trigger with a specific value referring to that motion-event associated with an event-path. As a finite path, every event-path has two ends: one is identified as its start and the other one as its end, because it is directed. Hence, the attributes @start, @mids, and @end are required attributes. Their values are *unspecified* if these locations are not explicitly mentioned.[7]

(5) Attribute-Value Specification for <moveLink>

```
  attributes = identifier, figure, ground, relType, [goalReached], [comment];
    {*The attributes in brackets [ ] are optional; others are required.*}
  identifier = mvL, positive integer;
  figure = IDREF; {*ID of a moving object*}
  ground = IDREF; {*ID of an event-path*}
  relType = CDATA | "traverses";
    {*CDATA allows other more specific values such as the motion-event involved
    than the general value "traverses".*}
  goalReached = "yes"|"no";
    {*If @goalReached is uncertain, then it is unspecified.*}
  comment = CDATA;
```

This specification conforms to the general triplet structure $<\eta, E, \rho>$, where η is represented by the value of the attribute @figure, E by the value of @ground, and ρ by that of @relType. Optional attributes such as @goalReached or @comment are freely allowed without violating the triplet structure of links.

Here is an example:

(6) a. Text: John flew to Miyazaki through Narita and Haneda.

   b. Markables Tagged:
   John$_{x1}$ flew$_{m1}$ $\emptyset_{ep1}$ pred="fly" to$_{sr1}$ Miyazaki$_{pl1}$ through$_{sr2}$ Narita$_{pl2}$ and Haneda$_{pl3}$.

   c. Annotated:
```
   <motion xml:id="m1" target="flew" pred="fly" tense="past" goal="#pl1"/>
   <eventPath xml:id="ep1" target="" trigger="#m1" start=""
     end="#pl1" mids="#pl2,#pl3" spatialRelator="#sr1,#sr2"/>
   <moveLink xml:id="mvL1" figure="#x1" ground="#ep1" relType="fly_through"
     goalReached="yes"/>
```

---

[7]Spatial relators such as *from*, *to*, and *through* just define the start, end, and mids of an event-path, without carrying any semantic content. Once the delimiting bounds of an event-path are marked up, the function of spatial relators is discharged.

As shown in (c), the annotation of an event-path, tagged <eventPath>, is treated as a complex entity structure referring to other entity structures just like link structures.[8]

3.3 Outline of Semantics

The semantics of revised ISO-Space is formulated on the basis of its abstract syntax, but its interpretation rules apply to the semantic interpretations of annotation structures as represented by a concrete syntax. Here is an example for the annotation structures represented in (4c). Each of the annotation structures is interpreted as a Discourse Representation Structure (DRS), as defined in Kamp and Reyle (1993)'s Discourse Representation Theory, through the interpretation function σ, as shown below:[9]

(7) DRSs:

Entity: $\sigma(John_{x1}) := [named(x, john), person(x)]$

Motion: $\sigma(flew_{m1}) := [fly(m_1), past(m_1), goal(\sigma_{pl1}, m_1)]$

Locations: $\sigma(Miyazaki_{pl1}) := [named(l_1, Miyazaki), airport(l_1)]$,

$\qquad \sigma(Narita_{pl2}) := [named(l_2, Narita), airport(l_2)]$,

$\qquad \sigma(Haneda_{pl3}) := [named(l_3, Haneda), airport(l_3)]$

Event-path: $\sigma(\emptyset_{ep1}) := [eventPath(r), triggers(m_1, r), endsAt(r, l_1), mids(r, <l_2, l_3>)]$

Link: $\sigma(mvL1) := [fly\_through(x_1, r), goalReached]$

The entity structures of the entity types *entity, motion, location*, and *event-path* represented in (4c) are each interpreted by σ as a DRS. The link structure corresponding to <moveLink> is interpreted as a DRS by combining the interpretations of those entity structures. All of the unbound variables are to be interpreted existentially and the commas interpreted as conjunctions. For the movement link, all these DRSs can be compositionally combined.

First, on the basis of neo-Davidsonian event semantics[10], which treats predicates as each applying to an event as an individual entity and with a list of participants in that event, we have the following interpretation of $traverses(x_1, p)$:

(8) Definition 1: $\forall\{x, r\}[traverses(x, r) \rightarrow \exists\{m, x\}[moves(m), mover(x, m), pathOf(r, m)]$

Second, *goalReached* is treated as a truth-value carrying proposition. Its interpretation requires a decomposition to predicates involving spatio-temporal properties:

(9) Definition 2:
$[goalReached \rightarrow \exists\{m, x, l, t\}[moves(m), mover(x, m), location(l), goal(l, m), time(t), terminatesAt(m, t),$
$locatedAt(x, <l, t>)]]$

This is interpreted as saying that the motion of moving terminated at the time t and at that time t the mover x was at the location l.[11]

goalReached may also be defined in terms of an event-path, as shown below:

(10) Definition 3:
$[goalReached \rightarrow \exists\{m, l, r\}[moves(m), goal(l, m), eventPath(r), triggers(m, r), endsAt(r, l), goal(l, m)]]$

This means that if a goal is reached, then there is a motion-event with a goal that triggers an event-path such that the goal matches the end of the event-path.

The attribute @goalReached is optional with its possible values, either "true" or "false". Consider:

(11) a. Lee$_{x1}$ climbed$_{m1}$ $\emptyset_{ep1}$ up to$_{sr1}$ [the peak of Mt. Halla]$_{pl1}$, but Kim$_{x2}$ couldn't $\emptyset_{m2}$ $\emptyset_{ep2}$.

---

[8] An annotation structure consists of entity structures and link structures. An entity structure is a pair $<m, s>$, where m is a markable and s, semantic information, while a link structure is a relation over entity structures, with its relation type specified.

[9] The notation used here can easily be converted into the box notation commonly used in DRT.

[10] See Davidson (1967) and Parsons (1991) and other related works.

[11] See Mani and Pustejovsky (2012) for the spatio-temporal interactions involving motions.

b.
```
<motion xml:id="m1" target="climbed" pred="climb" tense="past" goal="#pl1"/>
<eventPath xml:id="ep1" trigger="#m1" end="#pl1" spatialRelator="#sr1"/>
<moveLink xml:id="mvL1" figure="#x1" ground="#ep1" relType="climb_to"
goalReached="yes"/>
```

c.
```
<motion xml:id="m2" target="" pred="climb" tense="past" goal="#pl1"/>

<eventPath xml:id="ep2" trigger="#m2" end=""/>

<moveLink xml:id="mvL1" figure="#x2" ground="#ep2" relType="climb_to"

goalReached="no"/>
```

Lee succeeded in reaching the goal because the end of the event-path triggered by his climbing matched the goal of his climbing. Kim, on the other hand, failed to reach the goal, for the end of his climbing path was unspecified, failing to match the goal.[12]

4 Compatible Revision

4.1 Overview

As pointed out by Bunt et al. (2018), the notion of compatibility, related to semantic annotation schemes, works at three different levels: abstract syntax, concrete syntax, and semantics. Here we are concerned with compatibility at the semantic level. From an operational point of view, *semantic compatibility* is understood as follows:

(12) Given two versions, v_1 and v_2, of a semantic annotation scheme,
   v_1 is semantically compatible with v_2 only if the information annotated by v_1 is also annotated by v_2 independent of how it is annotated.

Applied to ISO-Space, the compatibility of its first edition with its revised edition means a one-way process can be defined for converting the annotations of the first edition to those according to the second edition. The revision may not invalidate the first edition of ISO-Space (2014) from a theoretical point of view, but when the new edition of an ISO standard is published, the first edition legally loses its status as an ISO standard.

In this paper we focus on the movement link (`<moveLink>`) and entity structures associated with it in the first edition of ISO-Space, presenting a procedure for reformulating them in the revised edition.[13] There are two steps to the conversion:

(13) i. Rename all of the path-related attributes in the movement link `<moveLink>` in ISO-Space (2014);
   ii. Move all of the path-related attributes to an `<eventPath>` restored in the revised version of ISO-Space.

Renaming attributes in a revision only affects the representation of annotation structures in some concrete format, but does not affect the semantics, although the range of attribute values may change. Changing the attribute name @beignPoint to @start, for example, only widens the range of their values from a point topossibly a line or an area. This allows to treat examples like "The car sped off Massachusetts Turnpike."

4.2 Renaming

The proposed renaming process is summarized in Table 1:
With an ID of a motion as value, the attribute @trigger remains the same in both of the versions. In the revised version, the attributes @source and @goal are renamed with path-related terms, @start and @end, respectively. The attribute @midpoint is renamed @mids, a more general term that allows its

---

[12]Kim's failure to reach the goal was made certain with the expression of *couldn't*. If it is uncertain, the optional attribute @goalReached is not marked up in `<moveLink>`.

[13]This procedure should be discussed in abstract terms, independent of representational issues, but is discussed in concrete terms to make it easier to understand what changes are being made.

Table 1: Renaming Attributes for <moveLink> in ISO-Space (2014)

ISO-Space (2014)	Revised	Possible values or Comments
IDprefix=mvl	IDprefix = "mvL"	
trigger	NOT CHANGED	ID of a <motion>
source	start	ID of a location (place or path)
goal	end	ID of a location @goal moves to <motion> as its attribute
midPoint	mids	IDs of locations
mover	figure	ID of a moving object
ground	NOT CHANGED	Values change to ID of <eventPath>
goalReached	NOT CHANGED	"yes" | "no"
pathID	REMOVED	incorporated into @mids
motionSignalID	REMOVED	incorporated into <eventPath>
comment	NOT CHANGED	CDATA

value to be a location which is either a place or a path, or a list of such locations. The attribute @mover took a more general name @figure as in other links. The attribute @ground remains the same, but has the ID of <eventPath> as value. The attribute @goalReached remains as an optional attribute in revised <moveLink> elements with its possible value listed as either "yes" or "no". Being optional, @goalReached may not be specified; if so, its value is interpreted as being "uncertain". The two attributes, @pathID and motionSignalID, are removed, but incorporated into @mids and <eventPath>, respectively.

4.3 Reallocation

Having modified the names of some of the attributes in <moveLink> in ISO-Space (2014), all of the five path-related attributes, @trigger, @start, @end, @mids and @spatialRelator, some of which are renamed, are reallocated from <moveLink> in the first edition to <eventPath> in the revised edition. The remaining four attributes, @figure, @ground, @goalReached, and @comment remain in the movement link <moveLink> with an additional attribute @relType introduced. The three attributes @figure, @ground, and @relType are required to be specified, conforming to the general link structure laid down by the ISO standard 2017-6 Principles of semantic annotation. The attributes @goalReached and @comment are optional, as licensed by these principles.

Table 2 shows how these attributes are reallocated:

Table 2: Reallocation of Attributes in revised ISO-Space

ISO-Space (2014)	Revised		
<moveLink>	<eventPath>	<moveLink>	<motion>
IDprefix="mvl"	IDprefix="ep"	IDprefix="mvL"	IDprifix="m"
[trigger]	trigger		
[source]	[start]		
[goal]	[end]		[goal]
[midPoint]	[mids]		
[mover]		figure	
[ground]		ground	
		relType	
[goalReached]		[goalReached]	
[pathID]			
[motionSignalID]	[spatialRelator]		[manner]
[comment]	[comment]	[comment]	[comment]

Note 1: The attributes in [ ] are optional.

The right-most column shows how the entity structure representation <motion> is modified. There are two attributes @goal and @manner introduced to it. The attribute @*goal* has an ID of a location as its possible value. The value @goal may be the same as that of @end for <eventPath>. Then the value of @goalReached for <moveLink> is "yes"; otherwise, it is "no" or "uncertain", depending other cues. If the value is "uncertain", then @goal is not specified.

The attribute @manner annotates information on the means of a trans-locational motion-event not through <moveLink>, as in the first 2014 edition of ISO-Space, but directly on the entity structure representation <motion>. This allows the removal of the manner-type <motionSignal> from the first edition. Except for these two newly introduced attributes, the original list of attributes for <motion> remains the same in revised ISO-Space just as in the first edition.

4.4 Semantic Compatibility Sketched

For the interpretation of each movement link, tagged <moveLink>, of ISO-Space (2014), we assume the following tuple as standing for a list of basic (discourse) entity types:

(14) $<D, L, m, r>$, where

D a set of discourse entities that include so-called spatial entities, represented by x_1, x_2, etc.;

L a set of locations, l_1, l_2, etc., or sequences of locations that may include a static path;

m is a motion;

r a dynamic route, called *event-path*.

This specifies variables for each of the entity types.

Then, associated with the attribute specification of <moveLink> in the concrete syntax of ISO-Space (2014), we have the following interpretations as DRSs:

(15) a. Given:

```
attributes = identifier, [trigger], [mover], [source], [goal], [midPoint],
[ground], [goalReached], [pathID], [motionSignalID], [comment];
```

b. For $motion(m_i)$ and $eventPath(r)$,[14]

$\sigma(\texttt{trigger}_{mi}) := triggers(m_i, r)$;

$\sigma(\texttt{mover}_{sei}) := [mover(x_i, m_i), eventPath(r), traverses(x_i, r)]$;

$\sigma(\texttt{source}_{pli}) := startsAt(r, l_i)$;

$\sigma(\texttt{goal}_{plj}) := [goal(l_j, m_j), endsAt(r, l_j)]$ if goalReached="yes";

$\sigma(\texttt{goal}_{plj}) := goal(l_j, m_i)$ if goalReached="no" or "uncertain";

$\sigma(\texttt{midPoint}_{\{pl_1, pl_2, \ldots\}}) := mids(r, <l_1, l_2>)$;

$\sigma(\texttt{pathID}_{pi}) := [path(l_i), overlaps(r, l_i)]$.

c. By combining them into one DRS together with $[motion(i), eventPath(r)]$, we obtain the overall DRS $\sigma(mvli)$ of the movement link.

All of the DRSs here reflect Axiom (1a) on event-paths and Definitions (1-3) of *goalReached*. The whole process given above makes the DRSs compatible with revised ISO-Space.

Here is an example:

(16) a. ISO-Space (2014):

John$_{se3}$ drove$_{m3}$ to$_{ms4}$ Worecester$_{pl3}$ on$_{ss3}$ [Massachusetts Turnpike]$_{p1}$.

b. Annotation:

```
<moveLink xml:id="mvl3" trigger="m3" mover="se3" goal="pl3"
    goaReached="true" motionSignalID="ms4" pathID="p1"/>
```

c. Interpretation of each of the entity structures:

$\sigma(\text{John}_{se3}) := [named(x_3, John), person(x_3)]$

$\sigma(\text{drove}_{m3}) := [drive(m_3), past(m_3)]$

$\sigma(\text{Worcester}_{pl3}) := [named(l_3, Worcester), city(l_3)]$

$\sigma(\text{MassachusettsTurnpike}_{p1}) := [named(l_4, Massachusetts\,Turnpike), highway(l_4)]$

---

[14]The domain of σ is a (possibly singleton) set of attribute-value pairs associated with annotation structures.

d. Interpretation of the movement link structure with an event-path variable r:

$$\sigma(mvl3) := [[triggers(m_3, r), mover(x_3, m_3), eventPath(r), drives\_through(x_3, r)],$$
$$[goal(l_3, m_3), endsAt(r, l_3), path(l_4), overlaps(l_4, r)]]^{15}$$

The interpretation $\sigma(mvl3)$ of ISO-Space (2014) above is considered as conveying the information obtained jointly from the interpretation of an event-path and that of the revised movement link in its revised edition. This is validated by Axiom (1a) and the interpretation of the proposition $goalReached$.

5 Concluding Remarks

Revision should not invalidate all of the costly past work. As discussed by Bunt et al. (2018) in this volume, compatibility is a requirement for revision. Such compatibility, especially as understood at the semantic level, guarantees the preservation of information in the process of revision. This paper has tried to show how such a requirement is a desirable option as compatibility of ISO-Space (2014) with its revised edition, by presenting a way of deriving compatible semantic forms on the basis of Axiom (1a) from unrevised annotations. Although we have shown it in this paper, the revision of the movement link (`<moveLink>`) has been required by other independent reasons such as its conformity to and its interoperability with other parts of the ISO 24617 standard on semantic annotation framework, as discussed in Lee (2012), Lee (2016), Pustejovsky and Lee (2017), and Lee (2018).

Other modifications than that of `<moveLink>` have been made in the revised edition of ISO-Space (ISO, 2014b). The measure link, tagged `<mLink>`, is such a case.[16] The modification of `<mLink>` as well as other parts in ISO-Space is not as complicated as the revision of `<moveLink>`. We thus assume that the conversion of the specifications for other entity and link structures in the first edition into those of its revised edition can be achieved relatively easily.

Acknowledgements

Thanks to Roland Hausser for the useful discussion of downward vs. upward compatibility, Tianyong Hao for reading a preliminary version with comments, and anonymous reviewers for their constructive and detailed comments.

References

Bunt, Harry. 2010. A methodology for designing semantic annotation languages exploiting semantic-syntactic ISO-morphisms. In Alex C. Fang, Nancy Ide, and Jonathan Webster (eds.), *Proceedings of the Second International Conference on Global Interoperability for Language Resources* (ICGL2010), pp.29-46. Hong Kong.

Bunt, Harry. 2011. Abstract syntax and semantics in semantic annotation, applied to time and events. Revised version of Introducing abstract syntax + semantics in semantic annotation, and its consequences for the annotation of time and events. In E. Lee and A. Yoon (eds.), *Recent Trends in Language and Knowledge Processing*, pp.157-204. Hankukmunhwasa, Seoul.

Bunt, Harry, Volah Petukhova, Andrei Malchanau, and Kars Wijnhoven. 2016. The Tilburg DialogBank corpus. *Proceedings of 10th Edition of the Language Resources and Evaluation Conference* (LREC2016), pp. xx-yy. May 2016, Portorož, Slovenia.

Bunt, Harry, Emer Gilmartin, Simon Keizer, Volha Petukhova, Catherine Pelachaud, Laurent Prévot and Mariët Theune. 2018. Downward compatible revision of dialogue annotation. In Harry Bunt (ed.), *Proceedings of the 14th Joint ACL–ISO Workshop on Interoperable Semantic Annotation (isa-14)*, pp. xx–yy. Workshop of COLING 2018, August 25, 2018, Santa Fe, NM, U.S.A.

Davidson, Donald. 1967. The logical form of action sentences. In N. Rescher (ed.), *The Logic of Decision and Action*, pp. 81120. University of Pittsburgh Press, Pittsburgh.

Kamp, Hans, and Uwe Reyle. 1993. *From Discourse to Logic: Introduction to Modeltheoretic Semantics of Natural Language, Formal Logic and Discourse Representation Theory (Studies in Linguistics and Philosophy)*. Kluwer, Dordrecht.

---

[15] `motionSignalID` is not translated.

[16] See Lee (2015), Hao et al. (2017), and Hao et al. (2018).

Hao, Tiyanong, Yunyan Wei, Jiaqi Qiang, Haitao Wang, and Kiyong Lee.. 2017. The representation and extraction of quantitative information. In Harry Bunt (ed.), *Proceedings of the 13th Joint ACL–ISO Workshop on Interoperable Semantic Annotation (isa-13)*, pp. 74–83. Workshop of IWCS 2017, September 19, 2017, Montpellier, France.

Hao, Tiyanong, Haotai Wang, Xinyu Cao, and Kiyong Lee. 2018. Annotating measurable quantitative information for an ISO standard. In Harry Bunt (ed.), *Proceedings of the 14th Joint ACL–ISO Workshop on Interoperable Semantic Annotation (isa-14)*, pp. xx–yy. Workshop of COLING 2018, August 25, 2018, Santa Fe, NM, USA.

ISO. 2012. *ISO 24617–1 Language resource management – Semantic annotation framework (SemAF) – Part 1: Time and events.* International Organization for Standardization, Geneva

ISO. 2014a. *ISO 24617–4 Language resource management – Semantic annotation framework (SemAF) – Part 7: Semantic roles (SemAF-SR).* International Organization for Standardization, Geneva.

ISO. 2014b. *ISO 24617–7 Language resource management – Semantic annotation framework (SemAF) – Part 7: Spatial information.* International Organization for Standardization, Geneva.

ISO. 2016. *ISO 24617-6 Language resource management - Semantic annotation framework (SemAF)- Part 6: Principles of semantic annotation.* International Organization for Standardization, Geneva.

ISO/IEC. 1996. *ISO/IEC 14977 Information technology - Syntactic metalanguage - Extended BNF.* International Organization for Standardization and International Electrotechnical Commission, Geneva.

Lee, Kiyong. 2012. Interoperable spatial and temporal Annotation Schemes. In Harry Bunt, Manuel Alcantara–Plá, and Peter Wittenburg (eds.), *Joint ISA-7 Workshop on Interoperable Semantic Annotation (isa–7), SRSL-3 Workshop on Semantic Representation for Spoken Language, and I2MRT Workshop on Multimodal Resources and Tools*, pp. 61–68. LREC 2012 workshop, 26–27 May 2012, Istanbul, Turkey.

Lee, Kiyong. 2015. The semantic annotation of measure expressions in ISO standards. In Harry Bunt (ed.), *Proceedings of the 11th Joint ACL–ISO Workshop on Interoperable Semantic Annotation (isa–11)*, pp. 55–66. Workshop at the 11th International Conference on Computational Semantics (IWCS 2015), April 14, 2015, Queen Mary University of London London, UK.

Lee, Kiyong. 2016. An abstract syntax for ISOspace with its `<moveLink>` reformulated. In Harry Bunt (ed.), *Proceedings of the LREC 2016 Workshop, 12th Joint ACL–ISO Workshop on Interoperable Semantic Annotation (isa-12)*, pp. 28–37. Workshop of LREC 2016, May 23–28, 2016, Portorož, Slovenia.

Lee, Kiyong. 2018. Revising ISO-Space for the semantic annotation of dynamic spatial information in language. *Language and Information* 22.1, 221–245. The Korean Society for Language and Information.

Mani, Inderjeet, and James Pustejovsky. 2012. *Interpreting Motion: Grounded Representations for Spatial Language.* Oxford University Press, Oxford.

Parsons, Terence. 1991. *Events in the Semantics of English: A Study in Subatomic Semantics.* The MIT Press, Cambridge, MA.

Pustejovsky, James. 2017. ISO–Space: Annotating static and dynamic spatial information. In Nancy Ide and James Pustejovsky (eds.), *Hanbook of Linguistic Annotation*, pp. 989–1024. Springer, Berlin.

Pustejovsky, James, Jessica L. Moszkowicz, and Marc Verhagen. 2010. ISO-Space Specification: Version 1.3 (October 5, 2010). includes discussion notes from the Workshop on Spatial Language Annotation, the Airlie Retreat Center, VA, September 26-29, 2010.

Pustejovsky, James and Zachary Yocum. 2008. Capturing motion in ISO-SpaceBank. In Harry Bunt (ed.), *Proceedings of the 9th Joint ACL–ISO Workshop on Interoperable Semantic Annotation (isa-9)*, pp. 25-34. Potsdam, Germany

Pustejovsky, James, and Kiyong Lee. 2017. Enriching the notion of path in ISOspace. In Harry Bunt (ed.), *Proceedings of the 13th Joint ACL–ISO Workshop on Interoperable Semantic Annotation (isa–13)*, pp. 134–139. September 19, 2017, Montpellier, France.

Chat, Chunk and Topic in Casual Conversation

Emer Gilmartin
ADAPT Centre
Trinity College Dublin
`gilmare@tcd.ie`

Carl Vogel
School of Computer Science and Statistics
Trinity College Dublin
`vogel@tcd.ie`

Abstract

Casual conversation does not follow a highly interactive 'ping-pong' structure but rather develops as a sequence of 'chat' and 'chunk' phases. Chat phases are highly interactive stretches amenable to Conversation Analysis, while chunk phases present as longer monologic stretches where one speaker dominates. Chunk phases can often be described in terms of genre, often manifesting as narrative. We describe an annotation scheme for chat and chunks, the chat and chunk annotation performed on six long (c. 1 hour) multiparty casual conversations, and outline plans to compare these chat and chunk annotations to topic annotations on the same data.

1 Introduction

Casual conversation, where participants talk 'for the sake of talking' rather than using spoken interaction to perform a practical task such as the purchase of a pizza, is fundamental to human social life. Dialog technology, particularly in the domains of healthcare, education, and entertainment is starting to focus on modelling such conversation in order to create more realistic dialog agents. Successful applications will require knowledge of the characteristics of such talk and annotated data to underpin modelling. Practical, 'task-based' or instrumental talk has been well studied and there exist several corpora of such interactions, including the ICSI and AMI meeting corpora, and the MapTask and Lucid Diapix 'knowledge gap task' corpora (Janin et al., 2003; McCowan et al., 2005; Anderson et al., 1991; Baker and Hazan, 2011). Casual social or interactional talk is less well studied, and existing corpora of such interactions tend to be collections of relatively short dyadic conversations or first encounters, such as the Cardiff Conversational Database, and the Spontal and Nomco corpora (Aubrey et al., 2013; Edlund et al., 2010; Paggio et al., 2010). However, much casual talk is multiparty and can last for extended periods. Casual talk has been described in terms of multi-turn phases of chat/chunk, and in terms of successive topics. Both descriptions provide a view of casual conversation above the utterance level – a level of granularity useful in understanding casual talk and in designing artificial talk. In this paper, we describe ongoing work on multiparty casual conversation. We briefly overview casual conversation in terms of its form and function, describe the annotation of chat and chunk phases in a dataset of such conversations, and discuss plans to contrast these annotation with annotations of topic made on the same data.

2 Casual Conversation - Chat, Chunks, and Topic

Casual conversation occurs whenever humans gather (Malinowski, 1923). Examples include short conversations when people meet, intermittent talk between workers on topics unrelated to the job, or longer dinner table or pub conversations. The duration of such interactions can vary from short 'bus stop' conversations to ongoing interactions which lapse and start again over several hours. Such talk is thought to build social bonds and avoid unfriendly or threatening silence, rather than simply to exchange information (Jakobson, 1960; Brown and Yule, 1983; Dunbar, 1998). In task-based or instrumental encounters, participants assume clear pre-defined roles ('customer-salesperson', 'teacher-student') which can strongly influence the timing and content of their contributions, even if roles vary over the course of an encounter. However, in casual talk, participants have equal speaker rights and can contribute at any time (Cheepen, 1988, p. 90). The form of such talk is also different to that of task-based exchanges –

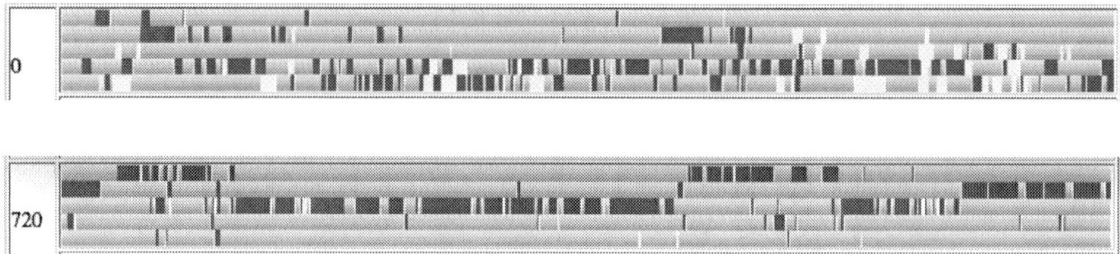

Figure 1: Examples of chat (top) and chunk (bottom) phases in two stretches from a 5-party conversation in the dataset. Each row denotes the activity of one speaker across 120 seconds. Speech is dark grey, and laughter is white on a light grey background (silence. The chat frame, taken at the beginning of the conversation (running from 0 to 120 seconds), can be seen to involve shorter contributions from all participants with frequent laughter. The chunk frame, taken from later in the conversation, running from 720 to 830 seconds, shows longer single speaker stretches.

with less reliance on question-answer sequences and more on commentary, storytelling, and discussion (Thornbury and Slade, 2006; Wilson, 1989). Instrumental and interactional exchanges differ in duration; task-based conversations are bounded by task completion and tend to be short, while casual conversation can go on indefinitely. In terms of structure greater than the utterance level, casual conversation seems to proceed in phases (Laver, 1975; Ventola, 1979), often beginning with ritualised opening greetings, light uncontroversial small talk, and in longer conversations more informative centre phases (consisting of sequential but overlapping topics), and then back to ritualised leave-takings (Ventola, 1979). Slade and Eggins describe sequences of 'chat' and 'chunk' elements in casual conversation (Eggins and Slade, 2004, p. 230). Chunks are segments where (i) 'one speaker takes the floor and is allowed to dominate the conversation for an extended period', and (ii) the chunk appears to move through predictable stages – that is, it is generic. 'Chat' segments are highly interactive and managed locally, turn by turn, as several participants contribute utterances with many questions and short comments. Chat frequently occurs at the start of a conversation and is often used to 'break the ice' among strangers involved in casual talk, (Laver, 1975). As the conversation progresses, chat phases are interspersed with chunk phases. The 'ownership' of chunks seems to pass around the participants in the talk, with chat linking one chunk to the next (Eggins and Slade, 2004). In a study of conversational data collected during workplace coffee breaks, Slade found that around fifty percent of all talk could be classified as chat, while the rest comprised longer form chunks from the following genres: storytelling, observation/comment, opinion, gossip, joke-telling and ridicule. Figure 1 shows examples drawn from our data of typical chat and chunk phases in a 5-party conversation, produced from annotations made using the scheme described in Section 3.1 below.

Topic is often used to segment conversations at a level above the utterance. The notion of topic in discourse has been studied extensively but a concise definition is difficult to find. Topic has been described at sentence level and discourse level (Lambrecht, 1996; Van Dijk, 1977), and as a manifestation of speakers' intentions (Passonneau and Litman, 1997). For the present work, we consider topic in the sense of the 'aboutness' of a stretch of talk or coherent segment of discourse about the same thing – what is being talked about. In terms of topic, task-based interactions often have the contents of the conversation pre-defined. A meeting has an agenda and it is perfectly normal for the chairperson to impose topics for discussion, while the task of buying a pizza imposes what is talked about during the transaction (toppings, price). In casual conversation there is no chairperson and topics are often introduced by means of a statement or comment by a participant which may or may not be taken up by other participants. Thus topic shifts or changes may suceed or fail and cannot be predicted as easily prior to the conversation or mandated by any one participant. The goal of this work is to explore how casual talk can be segmented into stretches of chat and chunk phases or into topics, how easily these phenomena can be annotated, and any correlations between the two.

Corpus	Participants	Gender	Duration (s)
D64	5	2F/3M	4164
DANS	3	1F/2M	4672
DANS	4	1F/3M	4378
DANS	3	2F/1M	3004
TableTalk	4	2F/2M	2072
TableTalk	5	3F/2M	4740

Table 1: Source corpora and details for the conversations used in dataset

3 Data and Annotation

We base our work on a set of 6 long (c. 1 hour) multiparty conversations, from the D64, DANS and TableTalk corpora (Oertel et al., 2010; Hennig et al., 2014; Campbell et al., 2006). Table 1 shows details of participant numbers, gender, and conversation duration for each of the six conversations, which were chosen to have a balance of participant numbers.

All of the conversations were recorded in a living room setting or around a table, where participants were instructed to speak or not as the mood took them. As these conversations were face to face and multiparty, automatic segmentation or transcription was not possible, and thus the recordings were hand segmented at the intonational phrase level and transcribed. Details of the dataset and annotation can be found in (Gilmartin et al., 2018b). Below we describe the annotation of chat and chunk phases in some detail and more briefly describe the topic annotation being carried out on the data.

3.1 Annotation of Chat and Chunk Phases

Chat and chunk phases were marked using an annotation scheme devised from the definitions of chat and chunk phases given in (Eggins and Slade, 2004, p. 230), and the descriptions given by Slade of her PhD work on transcripts of chat and chunk phases in casual talk (Slade, 2007). For an initial classification, conversations were divided by first identifying the 'chunks' and considering everything else 'chat'. This was done using the first, structural part of Slade and Eggins' definition of a chunk as 'a segment where one speaker takes the floor and is allowed to dominate the conversation for an extended period.' (Eggins and Slade, 2004). The following guidelines were created to aid in the placing of chat/chunk boundaries.

Start   A chunk starts when a speaker has established himself as leading the chunk. So, in a story, the speaker will be starting the story, and the story will be seen to go on. This guideline is necessarily vague as Slade and Eggins' definition does not give a fiure for 'an extended period'

Stop   To avoid orphaned sections, a chunk is ended at the moment the next element (chunk or chat) starts.

Aborted   In cases where a story is attempted, but aborted before it is established, this is left as chat. In cases where there is a diversion to another element mid-story, for example, and a return later, all three elements are annotated as though they were single chunks/stretches of chat but the chunks are given the same title with indices to distinguish them. For example, if Speaker A was midway through a story about a football match she'd seen in Barcelona, and a short chat developed around the city of Barcelona, after which Speaker A resumed and completed her story, the segments could be marked FootballStoryA1, BarcelonaChat, FootballStoryB

Overlap   Sometimes a new chunk begins where a previous chunk is still tailing off. In these cases the new chunk onset is placed where the new chunk starts, and serves as the closure of the old chunk.

Generic labels	
Type	Chunk: x, Chat: o
Ownership	mark with corresponding speaker code from transcript - a, b,... for chat - z
Story	S Can be further marked with codes denoting subtypes: Narrative (N), Anecdote (A), Exemplum (E), Recount (R)
Observation/Comment	C
Opinion	O
Gossip	G

Table 2: Labelling scheme for chunks

Once the chunk was identified, it could be classified by genre. This process was aided by the taxonomy of the stages of various types of story, given by Eggins and Slade in (Eggins and Slade, 2004) For annotation, a set of codes for the various types of chunk and chat was created. Each code is a hyphen-separated string containing at least a Type signifier for chat or chunk, an Ownership label, and optional subelements further classifying the chunks as shown in Table 3.1.

A Conversational Analysis (CA) style transcription for each conversation was generated from the Praat textgrids used in the segmentation and transcription process. These transcriptions had different coloured text for utterances produced by each participant. Annotators found this presentation easy to read, and found the colour coding useful in distinguishing turns. The resulting transcriptions were read by two annotators and onset and offset of chunks roughly marked. The type of chunk was then decided. The temporal boundaries of each chunk were then marked off more exactly in Praat. Intervals were labelled using the code shown in Table 3.1, marking type of phase (chat - o or chunk - x), subtype of phase (narrative, story, discussion..), name of phase (roughly equivalent to the topic under discussion), and phase 'owner' (main speaker in chunks and everyone in chat phases). As an example, the code **x_s_g_cats** would denote a chunk phase where the main speaker is **g** and the chunk, which was in story form, was about cats. A total of 213 chat and 358 chunk phases were identified across the six conversations. The topic annotation is ongoing. For the first pass of the topic annotation, two annotators are asked to mark the conversations in terms of 'aboutness', and advised to mark both central zones where topics are clear and points are topics changed. This methodology is based on work demonstrating that largely untrained or naive annotators demonstrate high levels of agreement when asked to segment by topic in meetings and conversations (Ries, 2001; Hearst, 1997), and on Schneider's observations on topic recall in casual conversation (Schneider, 1987). Below we briefly review the results of our analyses of chat and chunk phases in the data, which are more fully described in (Gilmartin et al., 2018a). We discuss how these results may be contrasted with topic data, and our plans for completion of this ongoing work.

4 Analysis of Chat and Chunk Phases

We contrasted the chat and chunk data in terms of phase duration, distribution of laughter and overlap, and how chat and chunk phases were distributed across conversations. Preliminary inspection of chat and chunk duration data (in seconds) showed that the distributions were unimodal but heavily right skewed, with a hard left boundary at 0. Log durations were near normal. The geometric means for duration of chat and chunk phases in the dataset were 28.1 seconds for chat and 34 seconds for chunks. The chat and chunk phase durations (raw and log) are contrasted in the boxplots in Fig 2, where it can be seen that there is considerably more variability in chat durations. Wilcoxon Rank Sum tests showed significant differences in the distributions of the untransformed durations for chat and chunk ($p < 0.01$). A Welch Two Sample t-test showed significant difference in log duration distributions ($p < 0.01$).

The findings on chunk duration are not speaker, gender or conversation specific in our preliminary experiments. Both laughter and overlap were found to be far more prevalent in chat than in chunk phases, reflecting the light and interactive nature of chat phases. We also investigated the frequency and

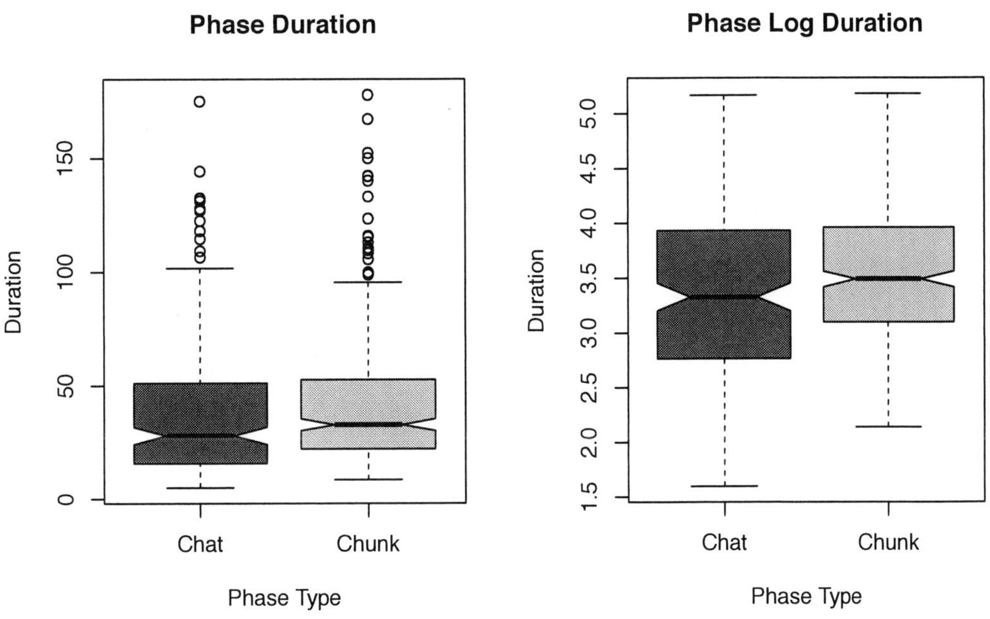

Figure 2: Boxplots of phase duration in Chat vs Chunk in raw and log transformed data

distribution of laughter in chat and chunk phases, finding that laughter accounts for approximately 9.5% of total duration of speech and laughter production in chat phases and 4.9% of total duration of speech and laughter production in chunk phases. Overlapping speech was also found to be more common in chat than in chunk phases. Table 3 shows the occupancy of the conversational floor for all conversations in chat and chunk phases. The number of speakers ranges from 0 (global silence), 1 (single speaker), 2 (2 speakers in overlap) to n-1 where n is the number of speakers in the conversation.

No. Speaking	Chat	Chunk
0	25.75%	22.14%
1	61.58%	72.27%)
2	11.88%	5.25%
3+	0.73%	0.42%

Table 3: Floor occupancy in percentage (seconds in brackets) in chat and chunk for all conversations

We observed more chat at conversation beginnings, with chat predominating for the first 8-10 minutes of conversations. As the conversation develops, chunks start to occur much more frequently, and the structure is an alternation of single-speaker chunks interleaved with shorter chat segments. Figure 3 shows the probability of a chunk phase being followed by chat or by chunk as conversation continues (only chunk phases can be followed by chat). There is a greater tendency for the conversation to go directly from chunk to chunk the longer the conversation continues, perhaps reflecting 'story swapping'.

5 Discussion and Work in Progress

The chunk duration distribution may indicate a natural preference of around half a minute for the time one speaker should dominate a conversation. It will be very interesting to compare this with the topic annotations, to see if topic length is comparable. Laughter has been shown to appear more often in social talk than in meeting data, and to happen more around topic endings and topic changes (Gilmartin et al.,

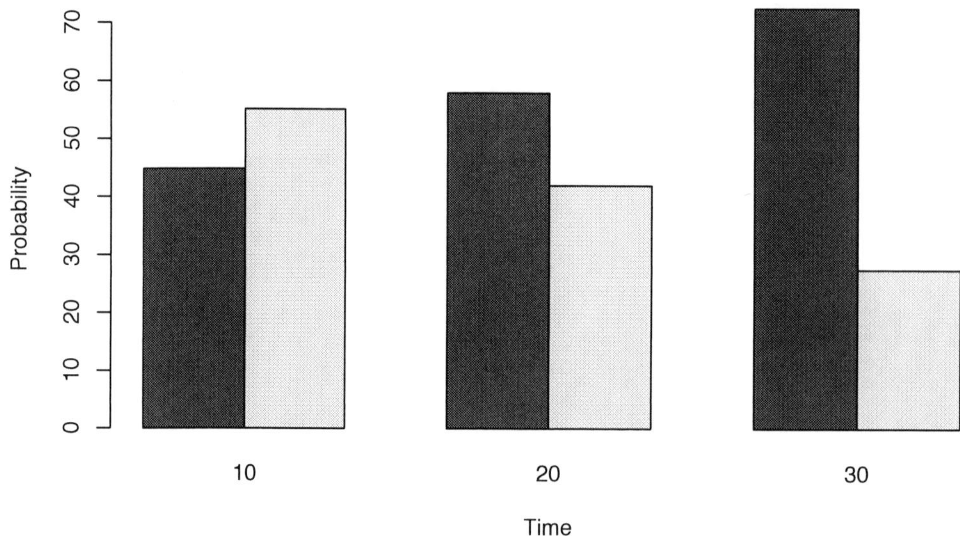

Figure 3: Probability of chunk-chunk transition (black) and chunk-chat transition (grey) in ten-minute bins for first 30 minutes of conversation

2013; Bonin et al., 2012). This is consistent with observations on chat and chunk phases – laughter is more common in chat phases which often provide a 'buffer' between single speaker chunks. The structure of chat following chunks is also consistent with Schneider's description of 'idling' phases at the end of topics, where speakers contribute short utterances referring back to previous content rather than committing to starting a new topic. In terms of the distribution of phases across conversations, chat was more common at the start of the multiparty conversations studied, in line with descriptions of casual conversation in the literature, where the initial stages comprise light interactive talk. Chunk phases become more prevalent as conversation continues. These observations lead to the interesting question of whether, once the conversation is well established, the extent of topics may correlate with the stretch from the beginning of one chunk to the beginning of the next chunk, with any intervening chat reflecting the decay of one topic and the process of starting the next. We intend to investigate this question using the topic annotation currently under way on the data.

6   Conclusion

We have described ongoing research into the 'superstructure' of multiparty casual talk. Our preliminary chat and chunk annotations show that these phases are significantly different in structure, and raise interesting questions on how chat/chunk structure may link to topic distribution. We are hoping to answer these questions in the near future. In addition to the better understanding of conversational structure we hope to gain, this work has practical implications. Automatic annotation of topic without transcripts is not possible, and transcripts of multiparty dialog are often of poor quality. It is often practically and ethically difficult to produce or obtain accurate knowledge of what is being said, but it may be possible to record that speech is happening. As chat and chunk phases may be largely described in terms of the temporal distribution of speech and silence among participants, if there are correlations between chat/chunk phases and topic distribution, such knowledge could be used to better follow the progress of casual talk, and ultimately model such interactions for a number of useful applications.

Acknowledgements

This work is supported by Science Foundation Ireland (Grant 13/RC/2106) and the ADAPT Centre (www.adaptcentre.ie) at Trinity College, Dublin.

References

A.H. Anderson, M. Bader, E.G. Bard, E. Boyle, G. Doherty, S. Garrod, S. Isard, J. Kowtko, J. McAllister, J. Miller, et al. 1991. The HCRC map task corpus. *Language and speech*, 34(4):351–366.

A. J. Aubrey, D. Marshall, P. L. Rosin, J. Vandeventer, D. W. Cunningham, and C. Wallraven. 2013. Cardiff Conversation Database (CCDb): A Database of Natural Dyadic Conversations. In *Computer Vision and Pattern Recognition Workshops (CVPRW), 2013 IEEE Conference on*, pages 277–282.

Rachel Baker and Valerie Hazan. 2011. DiapixUK: task materials for the elicitation of multiple spontaneous speech dialogs. *Behavior research methods*, 43(3):761–770.

Francesca Bonin, Nick Campbell, and Carl Vogel. 2012. Laughter and topic changes: Temporal distribution and information flow. In *Cognitive Infocommunications (CogInfoCom), 2012 IEEE 3rd International Conference on*, pages 53–58. IEEE.

Gillian Brown and George Yule. 1983. *Teaching the spoken language*, volume 2. Cambridge University Press.

N. Campbell, T. Sadanobu, M. Imura, N. Iwahashi, S. Noriko, and D. Douxchamps. 2006. A multimedia database of meetings and informal interactions for tracking participant involvement and discourse flow. In *Proceedings of LREC 2006*, pages 391–394, Genoa, Italy.

Christine Cheepen. 1988. *The predictability of informal conversation*. Pinter London.

R. Dunbar. 1998. *Grooming, gossip, and the evolution of language*. Harvard Univ Press.

Jens Edlund, Jonas Beskow, Kjell Elenius, Kahl Hellmer, Sofia Strömbergsson, and David House. 2010. Spontal: A Swedish Spontaneous Dialogue Corpus of Audio, Video and Motion Capture. In *Proceedings of LREC 2010*, pages 2992–2995, Malta.

S. Eggins and D. Slade. 2004. *Analysing casual conversation*. Equinox London.

Emer Gilmartin, Francesca Bonin, Carl Vogel, and Nick Campbell. 2013. Laugher and Topic Transition in Multiparty Conversation. In *Proceedings of the SIGDIAL 2013 Conference*, pages 304–308, Metz, France. Association for Computational Linguistics.

Emer Gilmartin, Christian Saam, Carl Vogel, Nick Campbell, and Vincent Wade. 2018a. Just talking - modelling casual conversation. In *Proceedings of the SIGDIAL 2018 Conference*, pages 51–59, Melbourne, Australia. Association for Computational Linguistics.

Emer Gilmartin, Carl Vogel, and Nick Campbell. 2018b. Chats and Chunks: Annotation and Analysis of Multiparty Long Casual Conversations. In *Proceedings of LREC 2018*, pages 1964–1970.

Marti A Hearst. 1997. Texttiling: Segmenting text into multi-paragraph subtopic passages. *Computational linguistics*, 23(1):33–64.

Shannon Hennig, Ryad Chellali, and Nick Campbell. 2014. The D-ANS corpus: the Dublin-Autonomous Nervous System corpus of biosignal and multimodal recordings of conversational speech. In *Proceedings of LREC 2014*, pages 3438–3443, Reykjavik, Iceland.

Roman Jakobson. 1960. Closing statement: Linguistics and poetics. *Style in language*, pages 350–377.

Adam Janin, Don Baron, Jane Edwards, Dan Ellis, David Gelbart, Nelson Morgan, Barbara Peskin, Thilo Pfau, Elizabeth Shriberg, and Andreas Stolcke. 2003. The ICSI meeting corpus. In *Acoustics, Speech, and Signal Processing, 2003. Proceedings.(ICASSP'03). 2003 IEEE International Conference on*, volume 1, pages I–364.

Knud Lambrecht. 1996. *Information structure and sentence form: Topic, focus, and the mental representations of discourse referents*, volume 71. Cambridge University Press.

John Laver. 1975. Communicative functions of phatic communion. In *Organization of behavior in face-to-face interaction*, pages 215–238. Mouton The Hague.

B. Malinowski. 1923. The problem of meaning in primitive languages. *Supplementary in the Meaning of Meaning*, pages 1–84.

Iain McCowan, Jean Carletta, W. Kraaij, S. Ashby, S. Bourban, M. Flynn, M. Guillemot, T. Hain, J. Kadlec, and V. Karaiskos. 2005. The AMI meeting corpus. In *Proceedings of the 5th International Conference on Methods and Techniques in Behavioral Research*, volume 88, page 100.

Catharine Oertel, Fred Cummins, Jens Edlund, Petra Wagner, and Nick Campbell. 2010. D64: A corpus of richly recorded conversational interaction. *Journal on Multimodal User Interfaces*, pages 1–10.

Patrizia Paggio, Jens Allwood, Elisabeth Ahlsen, and Kristiina Jokinen. 2010. The NOMCO multimodal Nordic resource - goals and characteristics. In *Proceedings of LREC 2010*, pages 19–21, Malta.

Rebecca J. Passonneau and Diane J. Litman. 1997. Discourse segmentation by human and automated means. *Comput. Linguist.*, 23(1):103—139.

Klaus Ries, 2001. *Segmenting Conversations by Topic, Initiative, and Style*, page 51—66. Lecture Notes in Computer Science. Springer, Berlin, Heidelberg.

Klaus Peter Schneider. 1987. Topic selection in phatic communication. *Multilingua*, 6(3):247–256.

Diana Slade. 2007. *The texture of casual conversation: A multidimensional interpretation*. Equinox London.

Scott Thornbury and Diana Slade. 2006. *Conversation: From description to pedagogy*. Cambridge University Press.

Teun A Van Dijk. 1977. Sentence topic and discourse topic. *Papers in Slavic philology*, 1:49–61.

Eija Ventola. 1979. The structure of casual conversation in English. *Journal of Pragmatics*, 3(3):267–298.

John Wilson. 1989. *On the boundaries of conversation*, volume 10. Pergamon Oxford.

Annotation of the Syntax/Semantics interface as a Bridge between Deep Linguistic Parsing and TimeML

Mark-Matthias Zymla

University of Konstanz

`Mark-Matthias.Zymla@uni-konstanz.de`

Abstract

This paper presents the development of an annotation scheme for the syntax/semantics interface that may feed into the generation of (ISO-)TimeML style annotations. The annotation scheme accounts for compositionality and calculates the semantic contribution of tense and aspect. The annotation builds on output from syntactic parsers and links information from morphosyntactic cues to a representation grounded in formal semantics/pragmatics that may be used to automatize the process of annotating tense/aspect and temporal relations.

1 Credits

We gratefully acknowledge funding from the Nuance Foundation. We also thank collaborators from the *Infrastructure for the Exploration of Syntax and Semantics (INESS)* and the *ParGram* projects.

2 Introduction

In this paper we report on the progress of a project concerned with the development of a novel annotation scheme for tense/aspect. This annotation scheme is designed to interact with morphosyntactic information that is the result of deep parsing. It is also designed to be crosslinguistically applicable and was first introduced in (Zymla, 2017a; Zymla, 2017b).

The annotation scheme is designed to be applied to linguistically parsed input, i.e. syntactic treebanks. In particular, we work with analyses resulting from deep syntactic parsing within the ParGram effort (Butt et al., 2002), which includes a wide variety of different types of languages. In addition to working with data from the ParGramBank (Sulger et al., 2013), we adapted crosslinguistically applicable testsuites found in (Dahl, 1985). Furthermore, we began experimenting with application of the annotation scheme to a treebank based on the TempEval-3 TimeML corpus (UzZaman et al., 2013).[1] Our annotation scheme is also compatible with representations resulting from universal dependency grammars (section 4).

The annotation scheme goes beyond the effort presented by Ramm et al. (2017) in that it can interact with both deep linguistic parsers as well as the shallower dependency parsers solely utilized by Ramm et al. (2017). It is also generally cross-linguistically applicable, rather than being restricted to the closely related European languages English, German and French. Furthermore and most importantly it allows for the annotation and dynamic calculation of the semantics and pragmatics of tense/aspect that go beyond the individual morphosyntactic cues.

---

[1]The treebanks are available at `http://clarino.uib.no/iness` (Rosén et al., 2012)

However, our annotation scheme is not aimed at replacing existing standardized annotations schemes such as (ISO)-TimeML (Pustejovsky et al., 2003), but rather aims at bridging a gap between TimeML style annotations and the actual morphosyntactic cues about tense/aspect found crosslinguistically. The original TimeML corpora (TimeBank (Pustejovsky et al., 2003)) and TempEval3 (UzZaman et al., 2013)) provide semantic annotation in terms of temporal links. However, it is difficult to test predictions concerning the mapping from form to meaning based on the syntax/semantics interface provided in TimeML.

A notable innovation of the annotation scheme presented here is that it distinguishes between several layers of semantic (and pragmatic) reasoning by calculating annotations at three different tiers. In the first two tiers abstract meaning concepts are calculated directly from the morphosyntactic input. Tier 3 then relates the calculated semantic concepts to the actual (explicit or implicit) temporal context. This dynamic annotation scheme consists of two parts: the syntax/semantics interface, a rule-based system that maps syntactic information onto abstract semantic properties and, secondly, a layer that describes the temporal ordering of eventualities. This is explained in detail in section 3.

The subordinated goal in this paper is to explore the benefits of a bi-directional pipeline between TimeML corpora and our annotation scheme. For this pipeline we take inspiration from the Reichenbachian Tense Markup Model (RTMML) (Derczynski, 2016) and other work whose goal is to incorporate (neo-)Reichenbachian tense semantics, e.g., Gast et al. (2016). This means that we provide a semantic annotation that restricts the relations between speech time, reference time and run time of any given event expressed by a verb form (section 5).

The goals of our project are thus two-fold: The first goal, which has been in the focus of the project up to now, is to provide a cross-linguistically valid annotation scheme for the syntax/semantics interface that takes into account the current state of the art with respect to formal semantics (see Tonhauser (2015) for an overview). The current goal is to improve upon the linguistically motivated temporal relation typing and to thus contribute to the growing system of ISO-compliant temporal annotations.

3 Development of the Annotation Scheme

Our annotation scheme is loosely based on the Reichenbachian tradition (Reichenbach, 1947). In the Reichenbachian framework tenses are categorized by means of three different kinds of points/intervals in time. First, the speech time S corresponds to the moment of utterance. Second, the reference time R encodes a time a given utterance refers to. Third, the event time E describes the time during which an event takes place. Example (1) illustrates a subset of the tenses proposed in Reichenbach's system. In simple tenses the reference time and the event time overlap and are related to the speech time in a straightforward fashion via *anteriority*, *posteriority* or *overlap*. The need for the reference time especially arises due to constructions such as the *past perfect*, which is used when talking about events that happened before a certain point in the past. The Reichenbachian system treats the past perfect as one tense. To achieve a more flexible system, it can be translated into an interval calculus, where E,R and S are intervals $t, ...t^n$ and the relations $(\prec, -)$ between these points are what we define as tenses (Comrie, 1985). Thus, the annotation of the past perfect results in two separate tenses with a specific relative order – a result of the underlying semantic composition — as shown in the XML annotation of the semantic representation (2) in terms of temporal relations (trel).[2]

---

[2]TimeML utilizes TLINKs to express temporal relations between elements (events,temporal expressions). However, our `trels` are distinct from TLINKS. There are two main reasons: i) the `trels` may express sets of relations (see *future perfect*), ii) the `trels` may express a relation between variables and/or concrete temporal elements.

(1)   simple past: $E - R \prec S$ past perfect: $E \prec R \prec S$

     simple present: $S - E - R$ present perfect: $E \prec S - R$

     simple future: $S \prec E - R$ future perfect: $S \prec E \prec R,\, S - E \prec R,\, E \prec S \prec R$

(2)   **Sample annotation – Representation**

    a.   (Yes), I <u>had met</u> Peter.

```
<doc time="now"/>
<timeref xml:id="t0" target="doc_time"/>
<timeref xml:id="t1" target="#token2"
 tense abstract="past" semantics="r2"/>            had

<event xml:id="e1" target="#token3">             met
<!-- conceptual description -->
<concepts xml:id="c0">
<tense="past"/> ... </concept></event>
<!-- temporal realization -->
<trel xml:id="r1" relation="e1<t1"/>             E < R
<trel xml:id="r2" relation="t1<t0"/>             R < S
```

At the center of the annotation scheme is the mapping from syntax to semantics. The first layer of the annotation maps morphosyntactic elements onto abstract semantic exponents (Tier 1) as per the tense system introduced above. For example, the overt morphosyntactic cues express past in (3a), present in (3b) and non-past in (3c).[3] In a second layer, semantic components can be combined to construct new meanings not (necessarily) encoded in the parts they were derived from (mimicking compositionality, but more powerful) in a rule-based system (Tier 2). This is necessary for examples like (4b), which presupposes that the verbal predicate is directly or indirectly pluralized (NUM pl). In this case, (4b) is pluralized indirectly by virtue of the plural object.

Tiers 1 and 2 form a set of implication rules. These rules generate abstract meanings, in the sense that they are not yet anchored to a time line. (4b) is analyzed as a habitual imperfective in (4b), while (4c) is non-past with an explicit reference time introduced by the adverbial 'tomorrow' ((4c)). This reference time is integrated in Tier 3, which weaves the Tier 1 and 2 information into the explicit and implicit context. Tier 3 also serves as the locus for pragmatic reasoning and contains so-called compatibility rules since it relies on the compatibility of the overt morphosyntactic cues and the given context.

(3)   a. John <u>left</u>.   b. John <u>build-s houses</u>.   c. John <u>komm-t morgen an.</u>
                                                            John arrive-Pres tomorrow

(4)   a.   TENSE past $\rightarrow$ TEMP-REF 'past' : $\lambda t.t \prec t_0$ Tier 1

    b.   TENSE pres : $\lambda t.t \circ t_0 \wedge$ NUM 'pl' : $\lambda e.pl(e) \rightarrow$
       ASPECT 'imperfective' $\wedge$ A-RESTR 'habitual'[4]   Tier 2

    c.   TEMP-REF 'non-past' : $\lambda t.t \nprec t_0 \wedge$ TIMEREF tomorrow(t_1) $\otimes$
       TEMP-REF 'tomorrow' : $\lambda t.t \nprec t_0 \wedge t \subset t1$ Tier 3

The annotation scheme was developed with two goals: First, to provide a representation of temporal semantic properties in compliance with formal linguistic research. Second, to provide a framework for the research on crosslinguistic semantic variation. We push the idea behind parallel treebanks as for example in the ParGram project (Butt et al., 2002) and the alignment of parallel corpora based on

---

[3] All rules are language specific and illustrate cross-linguistic variation in the mapping from form to meaning. $\rightarrow$ = implication rule, $\otimes$ = compatibility rule; TENSE = morphological tense, TEMP-REF = semantic tense, NUM = semantic verbal number, ASPECT = Viewpoint, A-RESTR = viewpoint interpretation (e.g., progressive, habitual ...).

[4] We omit a formal representation for reasons of space. See (Ferreira, 2016).

their morphosyntax, semantics and pragmatics. As of now, parallel corpora are mostly aligned based on morphosyntactic properties. However, our annotation of the syntax/semantics and pragmatics interface allows for a more fine-grained alignment and thus provides a valuable way forward for cross-linguistic research based on semantically parallel corpora.

4   Normalization Across Syntactic Parsers

One of our main goals is to provide a pipeline between a semantic annotation and syntactic treebanks. For this purpose, we work with an explicit syntax and semantics. We exemplify this in terms of representations derived from the deep linguistic XLE parsers based on LFG (Lexical Functional Grammar), in particular the f(unctional)-structure, which is a syntactic representation that encodes grammatical functions (subject, object, complement) and functional information (e.g., tense, aspect, mood) (Crouch et al., 2017; Bresnan et al., 2015). We can also work with universal dependencies (UD)[5], where dependencies correspond to grammatical functions in LFG and UD features correspond to functional information. The two representations are illustrated in Figure 1 (UD on the left, LFG on the right). Both of these syntactic structures are mappable onto a conceptually equivalent computational structure. We work with a normalization whereby each token of the UD parse corresponds to an entry in a hashmap which contains a list of dependencies and/or features as value. Figure 1 illustrates the normalization of the UD structure adding UD morphosyntactic features.[6]

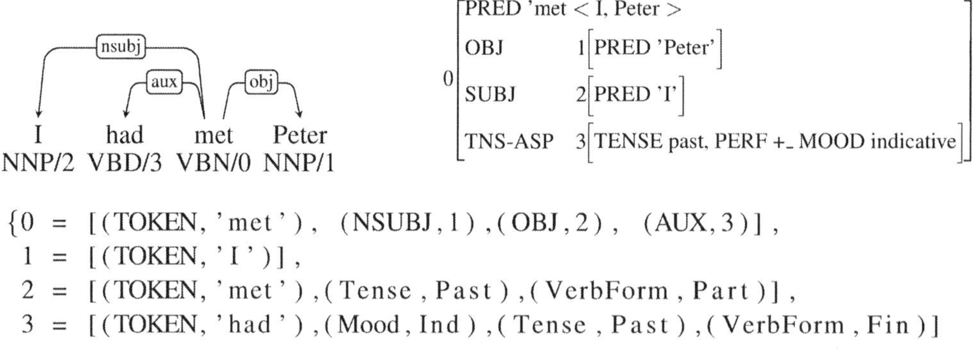

```
{0 = [(TOKEN,'met'), (NSUBJ,1),(OBJ,2), (AUX,3)],
 1 = [(TOKEN,'I')],
 2 = [(TOKEN,'met'),(Tense,Past),(VerbForm,Part)],
 3 = [(TOKEN,'had'),(Mood,Ind),(Tense,Past),(VerbForm,Fin)]
```

Figure 1: Universal dependency structure normalization

Sample annotation – Rules

```
#g AUX #h VerbForm Fin ∧ #h Tense Past →
(#h) TIMEREF past(t) : λt.t ≺ t₀
#g VerbForm Part ∧ #g Tense Past ∧  #g AUX (#h) TIMEREF past(t) →
(#g) TEMP-REF 'past' : λt'.t' ≺ t
```

Figure 2: UD structure annotation

Based on this internal structure the INESS query language (Rosén et al., 2012) that is used to identify syntactic paths in treebanks has been modified to identify elements for annotation. The object of annotation are (sets of) syntactic properties which are expressed in terms of tree paths from the verbal spine

---

⁵http://universaldependencies.org/. We use the Stanford CoreNLP parser (Chen and Manning, 2014)

⁶The idea of the normalization is based on Unhammer (2010). It does not map f-structures and dependency structures on to a formally equal representation, but onto a representation that may be annotated in the same manner. The endeavor of translating f-structures faithfully to dependency structures is discussed in Meurer (2017).

(the root element) to the appropriate morphosyntactic feature. In Figure 2 partial syntactic structures (UD heads, f-structures) are identified via variables (`#g-#o`). For example the expression `#g AUX #h VerbForm Fin` refers to any UD head which stands in an `AUX` relation with another head with the UD feature `VerbForm Fin`. Inside a single rule query variables retain their instantiation, thus the second conjoint of the first rule in Figure 2 can be abbreviated. Semantic elements are associated with a specific head, e.g., `(#h) TIMEREF past(t)`:$\lambda t.t \prec t_0$ tells us that each distinct head that is bound by the variable `#h` (in this case only one if we only consider the sentence in Figure 1) introduces a temporal variable that is restricted to a time that is in the past of the speech time t_0. The second rule in Figure 2 introduces a second tense that is relative to the auxiliary tense.

5 Treebank Annotation — Worked Examples

Table 1 shows statistics on our material with respect to languages, number of sentences, rules (Tier 1 and Tier 2) and compatibilities (Tier 3) for our work concerning just the past tense. Overall 764 sentences in 10 languages were considered. Table 1 shows that the complexity of the syntax/semantics interface with regard to past tense is straightforward in terms of implication rules. However, most sentences are contextually further restricted explicitly (e.g., via temporal modifiers) or implicitly (via context).

The annotation scheme was first developed through sentence level annotations with the idea to provide a qualitatively sound and comprehensive semantic annotation of linguistic categories. For this purpose we produced a treebank based on the typological work by Dahl (1985).

	Total	German	Italian	Polish	Urdu	Indonesian
Sentences	196	56	50	45	47	48
Implication rules	9	3	3	1	3	2
Compatibilities	191	45	39	34	36	37

Table 1: Annotation of the Past Tense

The annotation consists of two sets of rules with different felicity conditions to distinguish semantic and pragmatic processes. Implication rules provide more general but robust meanings derived from the morpho-syntactic input and semantic construction rules (Tier 1 and 2), while compatibility rules anchor meanings in the implicit and explicit context (Tier 3). From another perspective, semantic (i.e. Tier 1 and Tier 2) rules cover meaning grammaticalized in linguistic categories and compatibility (i.e. Tier 3) rules define restrictions implicit in the context or stated by lexical elements (i.e. temporal modifiers). Consequently, Tier 1 and Tier 2 rules generate a context independent, abstract semantic representation that is mapped onto actual contexts by means of the third tier.

Our data shows that two main Reichenbachian relations are relevant: $E \prec S$ and $E \prec R \prec S$. These are a simple temporal backshift of an event (E) or an iterated backshift which situates the event in the past of a past reference point (R).[7] German and Italian express the simple past in two variants: past tense or present perfect morphology. Urdu distinguishes between perfective and past tense morphology (hence the difference in f-structural analysis). Indonesian usually does not specify tense morphologically and requires contextual inferences, but optionally uses perfect auxiliaries to express semantic past tense and iterated past tense.

In (5) a slice of the possible cross-linguistic variation in the expression of the iterated backshift $E \prec$

---

[7] $E, R \prec S$ (simple past) and $E \prec R, S$ (present perfect) are subsumed under under $E \prec S$.

$R \prec S$ is illustrated.[8] Both English (5a) and Urdu (5b) may be considered variants of the prototypical *past perfect*. In contrast, tenseless Indonesian (5c) only optionally employs iterated perfect markers.

(5) [Q: When you came to this place a year ago, did you know Peter?]

    a. (Yes), I <u>had met</u> Peter. $\left[\text{TNS-ASP}\ \left[\text{TENSE past, PERF +}\right]\right]$

    b. (hãã), mãĩ piter=se <u>milaa</u> <u>thaa</u>. $\left[\text{TNS-ASP}\ \left[\text{TENSE past, ASPECT prv}\right]\right]$
        (yes), I   Peter=with meet.Perf be.Past

    c. (ya), saya <u>sudah</u> <u>pernah</u> ber-temu dengan Peter $\left[\text{TNS-ASP}\ \left[\text{PERF +}\right]\right]$
        (yes), 1st already ever   MID-meet with   Peter

```
<timeref xml:id="t3" target="#token15"/>                had

<event xml:id="e2" target="#token16">                  met
<!-- conceptual description ... --> </event>

<trel xml:id="r3" relation="e2≺t3"/>
<trel xml:id="r4" relation="t3≺t0"/>
<trel xml:id="r5" relation="t3=t2" />
```
$$E \prec R$$
$$R_{met} \prec S$$
$$R_{met} = R_{came}$$

Our annotation system takes the possibility of cross-linguistic morphosyntactic variation into account by providing a combination of "translational" (Tiers 1 and 2) and inferencing rules (Tier 3). These rules calculate a formal semantic representation of temporal relations from information provided by deep linguistic parsers like the LFG systems or from UD representations. For Urdu and English, the morphosyntactic cues themselves provide a clear reading of iterated backshift (past perfect). In contrast, these temporal relations must be calculated via inferencing depending on the previous context for the tenseless language Indonesian. However, the end result is parallel in its meaning as expected.

6   Summary and Conclusion

Overall, our annotation scheme provides insights into the syntax/semantics interface by specifying rules as to how morphosyntactic material expresses semantic tense/aspect categories directly and indirectly across languages. This allows for an abstraction over distinct morphosyntactic material with respect to semantic analysis and is an important requirement for a crosslinguistically valid annotation of the syntax/semantics interface. Currently, there are two main approaches to integrating semantic annotations of tense/aspect into TimeML. First, encode semantic variables directly as TIMEX in the annotation (Gast et al., 2016). Second, use a tense/aspect annotation that is independent of the TimeML standard (but compliant with the relevant ISO norms) that serves as a preprocessing step (Derczynski, 2016). In the spirit of the latter, we have developed a neo-Reichenbachian annotation. The system consists of three tiers, whereby the first two tiers comprise of default (Tier 1) and constructed (Tier 2) meanings generated from a robust rule system. The role of the Tier 3 annotation is to resolve ambiguities to the point where explicit TimeML compliant temporal relations may be specified – a process that at this point still requires human assistance. In sum, we present a system that provides: i) crosslinguistically motivated insights into semantic properties of tense/aspect; ii) the possibility of systematically abstracting over crosslinguistic variation; iii) a bridge between deep linguistic parsing and interoperable semantic annotation schemes such as TimeML. This allows us to broaden the research perspectives for qualitative linguistic research by providing tools that allow for the quantitative testing of qualitative predictions.

---

[8] PERF + = perfect construction; prv = perfective; MID = middle voice

References

[Bresnan et al.2015] Joan Bresnan, Ash Asudeh, Ida Toivonen, and Stephen Wechsler. 2015. *Lexical-functional syntax*, volume 16. John Wiley & Sons.

[Butt et al.2002] Miriam Butt, Helge Dyvik, Tracy Holloway King, Hiroshi Masuichi, and Christian Rohrer. 2002. The Parallel Grammar Project. In *Proceedings of the 2002 Workshop on Grammar Engineering and Evaluation*, volume 15, pages 1–7. Association for Computational Linguistics.

[Chen and Manning2014] Danqi Chen and Christopher Manning. 2014. A Fast and Accurate Dependency Parser Using Neural Networks. In *Proceedings of the 2014 Conference on Empirical Methods in Natural Language Processing*, pages 740–750.

[Comrie1985] Bernard Comrie. 1985. *Tense*, volume 17. Cambridge University Press.

[Crouch et al.2017] Dick Crouch, Mary Dalrymple, Ronald M. Kaplan, Tracy Holloway King, John T. Maxwell III, and Paula Newman, 2017. *XLE Documentation*. Palo Alto Research Center.

[Dahl1985] Östen Dahl. 1985. *Tense and Aspect Systems*. Oxford: Blackwell.

[Derczynski2016] Leon RA Derczynski. 2016. *Automatically Ordering Events and Times in Text*, volume 677. Springer.

[Ferreira2016] Marcelo Ferreira. 2016. The Semantic Ingredients of Imperfectivity in Progressives, Habituals, and Counterfactuals. *Natural Language Semantics*, 24(4):353–397.

[Gast et al.2016] Volker Gast, Lennart Bierkandt, Stephan Druskat, and Christoph Rzymski. 2016. Enriching TimeBank: Towards a More Precise Annotation of Temporal Relations in a Text. In *Proceedings of the Tenth International Conference on Language Resources and Evaluation (LREC 2016)*, Paris, France, May. European Language Resources Association (ELRA).

[Meurer2017] Paul Meurer. 2017. From LFG Structures to Dependency Relations. *Bergen Language and Linguistics Studies*, 8(1).

[Pustejovsky et al.2003] James Pustejovsky, Patrick Hanks, Roser Sauri, Andrew See, Robert Gaizauskas, Andrea Setzer, Dragomir Radev, Beth Sundheim, David Day, and Lisa Ferro. 2003. The Timebank Corpus. In *Corpus Linguistics*, volume 2003, page 40. Lancaster, UK.

[Ramm et al.2017] Anita Ramm, Sharid Loáiciga, Annemarie Friedrich, and Alexander Fraser. 2017. Annotating Tense, Mood and Voice for English, French and German. *Proceedings of ACL 2017, System Demonstrations*, pages 1–6.

[Reichenbach1947] Hans Reichenbach. 1947. The Tenses of Verbs. *Elements of Symbolic Logic*, pages 287–298.

[Rosén et al.2012] Victoria Rosén, Koenraad De Smedt, Paul Meurer, and Helge Dyvik. 2012. An Open Infrastructure for Advanced Treebanking. In Jan Hajič, Koenraad De Smedt, Marko Tadić, and António Branco, editors, *META-RESEARCH Workshop on Advanced Treebanking at LREC2012*, pages 22–29.

[Sulger et al.2013] Sebastian Sulger, Miriam Butt, Tracy Holloway King, Paul Meurer, Tibor Laczkó, György Rákosi, Cheikh M Bamba Dione, Helge Dyvik, Victoria Rosén, Koenraad De Smedt, Agnieszka Patejuk, Özlem Çetinoğlu, I Wayan Arka, and Meladel Mistica. 2013. ParGramBank: The ParGram Parallel Treebank. In *ACL*, pages 550–560.

[Tonhauser2015] Judith Tonhauser. 2015. Cross-Linguistic Temporal Reference. *Linguistics*, 1:129–154.

[Unhammer2010] Kevin Brubeck Unhammer. 2010. LFG-based Constituent and Function Alignment for Parallel Treebanking.

[UzZaman et al.2013] Naushad UzZaman, Hector Llorens, Leon Derczynski, James Allen, Marc Verhagen, and James Pustejovsky. 2013. Semeval-2013 Task 1: Tempeval-3: Evaluating Time Expressions, Events, and Temporal Relations. In *Second Joint Conference on Lexical and Computational Semantics (* SEM), Volume 2: Proceedings of the Seventh International Workshop on Semantic Evaluation (SemEval 2013)*, pages 1–9.

[Zymla2017a] Mark-Matthias Zymla. 2017a. Comprehensive Annotation of Cross-Linguistic Variation in the Category of Tense. In *12th International Conference on Computational Semantics*.

[Zymla2017b] Mark-Matthias Zymla. 2017b. Cross-Linguistically Viable Treatment of Tense and Aspect in Parallel Grammar Development. In *Proceedings of the LFG17 Conference*. CSLI Publications.

A Dialogue Annotation Scheme for Weight Management Chat using the Trans-Theoretical Model of Health Behavior Change

Ramesh Manuvinakurike[1]*, **Sumanth Bharadwaj**[2]*, **Kallirroi Georgila**[1]
[1]Institute for Creative Technologies, University of Southern California
[1]`[manuvinakurike,kgeorgila]@ict.usc.edu`, [2]`first_last@yahoo.com`

Abstract

In this study we collect and annotate human-human role-play dialogues in the domain of weight management. There are two roles in the conversation: the "seeker" who is looking for ways to lose weight and the "helper" who provides suggestions to help the "seeker" in their weight loss journey. The chat dialogues collected are then annotated with a novel annotation scheme inspired by a popular health behavior change theory called "trans-theoretical model of health behavior change". We also build classifiers to automatically predict the annotation labels used in our corpus. We find that classification accuracy improves when oracle segmentations of the interlocutors' sentences are provided compared to directly classifying unsegmented sentences.

1 Introduction

Individuals seeking ways to modify their unhealthy lifestyles are interested in the personal experiences of other people who describe how they have changed their unfavorable health behavior (e.g., smoking, poor diet, overeating, etc.). Such experiences are shared as stories where a person who successfully changed their health behavior narrates the journey from an unfavorable to a more favorable lifestyle in a blog or posts in a public forum. There are thousands of such stories. But different stories may have a different impact depending on who reads them. Not every story is relevant to an individual, but rather only a few stories can successfully motivate and provide useful information to a specific reader. This is because people tend to be influenced more by stories related to their personal experiences (Manuvinakurike et al., 2014). Research has shown that such personalized stories delivered to individuals are effective in motivating people to change their unfavorable health behavior successfully (Houston et al., 2011).

People subscribe to the personal experiences of others and seek to gain motivation to change their unfavorable health behavior to an alternative favorable behavior. They do this by looking for the "right" processes that they can benefit from and include in their own lives, e.g., the following advice is suitable for a regular coffee drinker rather than someone who does not drink coffee: "drinking coffee in smaller portions helped me lose weight". A recent survey also showed that individuals trust the stories and experiences shared on the "internet" (by professional health advisers) more than the stories and experiences of a family member or friend (Fox, 2011). This is not so surprising as the plethora of stories available on the internet makes it easier for users to find the "right" story that they can relate to.

Such a phenomenon of sharing stories and experiences on the internet is typically observed in social health advice sharing forums where a user with an unfavorable health behavior submits a post describing their problem. This is followed by peers replying to the post with their own relatable stories or providing suggestions based on their personal experiences. Such forums offer users a platform to share their stories, and provide help and encouragement to other users. Seeking help in this way could prove to be effective in motivating people to change to a healthier lifestyle such as weight loss (Hwang et al., 2010). These forums are popular and continue to gain in popularity. However, while these forums are useful, a real-time conversation where users can engage in a session of question answering and experience sharing could potentially yield more benefits.

---

* Equal contribution.

There is growing interest in building conversational agents that can motivate users to change their health behaviors; see for example Rizzo et al. (2011). Such systems typically have expert-authored content. However, generating expert-authored content tailored to an innumerable number of users is a difficult (if not impossible) task. For this reason there are benefits in pursuing the development of automated chat bots that can engage users in a conversation about changing their health behaviors, and that can be trained on chat-based conversations between regular people (non-experts) who exchange information in order to help one another. It is important to note that we do not claim that such a chat bot could replace an expert but rather act as a companion that could assist users by providing useful pointers towards their goal.

Obesity continues to grow in epidemic proportions. A change in lifestyle could help the population, and this serves as a long-term motivation for our work. We envision agents conversing with and assisting humans by providing advice, stories, and tips that the individuals can benefit from. Once developed, these agents can be used to (i) motivate users to begin their weight loss journey; (ii) provide useful tips on lifestyle changes to users already contemplating to lose weight; (iii) provide advanced suggestions and tips to users already in the process of losing weight; (iv) provide encouragement by reminding users about their goals; and (v) help users maintain their target weight once their goal is reached. However, developing such agents is a challenging problem. The agents need to carefully diagnose the condition of the person seeking to change their health behavior. Based on a variety of constraints the agent has to offer relevant and beneficial advice. For instance, behavior change advice for weight loss to an individual who is obese and looking to lose weight will be very different from the tips offered to an individual who is looking to lose the last few pounds to reach a fat percentage of less than 10%.

Such a "recommendation system" can benefit from research in health behavior change psychology. Advising health behavior change has been studied in the literature of psychology, and various competing theories exist which act as guidebooks in providing the right advice to individuals. One such theory, that we make use of in this work, is called "trans-theoretical model of health behavior change" (Prochaska and Velicer, 1997). This theory has proven successful in modeling health behavior change in individuals and provides a model for such a process (Prochaska and Velicer, 1997; Johnson et al., 2008; Tuah et al., 2011; Mastellos et al., 2014). The theory also provides a mapping from the person's stage in the journey of health behavior change to the classes of actionable items that can be taken to progress from an unfavorable stage to a favorable stage. For example, if the person is contemplating a change in their eating habits but still has not fully committed to the change in their behavior, one of the better pieces of advice to offer to this person is raising the awareness of the ill effects of being on a poor diet. This type of advice would not be relevant to a person who is acting upon their diet plan and is fully aware of the ill effects of a poor diet.

Research in the field of health behavior psychology has been carried out extensively by studying weight loss behaviors in humans. Recently the trans-theoretical model of health behavior change has been used to guide research on virtual human agents for studying the motivation of individuals with regard to weight management (Bickmore et al., 2005; Bickmore and Giorgino, 2006; Bickmore et al., 2013; Manuvinakurike et al., 2014). Our approach is different from the approaches followed in these works. In our work we annotate human-human chats based on the trans-theoretical model whereas previous work used concepts from the trans-theoretical model to guide agent utterances that were authored by human experts. In our work, we develop a corpus containing typed chats between a human health behavior change seeker and a helper. The chat is annotated using labels motivated from dialogue research (Bunt et al., 2012) and the trans-theoretical model of health behavior change for weight management (Prochaska and Velicer, 1997).

Our contributions are as follows: (i) development of a corpus containing dialogues between peers in a weight loss advice seeking session set up as a role-play game between a help seeker and a help provider; (ii) a novel annotation scheme for annotating the corpus; and (iii) models for automatically classifying sentences to one of the annotation labels used in our corpus. The rest of the paper is organized as follows. We begin with describing the data collection methods and experiments in Section 2. We then describe the trans-theoretical model of health behavior change and our novel annotation scheme inspired by this

# users	52
# dialogues	26
# turns	309
# word tokens	1230
average # turns in a conversation	10

Table 1: Statistics of the corpus collected.

model in Section 3. Section 4 describes our classification experiments. Finally, we conclude and outline our plans for future work in Section 5.

2 Data Collection

By collecting chat data we can model not only phenomena based on the trans-theoretical model of health behavior change but also conversational phenomena (e.g., question answering, acknowledgments, etc.) which are usually absent in data from popular social media forum posts. In this work, we use a role-play scenario in a make-belief setting to collect our chat-based dialogue data.

Crowd-sourcing has recently emerged as a popular platform for collecting dialogue data. It has also been popular among researchers studying the health behavior change phenomenon (Créquit et al., 2018). We collect data using the Amazon Mechanical Turk (MTurk) crowd-sourcing platform. The task is set up as a role-play chat game between two turkers (users of MTurk). All the turkers got equal pay irrespective of the quality of their chat. The users on the MTurk are instructed that they will be either assigned the role of a "help seeker" (seeker) or "help provider" (helper). If they are assigned the role of the "help seeker", they are instructed to imagine a scenario where they are overweight and want to lose weight. They are required to have a conversation with their partner to seek help with their weight loss journey. They are also informed that they will be paired with a "help provider" who will assist them with tips to overcome their barriers and help them lose weight. If the users are assigned the role of a "help provider" they are instructed to play the role of a helper who needs to assist the "help seeker" with their goal of losing weight.

Initially we were skeptical about the quality of chat that would result from such a setup. Surprisingly, the chat conversations between the participants yielded very good quality interactions indicating that MTurk could be a good platform for collecting similar chat data sets. The quality of the interaction was measured subjectively. The users were instructed to be kind to one another, and were informed that any abuse would disqualify them from participating in the experiment. The users were also asked to maintain anonymity and not reveal their name or personally identifiable information as the chat data could be released to the public in the future. The users were from the United States and native English speakers. Further demographic information about age and gender were not collected to maintain their anonymity. Once collected, the chat data were annotated by experts using the annotation scheme described in Section 3. Table 1 shows the statistics of the data collected and Table 2 shows a snapshot of an example chat between a helper and a seeker.

3 Annotation

Our novel annotation scheme was designed to leverage the benefits of the trans-theoretical model (TTM), which provides a theoretical framework for modeling the health behavior change process. The TTM also provides the framework for recommending activities to users based on their current stage in the journey of health behavior change. One of the goals of this annotation framework is to leverage the TTM's stages of change and processes of change.

It is important to identify the seeker's current stage of change in order to offer theoretically motivated activity suggestions belonging to one of the processes of change also annotated in the data. Likewise, it is also important to identify the processes for change recommended by the helper which form the activities that can be leveraged to motivate the seeker.

role	chat
helper	[Greeting : Hello]
seeker	[Greeting : Hello]! [Action : Just started my weight loss journey [TimeFrame : a couple months ago]]
helper	[acknowledge : Thats fantastic!] [question : How is it going thus far?]
...	
seeker	[Contemplation : [goal : Id like to get down to 225]]
seeker	[Contemplation : [SR : Ive been around [currWeight : 245-250] for [TimeFrame : years] now]]
helper	[acknowledge : That makes sense!] [question : How much weight have you lost [TimeFrame : thus far?]]
seeker	[Action : About 12 lbs]
...	
seeker	[Action : [question : How did you [SeLi : motivate yourself to work out?]]]
helper	[Action : [SeLi : My motivation always came from changing things up]]
helper	[Action : When [Lifestyle-undes : my music was no longer motivating], I found new music]
helper	[CC : [Lifestyle-undes : When I got bored of some exercises], I found new ones to try]
helper	[Action : [CC : When [Lifestyle-undes : I got sick of my [good-diet : diet]], I found [good-diet : new foods]]]
helper	[Action : [SeLi : That always helped me to keep from feeling stuck]]
seeker	[acknowledge : I can see how that would make a difference]
seeker	[Preparation : [Lifestyle-undes : I tend to stick to one thing, but after [TimeFrame : a couple weeks], my motivation dies out]]
helper	[question : If your free time was at night before, what do you think about trying morning workouts for something new?]
seeker	[acknowledge : That could work]. [Lifestyle-undes : Im a little lethargic in the morning]
seeker	[Contemplation : [Lifestyle-undes : Not exactly I morning person.] But I really dont have to think about getting on a treadmill - just have to do it]
helper	[acknowledge : Nothing a little [good-diet : coffee] cant fix] :)
seeker	[End : Hey thank you for the motivation today!]

Table 2: Example annotated chat interactions between a seeker and a helper exactly as they appear in the data set (with misspellings, lack of punctuation, etc.). SR: Self re-evaluation, SeLi: Self liberation, CC: Counterconditioning.

Section 3.1 describes the TTM and its relation to our work. We use the stages of change and processes of change defined by the TTM as dialogue act labels. We also use traditional dialogue act labels such as questions, greetings, etc. to track the user state.

3.1 Trans-Theoretical Model (TTM) of Health Behavior Change

The two concepts of the TTM that we adopt in this work are called "Stages Of Change" (SOC) and "Processes Of Change" (POC). One of the requirements for performing this kind of annotation is familiarity with the TTM. The annotators need to study the TTM closely. This is one of the limitations of annotating a large data set based on the TTM.[1] The goal of the annotator is to correctly identify the seeker's "stage of change" (point in the journey of weight loss where the seeker is) based on the information that the seeker provides to the helper and the "processes of change" (i.e., activities recommended by the helper

---

[1]Note that the SOC and POC can be identified deterministically by answering questions indicated in the TTM literature. This is something that we have not explored in our current work but keep in mind for our future work.

or indicated by the seeker). Below we describe the SOC and POC labels used in this work.

3.1.1 Stages Of Change (SOC)

The TTM places the users who want to change their health behavior into 5 stages, aptly called "Stages Of Change" (SOC). These stages are based on the individual's awareness and progress made during the health behavior change journey. They include changes from a stage where the individual is not aware that an unfavorable behavior needs to be changed to a stage where the change has been achieved and the individual is working towards avoiding a relapse back to the unfavorable health behavior. These 5 stages of change are:

i) Precontemplation: People in this stage do not wish or do not know how to change their behavior. In our study the users are instructed specifically to role-play an individual who wants to change their behavior, and thus this stage is not observed in our data.

ii) Contemplation: In this stage the users are planning to change their behavior (typically within the next 6 months). Typically the user of such a "health behavior change advice system" is in at least this stage or further.

iii) Preparation: In this stage the users are taking action to change their behavior (typically in a month) and are susceptible to the majority of the processes of change (see Figure 1).

iv) Action: In this stage the users have taken action to change their behavior and are making progress. They are no longer prone to advice about raising consciousness regarding the adverse effects of their unfavorable behavior.

v) Maintenance: In this stage the users have changed their behavior for at least 6 months and are working to avoid relapse.

We identify the appropriate SOC based on the goals described by the seeker. Table 2 shows an example where an individual states that the they have just started their "weight loss journey a couple of months ago" and hence places them in the "Action" SOC. Another example where the user says "I have been wanting to change my behavior soon" would place them in the "Contemplation" SOC. Such statements where users state their goals help the annotators place the seeker into one of the 5 SOC classes.

3.1.2 Processes Of Change (POC)

The "Processes Of Change" (POC) refer to covert and overt activities that users engage in to progress through the SOC (Prochaska and Velicer, 1997). There are totally 10 processes of change that we use in this work:

1. Consciousness raising: Attempt to seek out information concerning their problem behavior. Example: "strength training is supposed to be great for getting in shape".

2. Dramatic relief: Increased emotional experiences followed by reduced affect if an appropriate action can be taken. Examples: "I'm worried about my health", "if I go to 250, I'm done with life".

3. Substance use / Stimulus control: Use of medication/devices/surgery (external substance). Removes cues for unhealthy habits and adds prompts for healthier alternatives. Examples: "I have found success with one of those items that count your steps everyday", "I'm thinking of trying a fitbit".

4. Social liberation: Increase in social opportunities. Example: "me losing weight will help my tag team perform well at a team event".

5. Self re-evaluation: Cognitive and affective assessments of one's self-image. Example: "I want to look like a shark".

6. Helping relationships: Combine caring, trust, openness, and acceptance as well as support for the healthy behavior change. Examples: "I'll have to find a partner", "yeah my mom does zumba and wants me to go".

7. Counter conditioning: Substituting an unfavorable health behavior with a favorable one. Example: "juice has a lot of sugar but there are some different types of almond milks out there or even skim milk".

8. Reinforcement management: Consequences for taking steps in a particular direction. Example: "I do it by giving myself a cheat day only if I met my goals for the week".

9. Self liberation: The belief that one can change and the commitment and re-commitment to act on that belief. Examples: "believe it and have the dedication and you'll be able to succeed at it", "you have the

	Stages of change				
	Precontemplation	Contemplation	Preparation	Action	Maintenance
Consciousness raising	■	■	■		
Environmental re-evaluation	■	■	■		
Dramatic relief	■	■	■		
Helping relationships		■	■	■	
Social liberation		■	■	■	
Self liberation			■	■	
Self re-evaluation			■	■	
Stimulus control				■	
Substance use				■	
Counter conditioning				■	■
Reinforcement management				■	■

Figure 1: Relation between the SOC and POC typically observed in users changing their health behavior. The red block indicates that a POC (row label) is commonly used in a given SOC (column label) for progression, whereas an empty white box indicates that the a POC (row label) is not commonly used in a given SOC (column label) for progression (Prochaska and Velicer, 1997).

ability to lose whatever you want".

10. Environmental re-evaluation: Affective and cognitive assessments of how the presence or absence of a personal habit affects one's social environment. Example: "my brother's band team were coming to visit him and I wanted to lose weight to make him look good".

Relation between SOC and POC: Figure 1 shows the relation between the SOC and the POC in TTM[2]. In this work we annotate the SOC of the seeker and the POC mentioned by both the helper and the seeker. The POC annotations are designed to serve two purposes: (i) to equip future dialogue systems with the capability of providing suggestions based on the seeker's current SOC; and (ii) to track which POC were used by the seeker in the past or the seeker is aware of. The seekers in a given SOC are motivated to progress to the next stage by engaging in a POC. Generally, not all POC are suited for a given SOC. For instance, from Figure 1 we can observe that the POC "consciousness raising" is well suited for the individuals in the "Precontemplation", "Contemplation", and "Preparation" SOC. This is because further information about a behavior stops being useful for an individual in "Action" as the users in this SOC are already aware of the harmful effects of an unfavorable health behavior. This mapping between the SOC and POC is useful for identifying these labels in the data. However, it is important to keep in mind that the TTM provides the relations that we see in Figure 1 as a heuristic and not a rule to follow when performing the annotations. This implies that, while such a mapping is usually true, cases exist where a POC not indicated for a given SOC might be applicable.

3.2 "Other" Labels

We also identify "other" labels in the chat in order to facilitate better understanding of the seeker and helper behaviors. These labels are shown in Table 3. The table shows the labels, descriptions, and a relevant example. The labels include questions, greetings, end of the conversation markers, time information, etc.

We measured the inter-annotator agreement using Cohen's kappa. It was found to be 0.66 for POC, 0.81 for SOC, and 0.72 for other labels annotated in the corpus. The values were calculated at the sentence level. The numbers showed good agreement between 2 expert annotators who were well versed at the TTM concepts and annotated the same 2 dialogues (22 turns).

Shortcomings of the scheme: It was observed that a sentence could fall into multiple POC resulting in lower inter-annotator agreement, e.g., "my mom is helping me eat broccoli for a snack instead of chips", falls under both "helping relationships" and "counter conditioning". Such cases caused disagreements

---

[2]Figure 1 shows the "Stimulus control" POC that was not observed in our data.

Label	Description	Example
question	question	how much weight are you looking to lose?
greeting	represents a greeting	how are you this evening?
goal	weight loss goals	I got back down to 190
time-frame	duration in time	a few months
bad-diet	bad dietary choices	sugar, fat
good-diet	good dietary choices	vegetables
lifestyle-undesired	bad lifestyle choices	ate junk food
acknowledge	acknowledgments	yeah, I know
frequency	frequency of various behaviors	two days of the week
end	end of conversation	thank you
device	equipment that aids weight loss	fitbit
current-weight	current weight	I'm 250 lbs

Table 3: Additional "other" labels annotated in the data set.

between the annotators. In order to account for this, further annotation labels would be needed or the annotation scheme would have to support annotation of each sentence with all applicable labels. However, these changes would make it hard to develop an automated classifier.

4 Experiments

We performed machine learning experiments to automatically predict the annotation labels in our corpus. We build a separate classifier for SOC, POC, and "other" labels (3 classifiers in total). This is because these labels are annotated independent of one another. Each classifier could output one of the corresponding labels or a "null" label. We use logistic regression in Weka (Hall et al., 2009), and since no prior work exists a majority baseline for comparison. The data were preprocessed before the classification was performed. We used the NLTK toolkit for lemmatization (Loper and Bird, 2002) and removed stop words. The features that we used were just words. We report the results on 10-fold cross validation performed on the user sentences.

We predict the labels in two separate experiments: (i) "unsegmented" and (ii) "segmented". For both settings we use the same set of features. In the "unsegmented" version, we predict the classification labels using the complete sentences. Each complete sentence is forwarded to the 3 classifiers and each classifier outputs one of its corresponding labels or the "null" label. For the "segmented" approach we segment the sentences and use each segment as an input to each classifier. Again each classifier outputs one of its corresponding labels or the "null" label.

In the "segmented" approach we assume oracle (perfect) segmentation of the user sentences before classification. In future experiments we plan to perform the segmentation automatically and then predict the label. Note however that the annotations can overlap, which means that an "other" label can be inside a section of the sentence annotated with a SOC or POC label. Similarly, POC and SOC labels can overlap. Hence we use 3 types of segmentations the output of which would be forwarded to each one of the 3 classifiers. Let us consider an example:

[GREET{OTHER}: Hi there] [ACTION{SOC}: I would like to [GOAL{OTHER}: lose weight] but [SL{POC}: exercising] didn't help me much]

The segmentation for the SOC classifier would be:

SEG1: Hi there

SEG2: I would like to lose weight but exercising didn't help me much

The segmentation for the POC classifier would be:

SEG1: Hi there I would like to lose weight but

SEG2: exercising

SEG3: didn't help me much

The segmentation for the "other" label classifier would be:

Task	Unsegmented Majority Baseline	Unsegmented Classification Accuracy	Segmented Classification Accuracy
SOC prediction	0.37	0.44	0.48
POC prediction	0.25	0.41	0.49
Other label prediction	0.18	0.35	0.67

Table 4: Classification results. The differences between the unsegmented and the segmented accuracies as well as the differences between the unsegmented and segmented accuracies and the majority baseline are significant ($p < .05$).

SEG1: Hi there
SEG2: I would like to
SEG3: lose weight
SEG4: but exercising didn't help me much

Table 4 shows our results for each classifier: "unsegmented" majority baseline and accuracy using the "segmented" and "unsegmented" approaches. We observe that the "segmented" approach results in higher classification accuracies.

5   Conclusion & Future Work

In this work we presented a novel annotation scheme for health behavior change motivation chat-based dialogues. Our annotation labels are grounded in the health behavior change psychology literature and are also complemented by standard annotation labels used in conversational data. We also performed automated classification experiments using 3 classifiers for classifying SOC, POC, and "other" labels respectively.

We hypothesize that the sparsity of our data negatively impacts classification accuracy. In a follow up experiment we aim to expand our data set by collecting more chat interactions. However, collection of large data sets can be an issue as our annotations require expert annotators. It will be fruitful to explore the possibility of extracting the annotation labels using crowd-sourcing by providing MTurk annotators with TTM-based questionnaires to guide their annotations. We also plan to extend this work by building a dialogue system that can play the role of the helper.

Acknowledgments

This work was partially supported by the U.S. Army; statements and opinions expressed do not necessarily reflect the position or policy of the U.S. Government, and no official endorsement should be inferred.

References

Timothy Bickmore and Toni Giorgino. 2006. Health dialog systems for patients and consumers. *Journal of Biomedical Informatics*, 39(5):556–571.

Timothy Bickmore, Amanda Gruber, and Rosalind Picard. 2005. Establishing the computer–patient working alliance in automated health behavior change interventions. *Patient Education and Counseling*, 59(1):21–30.

Timothy W. Bickmore, Daniel Schulman, and Candace Sidner. 2013. Automated interventions for multiple health behaviors using conversational agents. *Patient Education and Counseling*, 92(2):142–148.

Harry Bunt, Jan Alexandersson, Jae-Woong Choe, Alex Chengyu Fang, Koiti Hasida, Volha Petukhova, Andrei Popescu-Belis, and David R. Traum. 2012. ISO 24617-2: A semantically-based standard for dialogue annotation. In *Proceedings of LREC*, pages 430–437, Istanbul, Turkey.

Perrine Créquit, Ghizlène Mansouri, Mehdi Benchoufi, Alexandre Vivot, and Philippe Ravaud. 2018. Mapping of crowdsourcing in health: Systematic review. *Journal of Medical Internet Research*, 20(5):e187.

Susannah Fox. 2011. *The social life of health information.* Pew Internet & American Life Project Washington, DC.

Mark Hall, Eibe Frank, Geoffrey Holmes, Bernhard Pfahringer, Peter Reutemann, and Ian H. Witten. 2009. The WEKA data mining software: An update. *ACM SIGKDD Explorations Newsletter,* 11(1):10–18.

Thomas K. Houston, Jeroan J. Allison, Marc Sussman, Wendy Horn, Cheryl L. Holt, John Trobaugh, Maribel Salas, Maria Pisu, Yendelela L. Cuffee, Damien Larkin, et al. 2011. Culturally appropriate storytelling to improve blood pressure: A randomized trial. *Annals of Internal Medicine,* 154(2):77–84.

Kevin O. Hwang, Allison J. Ottenbacher, Angela P. Green, M. Roseann Cannon-Diehl, Oneka Richardson, Elmer V. Bernstam, and Eric J. Thomas. 2010. Social support in an internet weight loss community. *International Journal of Medical Informatics,* 79(1):5–13.

Sara S. Johnson, Andrea L. Paiva, Carol O. Cummins, Janet L. Johnson, Sharon J. Dyment, Julie A. Wright, James O. Prochaska, Janice M. Prochaska, and Karen Sherman. 2008. Transtheoretical model-based multiple behavior intervention for weight management: Effectiveness on a population basis. *Preventive Medicine,* 46(3):238–246.

Edward Loper and Steven Bird. 2002. NLTK: The natural language toolkit. In *Proceedings of the ACL Workshop on Effective Tools and Methodologies for Teaching Natural Language Processing and Computational Linguistics,* pages 63–70.

Ramesh Manuvinakurike, Wayne F. Velicer, and Timothy W. Bickmore. 2014. Automated indexing of internet stories for health behavior change: weight loss attitude pilot study. *Journal of Medical Internet Research,* 16(12).

Nikolaos Mastellos, Laura H. Gunn, Lambert M. Felix, Josip Car, and Azeem Majeed. 2014. Transtheoretical model stages of change for dietary and physical exercise modification in weight loss management for overweight and obese adults. *The Cochrane Library.*

James O. Prochaska and Wayne F. Velicer. 1997. The trans-theoretical model of health behavior change. *American Journal of Health Promotion,* 12(1):38–48.

Albert Rizzo, Belinda Lange, John G. Buckwalter, Eric Forbell, Julia Kim, Kenji Sagae, Josh Williams, JoAnn Difede, Barbara O. Rothbaum, Greg Reger, et al. 2011. SimCoach: An intelligent virtual human system for providing healthcare information and support. *International Journal on Disability and Human Development,* 10(4):277–281.

N. A. Tuah, Cressida Amiel, Samrina Qureshi, Josip Car, Balvinder Kaur, and Azeem Majeed. 2011. Transtheoretical model for dietary and physical exercise modification in weight loss management for overweight and obese adults. *Cochrane Database Syst Rev,* 10.

Annotating Measurable Quantitative Information in Language: for an ISO Standard

Tianyong Hao
South China
Normal University
Guangzhou, China
haoty@126.com

Haitao Wang
China National Institute
of Standardization
Beijing, China
wanght@cnis.gov.cn

Xinyu Cao
China National Institute
of Standardization
Beijing, China
caoxy@cnis.gov.cn

Kiyong Lee
Korea University
Seoul, Korea
ikiyong@gmail.com

Abstract

Measurable quantitative information (MQI) such as *165 cm* or *60 kg* that applies to the height or weight of an entity is quite common in ordinary language. Such information is abundant in scientific journals, technical reports or medical records that it constitutes an essential part of communicative segments of language in general. The processing of such information is thus required for successful language resource management. To facilitate such processing in a normalized way, this paper aims to specify a general markup language QML for the semantic annotation of MQI in language, while making it interoperable with other semantic annotation schemes that have been developed as ISO standards.

1 Introduction

Demands from industry and academic communities for a precise acquisition of measurable quantitative information from unstructured texts have increased. For example, as addressed in Hao (2016), the fast growing medical informatics research also needs to process a large amount of medical texts to analyze the dose of medicine, the eligibility criteria of clinical trial, the phenotype characters of patients, the lab tests in clinical records, etc. The demands require the reliable and consistent extraction and representation of measurable quantitative information.

This paper is aimed at developing a markup language QML as specifying a semantic annotation scheme for measurable quantitative information in language. As first proposed by Bunt (2010) and Bunt (2011), and then laid down as part of the principles of semantic annotation by ISO (2016), QML consists of an abstract syntax QML_{as}, a concrete syntax QML_{cs}, and a semantics. This paper focuses on developing an XML-based QML_{cs} that provides a format for representing annotation structures that consist of entity structures and link structures.

QML is being developed in the working environment of ISO/TC 37/SC 4/WG 2 Semantic Annotation. It thus aims at following the principles of semantic annotation laid down in ISO (2016) in general. It also follows the basic requirements of the linguistic annotation framework (LAF) (ISO, 2012a): (1) the normalization of MQI annotation is to be stated at the abstract level of annotation and (2) the standoff annotation format is to be adopted at the concrete level of serialization.

QML, as developed in this paper, is designed to be interoperable with other parts of ISO 24617 Language resource management - Semantic annotation framework (SemAF). It also utilizes various ISO standards on lexical resources and morpho-syntactic annotation frameworks. It aims at being compatible with other existing standards, especially ISO (2009) on quantities and units, while being applicable to TimeML (ISO, 2012b) for event-based temporal measures and to ISO-Space (ISO, 2014) for motion-related spatio-temporal measures.

2 Scope

The proposed markup language QML for quantitative information focuses on *measurable* quantitative information. If quantitative information is measurable, then it is expressible in unitized numeric terms such as *165 cm tall, sixty-five kilograms, 60 miles per hour, five books,* or *HbA1c between 5-7 %*. The extent of measurability is wider than that of countability; for example, the measures associated with objects that are referred to by mass nouns such as *whisky* or *gasoline* themselves are not countable measures, although bottles of whisky or gallons of gasoline are countable and measurable. Hence, the scope of QML includes countable measures as well as other types that are considered measurable.

The following three cases are, however, excluded from the scope of QML, although they may be considered as involving quantitative information in one way or another;

1. Pure mathematical equations or formulas for scientific calculations like *1+1=2* and *1 plus 1 equals 2*, pure numerical relation such as *2 is greater than 1*. They express (truth-functional) propositions involving numerical relations only.

2. Quantitative terms such as *a few miles* or *very far* are excluded either because the quantity is not expressed in explicitly numerical terms or because no unit is mentioned.

3. QML does not define what units are. Units are conventionally decided on, depending on their application domains. If needed, QML simply refers to ISO (2009) or more than a dozen of its subsequent parts on *quantities and units*, in which units are rigorously defined with respect to each application domain.

3 Specification of QML

3.1 Metamodel

The overall structure of QML is represented by a metamodel in Figure 1. This metamodel introduces: (1) communicative segments as input to the annotation of MQI, (2) from which markable expressions are extracted, and (3) four basic entity types: **entity, dimension, quantitative relation**, and **measure** with its two subtypes, **numeric** and **unit**, which are all anchored to markables. This metamodel also introduces (4) two relation types, measure link (<mLink>) and comparison link (<cLink>). Triggered by a dimension, each **measure link**, tagged <mLink>, relates a measure to an entity. Triggered by a quantitative relation, each **comparison link**, tagged <cLink> relates a measure to another or other more measures.

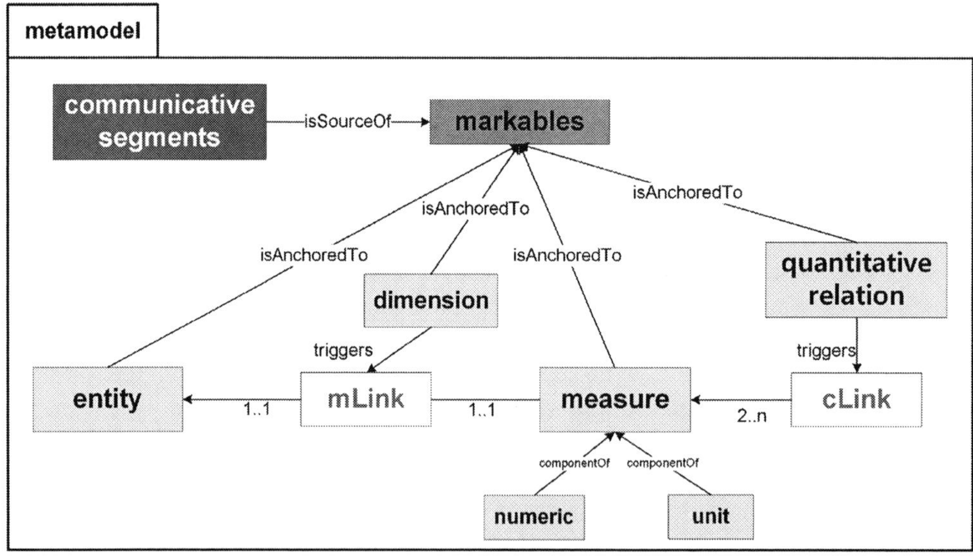

Figure 1: Metamodel of QML

3.2 Abstract syntax of QML (QML$_{as}$)

The abstract syntax specifies an annotation scheme in set-theoretical terms in an abstract way. The abstract syntax QML$_{as}$ for the semantic annotation of measurable quantitative information in communicative segments of language is a quintuple $<C, M, B, R, @>$ such that

1. C is a nonempty set of communicative segments;
2. M is a nonempty set of (possibly null) sequences of segments, called *markables*, from C;

3. B is a nonempty set of basic entity types, anchored to M, consisting of **entity, dimension, quantitative relation**, and **measure** with its two subtypes, **numeric** and **unit**.

4. R is a nonempty set of relation types that consists of **measure link** and **comparison link**.

5. @ is a set of assignments that specify the list of attributes and their value types associated with each of the basic entity types in B and each of the link types in R.

In the abstract syntax QML_{as}, @ is expressed in set-theoretic tuples. $@(measure)$ is, for instance, a tuple $<@target, @numeric, @unit>$, consisting of three required attributes such that $@target$ is an anchor to M, the value of $@numeric$ is REALS, and the value of $@unit$ is one of conventionally accepted unit values, provided their values are not complex. The entity types, $@numeric$ and $@unit$, treat complex numerics (e.g. '14.0 x 109') and units (e.g. 'km/hr'). As specified in ISO (2016), each link r in R is a triplet such that $@r = <\eta, E, \rho>$, where η is an entity structure, E a set of entity structures, and ρ a relation from η to E.

QML_{as} defines well-formed structures, called *annotation structures*, each of which consists of a list of entity structures, each associated with a basic entity type in B, and a list of link structures, each associated with a relation type in R. Semantics then operates on these structures.

3.3 Concrete syntax (QML_{cs})

3.3.1 Overall

Based on an abstract syntax, there can be several equivalent concrete syntaxes. The concrete syntax QML_{cs} is one of such syntaxes based on the abstract syntax QML_{as} as specified above. This concrete syntax QML_{cs} is XML-serialized. Each entity or link structure is represented by a structure, called *element*, consisting of a set of attribute-value pairs with a unique ID that has an attribute name `xml:id`. Each annotation structure is then a list of these structures, enclosed by the element, called *root element*.

Corresponding to each of the basic entity types and the link types in the abstract syntax QML_{as}, there is a unique element name, called *tag*, and a unique ID prefix for an XML-based concrete syntax QML_{cs}, as shown in Table 1. Each ID prefix is followed by a positive integer. For example, `"x25"` for `<entity>`. In XML, the attribute for ID is prefixed with `xml:id`.

Table 1: List of Tags in QML_{cs}

	Tags	**ID prefixes**	**Comment**
root	`<QI>`	qi	root tag
Basic entity types			
entity	`<entity>`	x	object to which a measure applies
dimension	`<dimension>`	d	triggers `<mLink>`
quantitative relation	`<qRelation>`	qr	triggers `<cLink>`
measure	`<measure>`	me	unitized numeric quantities only
numeric	`<num>`	nu	allows complex numeric quantities
unit	`<unit>`	u	allows complex units
Link types			
measure relation	`<mLink>`	mL	relates a measure to an entity
comparison relation	`<cLink>`	cL	relates a measure to another or other more measures

The specification of attribute assignments @ is defined with more specific data types in extended BNF (ISO/IEC, 1996) for the root in 3.3.2, entity types in 3.3.3, and link types in 3.3.4.

3.3.2 Attribute specification of the root `<QI>`

List 1: List of attributes for `<QI>` in extended BNF

```
attributes = identifier, target, [lang], [source], [comment];
target = IDREF | CDATA;
lang = CDATA; {* refer to ISO (2010) on language codes*};
```

```
source = CDATA;
comment = CDATA;
```

3.3.3 Attribute specification of the basic entity types

List 2: List of attributes for <entity> in extended BNF

```
attributes = identifier, target, type, [comment];
identifier = x + positive integer;
target = IDREF | CDATA;
type = CDATA; {*ontological types*}
comment = CDATA;
```

List 3: A list of attributes for <dimension> in extended BNF

```
attributes = identifier, target, type, [comment];
identifier = d + positive integer;
target = IDREF | CDATA;
type = CDATA; {*For example, "length", "width"*}
comment = CDATA;
```

List 4: A list of attributes for <qRelation> in extended BNF

```
attributes = identifier, target, type, [comment];
identifier = qr + positive integer;
target = IDREF | CDATA;
type = CDATA; {* mathematical operators, e.g., "greater than"*}
comment = CDATA;
```

List 5: A list of attributes for <measure> in extended BNF

```
attributes = identifier, target, num, unit, [comment];
identifier = me + positive integer;
target = IDREF | CDATA;
num = real numbers;
unit = CDATA | IDREF; {*IDREF refers to a complex unit*}
comment = CDATA;
```

3.3.4 Attribute specification of the link types

By ISO (2016), every link structure is of the form $<\eta, E, \rho>$ such that η is an entity structure, E is a set of entity structures, and ρ is a relation over them.[1] In QML_{cs}, we name the entity structure η "figure" and the set of entity structure E "ground" as in ISO-Space ISO (2014). There are two link types in QML_{as}, tagged <mLink> and <cLink> in QML_{cs}. Their attributes are specified as in List 6 and List 7.

List 6: A list of attributes for <mLink> in extended BNF

```
attributes = identifier, figure, relType, ground, [trigger], [comment];
identifier = mL + positive integer;
figure = IDREF; {*ID of <measure>*}
ground = IDREFS; {*IDS of <entity>s to which the value of <measure> applies*}
relType = CDATA; {*type of measure that depends on its application domain*}
trigger = IDREF; {*ID of <dimension>*}
comment = CDATA;
```

List 7: A list of attributes for <cLink> in extended BNF

```
attributes = identifier, relType, figure, ground, [trigger], [comment];
identifier = cL + positive integer;
relType = CDATA;
figure = IDREF; {*ID of <measure>*}
```

---

[1] An entity structure is a pair $<m, s>$, where m is a markable and s is semantic information annotated on m.

```
ground = IDREFS; {*IDS of <measure>s*}
trigger = IDREF; {*ID of <qRelation>*}
comment = CDATA;
```

3.4 Illustration of Concrete syntax (QML_{cs})

This clause illustrates how QML_{cs}) applies to the representation of measure quantitative information in language in general.[2]

Each of the steps of MQI annotation is illustrated with a sample textual data `"Mia is 165 cm tall."`

Step 1: Pre-processing: word-segmentation and anchoring

Before the semantic annotation of QML-cs applies to some specific language data, the data needs to be pre-processed, for instance, through word segmentation. The word segmentation of the sample data is represented inline as illustrated below.

```
(1) <wordSeg xml:id="ws1" target="#1a" lang="en">
    <w xml:id="w1">Mia</w>
    <w xml:id="w2">is</w>
    <w xml:id="w3">165</w>
    <w xml:id="w4">cm</w>
    <w xml:id="w5">tall</w>
    <punct xml:id="p1">.</punct>
    </wordSeg>
```

This can also be represented in a much simpler way:

```
(2) <wordSeg xml:id="ws1" target="#1a" lang="en">Mia_w1 is_w2 165_w3 cm_w4 tall_w5.
    </wordSeg>
```

Based on the word-segmentation data such as (1) or (2), markables are chosen and each assigned an appropriate entity type, as represented below.

```
(3) Mia_x1 is [165 cm]_me1 tall_d1.
```

Step 2:Annotation with quantitative information

Word-segmented and anchored data is then annotated with measurable quantitative information, as represented below.

```
(4) a. <wordSeg xml:id="ws1" target="#1a" lang="en" >Mia_w1 is_w2 165_w3 cm_w4
       tall_w5.</wordSeg>

    b. <QI xml:id="qi1" target="#ws1" lang="en">
       <entity xml:id="x1" target="#w1" type="person"/>
       <measure xml:id="me1" target="#w3,#w4" num="165" unit="cm"/>
       <dimension xml:id="d1" target="#w5" type="length" />
       <mLink xml:id="mL1" figure="#me1" ground="#x1" relType="length"
       trigger="#d1" />
       </QI>
```

With anthor sample data `"John is more than two meters tall."`, we show how a quantitative relation, tagged `<qRelation>`, triggers a comparison relation, tagged `<cLink>`, that relates a measure to another or other more measures. This annotation is interpreted as stating that the height of a person, named *John*, is represented

```
(5) a. <wordSeg xml:id="ws2" target="#1b" lang="en" >John_w1 is_w2 more_w3 than_w4
       two_w5 meters_w6 tall_w7.</wordSeg>

    b. <QI xml:id="qi2" target="#ws2" >
       <entity xml:id="x1" target="#w1" type="person" />
       <qRelation xml:id="qr1" target ="#w3, #w4" type="greaterThanOrEqual">
       <measure xml:id="me1" target=" " num="" unit=" " />
       {*The <measure xml:id="me1"> is a non-consuming tag which is understood as
       being anchored to an empty string of texual segments*}
```

---

[2]We intend to adopt the TEI-serialization as specified in TEI (2016) for QML_{cs}. As this stage, however, we have adopted a less embedded mode of representing XML-elements for annotation structures that consist of entity and link structures.

```
<measure xml:id="me2" target="#w5, #w6" num="2" unit="meters" />
<cLink xml:id="cL1" figure="#me1" ground="#me2" relType="
greaterThanOrEqual" trigger="#qr1" />
<dimension xml:id="d1" target="#w7" type="length" />
<mLink xml:id="mL1" figure="#me1" ground="#x1" relType="length"
trigger="#d1" />
</QI>
```

4   Concluding Remarks

Focusing on measurable quantitative information, this paper reports the most recent progress of specification of a markup language QML. We defined the extent of markables of QML and presented a metamodel to show its general structure. In addition, its abstract syntax and an XML-based concrete syntax were formulated with the specification of associated attributes expressed in extended BNF, which is considered expressively more powerful than commonly used data-type declarations (DTD) of XML. The proposed concrete syntax was briefly illustrated with two simple datasets. A fully developed QML is expected to be part of the ISO 24617 standards on semantic annotation for language resource management.

5   Acknowledgments

This paper is supported by grants from National Key R&D Program of China (2016YFF0204205, 2018YFF0213901), China National Institute of Standardization (522016Y-4681, 522018Y-5948, 522018Y-5941), and National Natural Science Foundation of China (No.61772146).

References

Bunt, Harry. 2010. A methodology for designing semantic annotation languages exploiting semantic-syntactic ISO-morphisms. In Alex C. Fang, Nancy Ide, and Jonathan Webster (eds.), *Proceedings of the Second International Conference on Global Interoperability for Language Resources* (ICGL2010), pp.29-46. Hong Kong.

Bunt, Harry. 2011. Abstract syntax and semantics in semantic annotation, applied to time and events. Revised version of Introducing abstract syntax + semantics in semantic annotation, and its consequences for the annotation of time and events. In E. Lee and A. Yoon (eds.), *Recent Trends in Language and Knowledge Processing*, pp.157-204. Hankukmunhwasa, Seoul.

ISO. 2009. *ISO 80000:2009(E) Quantities and units - Part 1: General.* The International Organization for Standardization, Geneva.

ISO. 2010. *ISO 639–1:20109(E) Codes for the representation of names of languages – Part 1: Alpha–2 code.* The International Organization for Standardization, Geneva.

ISO. 2012a. *ISO 24612:2012(E) Language resource management – Linguistic annotation framework (LAF).* The International Organization for Standardization, Geneva.

ISO. 2012b. *ISO 24617–1:2012(E) Language resource management – Semantic annotation framework (SemAF) – Part 1: Time and events.* The International Organization for Standardization, Geneva.

ISO. 2014. *ISO 24617–7:2014(E) Language resource management – Semantic annotation framework (SemAF) – Part 7: Spatial information.* The International Organization for Standardization, Geneva.

ISO. 2016. *ISO 24617-6:2016(E) Language resource management - Semantic annotation framework (SemAF)- Part 6: Principles of semantic annotation.* The International Organization for Standardization, Geneva.

ISO/IEC. 1996. *ISO/IEC 14977:1996(E) Information technology - Syntactic metalanguage - Extended BNF.* The International Organization for Standardization and the International Electrotechnical Commission, Geneva.

Lee, Kiyong. 2016. An abstract syntax for ISOspace with its `<moveLink>` reformulated. In Harry Bunt (ed.), *Proceedings of the LREC 2016 Workshop, 12th Joint ACL–ISO Workshop on Interoperable Semantic Annotation (ISA-12)*, pp. 28-37. May 23–28, 2016, Portorož, Slovenia.

Lee, Kiyong. 2015. The annotation of measure expressions in ISO standards. *Proceedings of the 11th Joint ACL-ISO Workshop on Interoperable Semantic Annotation (ISA-11)*

Hao, Tianyong, Wei, Yunyan, Qiang, Jiaqi, Wang, Haitao and Lee, Kiyong. 2017. The representation and extraction of quantitative information. *Proceedings of the 13th Joint ISO-ACL Workshop on Interoperable Semantic Annotation (ISA-13)*, pp. 74-83.

Hao, Tianyong, Liu, Hongfang, Weng, Chunhua. 2016. Valx: A system for extracting and structuring numeric lab test comparison statements from text. *Methods of Information in Medicine*. Vol. 55: Issue 3, pp. 266-275.

TEI. 2016. *TEI P5: Guidelines for Electronic Text Encoding and Interchange.* Text Encoding Intiative Consortium.

Improving String Processing for Temporal Relations

David Woods, Tim Fernando
ADAPT Centre
Computational Linguistics Group
School of Computer Science and Statistics
Trinity College Dublin, Ireland
dwoods@tcd.ie, tim.fernando@tcd.ie

Abstract

This paper presents a refinement of the superposition operation on strings which are used to represent temporal relation information such as is found in documents annotated with TimeML. Superposition is made demonstrably more efficient by interleaving generation with testing, rather than generating and then testing. The strings offer compact visual appeal while remaining an attractive option for computation and reasoning. Motivated by Freksa's semi-interval relations, a suggestion is also made for a potential method of representing partial information in these strings so as to allow for analysis at different granularities, and for more flexibility when dealing with cases of ambiguity.

1 Introduction

A string of n sets $\alpha_1\alpha_2 \cdots \alpha_n$ can be used to represent a sequence of events and time periods such that the linear order and inter-relations of the events are clearly apparent, while remaining compact. Such a string is read from left to right chronologically, with each α_i, $i \in \{1, 2, \ldots, n\}$, depicting one of n moments in time, and specifying the set of exactly those temporal propositions, or fluents, which hold simultaneously at that moment i. A fluent $a \in \alpha_i$ is understood to be occurring before another fluent $a' \in \alpha_j$ iff $i < j$ and $a' \notin \alpha_i$.

Note that these strings do not (necessarily) offer any information concerning real duration: a fluent may occur in several string positions, but this does not affect any interpretation of its duration, only its relation to other fluents, i.e. if the symbol a appears in both α_i and α_{i+1}, the event it stands for is not understood as being twice as long as if the symbol had only appeared in α_i. Fluents representing fixed time points may be used to give a sense of real time (e.g. $a =$ "5pm on 25th May 2018"). Because of this, a string in which $\alpha_i = \alpha_{i+1}$ for any $1 \leq i < n$ will not have its interpretation affected if either α_i or α_{i+1} are deleted. For example, the string $\{a\}\{a\}\{a, b\}\{b\}\{b\}$ is equivalent in interpretation to $\{a\}\{a, b\}\{b\}$. A string featuring these repetitions is said to *stutter*, and the process of removing stutter from a string is called *block compression* (Fernando, 2015; Woods et al., 2017).

Throughout this paper, each string position α_i will be drawn as a box, with $\boxed{}$ for the empty set $\varnothing$, allowing the strings to be read like strips of film. Events are treated as bounded intervals, such that they have a beginning and ending – this is represented through the use of bounding empty sets – although this assumption is not required by the string framework: the finite event a, drawn as $\boxed{}\boxed{a}\boxed{}$, as opposed to non-finite event a', drawn as $\boxed{a'}$.

By superposing multiple strings, large amounts of information may be condensed into a single string, which offers a timeline-like visual appeal. The strings may be used to encode and reason about interval relations, as in Allen (1983), and also to aid visualisation in the annotation process. It is hoped that this approach may be seen as complementary to existing graphical tools. In Section 3, a refinement is offered of the superposition operation discussed in Woods et al. (2017) which preserves relational information under reduct, and interleaves generation with testing of results for a more efficient calculation. A

potential extension of the framework is also shown in Section 4 such as to allow for incomplete information, and for Freksa (1992)'s semi-interval relations to be represented. This would enable reasoning over
partial or uncertain information, or in case coarser analysis was desired.

2   Motivation

Several attempts have been made to create a visualisation system which best represents the temporal
relations found in TimeML (TimeML Working Group, 2005; Pustejovsky et al., 2010), particularly for
use as an annotation aid, including Tango (Pustejovsky et al., 2003; Verhagen et al., 2006), using labelled
arcs in a directed graph, and T-BOX (Verhagen, 2005a), using relative placement of boxed temporal
propositions. A clear advantage of T-BOX is that it presents the information in a way that makes it easy
to quickly gain a sense of a document's overall temporal structure, due to its intuitive use of arrows,
box-inclusion, and stacking.

Using strings as a representational tool presents the same intuitive structure, with a timeline-like left-
to-right layout, but in a compact format which may also be used for computations, rather than being a
purely visual entity.

Although these strings may be used for other problems (see Fernando (2015)), one of their more
obvious uses is as a tool for the simultaneous visualisation of and reasoning about collections of Allen
(1983)'s interval relations, such as those which appear (slightly renamed) as TLINKs in documents
annotated with TimeML. A TLINK, or temporal link, is a tag featuring a pair of temporal entities, either
event instances or time periods, from the text of the document and a relation between them, which can
be translated to a string.

By way of example, taking a tag `<TLINK lid="15" relType="BEFORE" timeID="t86"`
`relatedToTime="t82"/>`[1] ($t86$ referring to a five year period, and $t82$ being the document creation time), it is straightforward to convert this to a string: find the Allen relation which corresponds to the `relType` attribute, then substitute a and a' in Table 1 with the values of `timeID` (or
`eventInstanceID`) and `relatedToTime` (or `relatedToEventInstance`), respectively, to
give "$t86$ before $t82$" – $\boxed{}\,\boxed{t86}\,\boxed{}\,\boxed{t82}\,\boxed{}$, which is interpreted as saying that the five year period occurred
before the document creation time. By converting all of a document's TLINKs to strings and superposing
them with one another, a picture begins to build up of the document's overall temporal structure.

As Derczynski (2016, p. 2) points out, the choice of representation for temporal relation types is
critical, as choosing the right relation for arbitrary pairs of events is difficult. By using these strings, an
annotator would be able to see the state of the document as a whole, and receive suggestions when there
are constraints on the possible relations they may choose, given other relations. For example, given "x
during y" – $\boxed{}\,\boxed{y}\,\boxed{x,y}\,\boxed{y}\,\boxed{}$ and "y during z" – $\boxed{}\,\boxed{z}\,\boxed{y,z}\,\boxed{z}\,\boxed{}$, there is only one possible relation between
x and z: "x during z" – $\boxed{}\,\boxed{z}\,\boxed{x,z}\,\boxed{z}\,\boxed{}$. In scenarios such as this, where there is only one possibility, the
system should be able to fill it in automatically, but in other cases, it might suggest to an annotator that
only a certain group of relations is feasible.

The ultimate goal here would be to achieve full temporal closure over the document. If the temporal
entities were (as in Tango) represented as nodes on a graph, and the relations between them as the
arcs, this would look like a fully connected graph, with an arc from every node to every other node.
Using strings instead, a single, timeline-like string would be computable, which would contain all of the
temporal relation information of the document. It would be possible to determine the relation between
any two (or more) events in a single operation, and to quickly examine subsections of the timeline, or
see the relative ordering of a specific subset of events (see reduct and projections, Section 3).

Reaching this somewhat lofty target in an automatic way seems unlikely, at least for now, as the
number of relations given in a typical document from TimeBank (Pustejovsky et al., 2006), the largest
corpus of documents annotated with TimeML, is far short of the total $N(N-1)/2$ (for N fluents) links
mentioned by Verhagen (2005b, p. 3), and in most cases, there is simply not enough information to
compute everything. See Section 4 for further discussion on this matter.

---

[1] Document ABC19980108.1830.0711.tml

One benefit the strings offer from an automation point of view is the ability to quickly determine inconsistent labellings in TimeML documents. If superposition of any two strings produces an empty language, then there is an incompatibility between them (e.g. "x before y" – $\boxed{\ \boxed{x}\ \boxed{\ }\ \boxed{y}\ }$ and "x after y" – $\boxed{\ \boxed{y}\ \boxed{\ }\ \boxed{x}\ }$), and there is a problem with the document. As some inconsistencies are only revealed through transitivities, superposing more than two strings will often present further issues.

Since the superposition operation would be used very frequently in any system that employed these strings for visualisation or computation, it is critical that it be made as efficient as possible.

3   Constraints for superposition of strings

Superposition in its simplest form is defined as the componentwise union of two strings of equal length:

$$\alpha_1\alpha_2\cdots\alpha_n \ \& \ \alpha_1'\alpha_2'\cdots\alpha_n' \ := \ (\alpha_1\cup\alpha_1')(\alpha_2\cup\alpha_2')\cdots(\alpha_n\cup\alpha_n') \tag{1}$$

for example

$$\boxed{a}\,\boxed{b}\,\boxed{c} \ \& \ \boxed{a}\,\boxed{a}\,\boxed{d} = \boxed{a}\,\boxed{a,b}\,\boxed{c,d} \tag{2}$$

This is extended to languages (sets of strings) L and L':

$$L \ \& \ L' \ := \ \bigcup_{n\geq 0} \{s \ \& \ s' \mid s \in L_n, \ s' \in L_n'\} \tag{3}$$

where L_n and L_n' are the sets of strings of length n in L and L', respectively.

In order to extend this operation further to strings of unequal lengths, it should first be said that s and s' are *bc-equivalent* if they block compress to the same string, that is $bc(s) = bc(s')$. The inverse of the block compression operation may be used to introduce stutter in the strings which are to be superposed, and generate an infinite language of bc-equivalent strings:

$$bc^{-1}(s) = \alpha_1^+\alpha_2^+\cdots\alpha_n^+ \qquad \text{if } s = bc(\alpha_1\alpha_2\cdots\alpha_n) \tag{4}$$

These languages are then superposed, and the results are block compressed to give a finite set, the *asynchronous superposition* of s and s' (noting that $bc(s) = bc(s') \iff s' \in bc^{-1}bc(s)$):

$$s \ \&_* \ s' \ := \ \{bc(s'') \mid s'' \in bc^{-1}bc(s) \ \& \ bc^{-1}bc(s')\} \tag{5}$$

For example:

$$\boxed{x}\,\boxed{z} \ \&_* \ \boxed{x}\,\boxed{y}\,\boxed{z} = \{\,\boxed{x}\,\boxed{x,y}\,\boxed{z}\,, \boxed{x}\,\boxed{x,y}\,\boxed{x,z}\,\boxed{z}\,, \boxed{x}\,\boxed{y,z}\,\boxed{z}\,, \boxed{x}\,\boxed{x,y}\,\boxed{y,z}\,\boxed{z}\,, \boxed{x}\,\boxed{x,z}\,\boxed{y,z}\,\boxed{z}\,\} \tag{6}$$

Interestingly, the thirteen Allen interval relations given in

$$\mathcal{AR} \ := \ \{<, >, d, di, f, fi, m, mi, o, oi, s, si, =\} \tag{7}$$

are represented by the asynchronous superposition

$$\boxed{\ \boxed{a}\ } \ \&_* \ \boxed{\ \boxed{a'}\ } = \{\mathcal{S}_R(a, a') \mid R \in \mathcal{AR}\} \tag{8}$$

with each string $\mathcal{S}_R(a, a')$ featuring one relation $a \, R \, a'$, as shown in Table 1.

R	$a\,R\,a'$	$\mathcal{S}_R(a,a')$	R^{-1}	$a\,R^{-1}\,a'$	$\mathcal{S}_{R^{-1}}(a,a')$
$<$	a before a'	$\boxed{a}\;\boxed{a'}$	$>$	a after a'	$\boxed{a'}\;\boxed{a}$
m	a meets a'	$\boxed{a}\,\boxed{a'}$	mi	a met by a'	$\boxed{a'}\,\boxed{a}$
o	a overlaps a'	$\boxed{a}\,\boxed{a,a'}\,\boxed{a'}$	oi	a overlapped by a'	$\boxed{a'}\,\boxed{a',a}\,\boxed{a}$
d	a during a'	$\boxed{a'}\,\boxed{a,a'}\,\boxed{a'}$	di	a contains a'	$\boxed{a}\,\boxed{a',a}\,\boxed{a}$
s	a starts a'	$\boxed{a,a'}\,\boxed{a'}$	si	a started by a'	$\boxed{a',a}\,\boxed{a}$
f	a finishes a'	$\boxed{a'}\,\boxed{a,a'}$	fi	a finished by a'	$\boxed{a}\,\boxed{a',a}$
$=$	a equals a'	$\boxed{a,a'}$			

Table 1: Allen interval relations in strings

It should be noted that neither the basic ($\&$) or asynchronous ($\&_*$) forms of superposition pay attention to the semantics of the strings on which they operate. For instance, in (2), there is no way to determine the actual relation between c and d, given the strings $\boxed{a}\,\boxed{b}\,\boxed{c}$ and $\boxed{a}\,\boxed{a}\,\boxed{d}$. Similarly, the strings $\boxed{x}\,\boxed{z}$ and $\boxed{x}\,\boxed{y}\,\boxed{z}$ suggest a contradiction in (6), since each contains a different relation between x and z, only one of which could be veridical at once.

An upper bound on the length of the strings to be generated when using inverse block compression is established as $n + n' - 1$ in Woods et al. (2017), where n and n' are the respective lengths of input strings s and s'. However, while this limit is an obvious and necessary improvement on generating the infinite language $\mathrm{bc}^{-1}\mathrm{bc}(s) \,\&\, \mathrm{bc}^{-1}\mathrm{bc}(s')$ in (5), further constraints are required in order for superposition to truly be effective.

Some additional notation is presented here which will prove helpful in describing the present issue and its solution. The following string will be used for demonstrative purposes, with $lt =$ "last Tuesday", $js =$ "John sleeps", $fa =$ "a fire alarm sounds":

$$\boxed{\;\boxed{lt}\,\boxed{lt,js}\,\boxed{lt,js,fa}\,\boxed{lt,js}\,\boxed{lt}\;} = \text{"John slept through the fire alarm last Tuesday"} \tag{9}$$

The *vocabulary* of a string s will be said to be the union of each of its components:

$$voc(s) := \bigcup_{i=1}^{n} \alpha_i \tag{10}$$

This makes s an $\mathrm{MSO}_{voc(s)}$-model,[2] interpreting each $a \in voc(s)$ as the set of string positions where a occurs. The vocabulary of (9) is $\{lt, js, fa\}$.

For any set A, the *A-reduct* of a string s is defined as the componentwise intersection of s with A (Fernando, 2016):

$$\rho_A(\alpha_1\alpha_2\cdots\alpha_n) := (\alpha_1 \cap A)(\alpha_2 \cap A)\cdots(\alpha_n \cap A) \tag{11}$$

resulting in a string $\rho_A(s)$ with vocabulary $voc(s) \cap A$. For example, setting $A = \{lt, fa\}$, the A-reduct of (9) is the string $\boxed{\;\boxed{lt}\,\boxed{lt}\,\boxed{lt,fa}\,\boxed{lt}\,\boxed{lt}\;}$.

A string s will also be said to *project to* another string s' if the $voc(s')$-reduct of s block compresses to s':

$$\mathrm{bc}(\rho_{voc(s')}(s)) = s' \tag{12}$$

For example, a string projects to itself precisely if it is stutterless. Additionally, a language L can be said to project to a string s' if every string $s \in L$ projects to s'. As an $\mathrm{MSO}_{voc(s)}$-model, a string s *satisfies* $a\,R\,a'$ if s projects to $\mathcal{S}_R(a,a')$

$$s \models a\,R\,a' \iff \mathrm{bc}(\rho_{\{a,a'\}}(s)) = \mathcal{S}_R(a,a') \tag{13}$$

---

[2] See Libkin (2004) for a discussion of Monadic Second-Order Logic.

and "a is a bounded interval in s" if s projects to $\boxed{\ \boxed{a}\ }$. The string in (9) can be said to satisfy, for instance, "lt contains fa", since it projects to the string $\boxed{\ \boxed{lt}\ \boxed{fa, lt}\ \boxed{lt}\ }$ ("The fire alarm sounded at some point last Tuesday"). It also satisfies "lt contains js", and "js contains fa", as well as the inverses of these three relations.

In general, every string in $s \ \&_* \ s'$ will project back to both s and s', provided $voc(s) \cap voc(s') = \varnothing$. However, if this condition of disjoint vocabulary does not hold, then $s \ \&_* \ s'$ need not preserve the projections. For example, the superposition of "x before y" – $\boxed{\ \boxed{x}\ \boxed{y}\ }$ and "y before z" – $\boxed{\ \boxed{y}\ \boxed{z}\ }$ should, presumably,[3] result in a language containing exactly one string, namely $\boxed{\ \boxed{x}\ \boxed{y}\ \boxed{z}\ }$ ("x happened before y did, which happened before z"). This string projects to both of the strings which made it, preserving that original information, and further projects to "x before z" – $\boxed{\ \boxed{x}\ \boxed{z}\ }$, demonstrating one of the transitivities of the Allen interval relations i.e. the possible relation(s) between a and a'', given $a \ R \ a'$ and $a' \ R' \ a''$.

Asynchronous superposition in its current form, in fact, will produce a language of 270 strings, five of which project to $\boxed{\ \boxed{x}\ \boxed{y}\ }$, five which project to $\boxed{\ \boxed{y}\ \boxed{z}\ }$, and just one ($\boxed{\ \boxed{x}\ \boxed{y}\ \boxed{z}\ }$) which projects to both. Of these 270 strings, 245 will project to $\boxed{\ \boxed{y}\ \boxed{y}\ }$, which is plainly invalid by the earlier assertion that only finite intervals should be expected (i.e. for any fluent $a \in voc(s)$, s should project to $\boxed{\ \boxed{a}\ }$). By requiring that the resulting language of a superposition can project back to each of its "parent" strings, it is ensured that the original information is not lost, and allows for the calculation of the transitivities which are essential to temporal reasoning in Allen (1983) and Freksa (1992).

In Woods et al. (2017, p. 130), the potential results of a superposition are generated and then tested, checking each one for validity (using an algorithm based on matching string positions). While this does produce the correct output, it involves extensive overgeneration, even in the most basic of cases. Here an approach is presented which interleaves testing with generation, ensuring that only valid results are generated at all.

Θ is fixed as an infinite set of fluents, and $Fin(\Theta)$ as the set of finite subsets of Θ, such that any string s is in $Fin(\Theta)^*$. Given $\Sigma, \Sigma' \in Fin(\Theta)$, a function

$$\&_{\Sigma, \Sigma'} : (Fin(\Theta)^* \times Fin(\Theta)^*) \to 2^{Fin(\Theta)^*} \tag{14}$$

is defined, mapping a pair $(s, s') \in Fin(\Theta)^* \times Fin(\Theta)^*$ of strings to a set $s \ \&_{\Sigma, \Sigma'} \ s' \subseteq Fin(\Theta)^*$ of strings as follows:

$$\epsilon \ \&_{\Sigma, \Sigma'} \ \epsilon := \{\epsilon\} \tag{15}$$

where ϵ is the empty string (of length 0)

$$\epsilon \ \&_{\Sigma, \Sigma'} \ s := \varnothing \ \text{ for } s \neq \epsilon \tag{16a}$$

$$s \ \&_{\Sigma, \Sigma'} \ \epsilon := \varnothing \ \text{ for } s \neq \epsilon \tag{16b}$$

and for $\alpha, \alpha' \in Fin(\Theta)$

$$\alpha s \ \&_{\Sigma, \Sigma'} \ \alpha' s' := \begin{cases} \{(\alpha \cup \alpha')s'' \mid s'' \in L(\alpha, s, \alpha', s', \Sigma, \Sigma')\} & \text{if } \Sigma \cap \alpha' \subseteq \alpha \text{ and } \Sigma' \cap \alpha \subseteq \alpha' \ \ \dagger \\ \varnothing & \text{otherwise} \end{cases} \tag{17}$$

where $L(\alpha, s, \alpha', s', \Sigma, \Sigma')$ is

$$(\alpha s \ \&_{\Sigma, \Sigma'} \ s') \ \cup \ (s \ \&_{\Sigma, \Sigma'} \ \alpha' s') \ \cup \ (s \ \&_{\Sigma, \Sigma'} \ s') \tag{18}$$

(from which it follows that any string in $s \ \&_{\Sigma, \Sigma'} \ s'$ has length less than $\text{length}(s) + \text{length}(s')$). If $\Sigma = \Sigma' = \varnothing$, then ($\dagger$) holds vacuously, and $\&_{\Sigma, \Sigma'}$ is functionally identical to the existant asynchronous superposition operation $\&_*$. Otherwise, ($\dagger$) can be used to prevent those invalid superpositions which do not project to both s and s'.

---

[3] The assumption here being that all occurrences of a fluent symbol, whether appearing in one string or several, refer to the same unique event or time period.

Proposition 1. *For all* $\Sigma, \Sigma' \in Fin(\Theta)$ *and* $s, s' \in Fin(\Theta)^*$, $s \,\&_{\Sigma,\Sigma'}\, s'$ *selects those strings from* $s \,\&_{\varnothing,\varnothing}\, s'$ *which project to both the* Σ-reduct *of* s *and the* Σ'-reduct *of* s'

$$s \,\&_{\Sigma,\Sigma'}\, s' = \{s'' \in s \,\&_{\varnothing,\varnothing}\, s' \mid bc(\rho_{voc(s) \cap \Sigma}(s'')) = bc(\rho_{\Sigma}(s)) \text{ and}$$
$$bc(\rho_{voc(s') \cap \Sigma'}(s'')) = bc(\rho_{\Sigma'}(s'))\} \tag{19}$$

Corollary 2. *For all* $s, s' \in Fin(\Theta)^*$ *that are stutterless, if* $\Sigma = voc(s)$ *and* $\Sigma' = voc(s')$, *then* $s \,\&_{\Sigma,\Sigma'}\, s'$ *selects those strings from* $s \,\&_{\varnothing,\varnothing}\, s'$ *which project to* s *and* s'

$$s \,\&_{\Sigma,\Sigma'}\, s' = \{s'' \in s \,\&_{\varnothing,\varnothing}\, s' \mid bc(\rho_{\Sigma}(s'')) = s \text{ and } bc(\rho_{\Sigma'}(s'')) = s'\} \tag{20}$$

Corollary 2 suggests that to preserve information under projection during superposition, *vocabulary constrained* superposition should be used:

$$s \,\&_{vc}\, s' := s \,\&_{voc(s),voc(s')}\, s' \tag{21}$$

Below, (22) shows a short worked example for $\boxed{\ x\ y\ } \,\&_{vc}\, \boxed{\ y\ z\ }$.[4]

$$(\boxed{\ } \cup \boxed{\ })(\boxed{\ x\ y\ }\,\&_{vc}\,\boxed{y\ z} \cup \boxed{x\ y}\,\&_{vc}\,\boxed{\ y\ z\ } \cup \boxed{x\ y}\,\&_{vc}\,\boxed{y\ z\ }) \tag{22a}$$

$$(\boxed{\ })(\varnothing \cup (\boxed{x} \cup \boxed{\ })(\boxed{x\ y}\,\&_{vc}\,\boxed{y\ z} \cup \boxed{y}\,\&_{vc}\,\boxed{\ y\ z\ } \cup \boxed{y}\,\&_{vc}\,\boxed{y\ z\ }) \cup \varnothing) \tag{22b}$$

$$(\boxed{\ x})(\varnothing \cup \varnothing \cup (\boxed{y} \cup \boxed{y})(\boxed{y}\,\&_{vc}\,\boxed{z} \cup \boxed{\ }\,\&_{vc}\,\boxed{y\ z} \cup \boxed{\ }\,\&_{vc}\,\boxed{z})) \tag{22c}$$

$$(\boxed{\ x\ y})(\varnothing \cup \varnothing \cup (\boxed{\ } \cup \boxed{z})(\boxed{\ }\,\&_{vc}\,\boxed{\ } \cup \epsilon\,\&_{vc}\,\boxed{z} \cup \epsilon\,\&_{vc}\,\boxed{\ })) \tag{22d}$$

$$(\boxed{\ x\ y\ z})((\boxed{\ } \cup \boxed{\ })(\boxed{\ }\,\&_{vc}\,\epsilon \cup \epsilon\,\&_{vc}\,\boxed{\ } \cup \epsilon\,\&_{vc}\,\epsilon) \cup \varnothing \cup \varnothing) \tag{22e}$$

$$(\boxed{\ x\ y\ z\ })(\{\epsilon\}) = \boxed{\ x\ y\ z\ } \tag{22f}$$

Compare the steps above with the procedure for asynchronous superposition. First, the padded forms of $\boxed{\ x\ y\ }$ and $\boxed{\ y\ z\ }$ must be generated, each of which are superposed together (in this case, 20×20 strings):

$$\{\boxed{\ \ \ \ x\ y\ \ } \,\&\, \boxed{\ \ \ \ y\ z\ }, \ldots, \boxed{\ x\ y\ \ \ \ } \,\&\, \boxed{\ y\ z\ \ \ \ }\} \tag{23}$$

Next, each of the resulting 400 strings is block compressed, to form a set of 53 possible strings:

$$\{\boxed{\ x,y\ y,z\ }, \ldots, \boxed{\ x,y\ \ y,z\ }\} \tag{24}$$

Finally, each of these strings is tested to ensure that it projects to both $\boxed{\ x\ y\ }$ and $\boxed{\ y\ z\ }$, reducing the set to $\{\boxed{\ x\ y\ z\ }\}$.

Below in Table 2 are some speed-tests comparing asynchronous superposition's generate-then-test approach against vocabulary constrained superposition, each run in the same test environment[5] with the same inputs. The correct strings are found by each algorithm, so the notable element here is simply the difference in time (the mean time of 1001 runs is given in milliseconds). Column 5 shows the percentage decrease in time to produce the final result from $\&_*$ to $\&_{vc}$, with a mean decrease over these six examples of 72.27%.

---

[4] It is worth mentioning that, although $\&_{vc}$ is written in each of (22), Σ and Σ' are fixed as $\{x, y\}$ and $\{y, z\}$, respectively, at the first step of this procedure.

[5] Node.js v10.0.0 (64-bit) on Ubuntu 16.04 using an Intel i7-6700 CPU with 16GB of memory.

s		s'		Time to $s \mathbin{\&_*} s'$	Time to $s \mathbin{\&_{vc}} s'$	Decrease in time
x	y	y	z	0.3207ms	0.0659ms	79.45%
x	y	y	x	0.3207ms	0.0180ms	94.39%
x	y	x	z	0.6124ms	0.2238ms	63.46%
x y		x	z	0.1528ms	0.1059ms	30.69%
x	y	u	v	22.4016ms	5.3616ms	76.07%
w w,x x	y	w	z	4.7403ms	0.4955ms	89.55%

Table 2: Comparison of $\&_*$ and $\&_{vc}$

Although these particular inputs are, for the most part, quite basic and arbitrarily chosen, they do illustrate how preventing the problematic strings as they are generated, as in vocabulary constrained superposition, is generally quicker than generating all of the syntactically possible strings then testing them for validity, as asynchronous superposition does. The mean percentage decrease for all pairs of strings $s \in \mathcal{S}_R(x, y)$ and $s' \in \mathcal{S}_R(y, z)$, with $R \in \mathcal{AR}$, is 34.11%. With $s \in \mathcal{S}_R(x, y)$ and $s' \in \mathcal{S}_R(u, v)$ the mean decrease is 64.51%, and with both strings $s, s' \in \mathcal{S}_R(x, y)$, it is 74.28%, which seems to suggest that there are large gains in efficiency to be made in the cases when $voc(s) \cap voc(s') = \varnothing$ and when $voc(s) = voc(s')$.

4 Beyond Allen's relations

While treating all temporal propositions as finite, bounded intervals makes it straightforward to represent Allen's interval relations as strings, the situation is more complicated when the data is incomplete (as it most often is). If a superposition results in a language of size > 1, it is impossible to narrow that set down to a single, correct string without further information. In this scenario, we are left with a number of possible strings, each representing a different timeline of the events, only one of which is veridical.

Taking an example from TimeBank,[6] two of the TLINKs are converted to their string representations, featuring three distinct event instances ($ei1$, $ei2$, and $ei12$):

```
<TLINK relType="IBEFORE" eventInstanceID="ei1" relatedToEventInstance="ei2"/>
```

$$\text{``}ei1 \text{ meets } ei2\text{''} - \boxed{\;\boxed{ei1}\;\boxed{ei2}\;} \qquad (25)$$

```
<TLINK relType="AFTER" eventInstanceID="ei12" relatedToEventInstance="ei1"/>
```

$$\text{``}ei12 \text{ after } ei1\text{''} - \boxed{\;\boxed{ei1}\;}\;\boxed{\;\boxed{ei12}\;} \qquad (26)$$

Superposing these two strings gives a language with five strings, each of which projects to one of a disjunction of the possible Allen relations between $ei2$ and $ei12$ (see Table 3).

s	$\mathrm{bc}(\rho_{\{ei2, ei12\}}(s))$	$ei2 \; R \; ei12$
$\boxed{ei1}\,\boxed{ei2}\,\boxed{ei2, ei12}$	$\boxed{ei2}\,\boxed{ei12, ei2}$	$ei2$ finished by $ei12$
$\boxed{ei1}\,\boxed{ei2}\,\boxed{ei2, ei12}\,\boxed{ei2}$	$\boxed{ei2}\,\boxed{ei12, ei2}\,\boxed{ei2}$	$ei2$ contains $ei12$
$\boxed{ei1}\,\boxed{ei2}\,\boxed{ei12}$	$\boxed{ei2}\,\boxed{ei12}$	$ei2$ meets $ei12$
$\boxed{ei1}\,\boxed{ei2}\,\boxed{ei12}$	$\boxed{ei2}\,\boxed{ei12}$	$ei2$ before $ei12$
$\boxed{ei1}\,\boxed{ei2}\,\boxed{ei2, ei12}\,\boxed{ei12}$	$\boxed{ei2}\,\boxed{ei2, ei12}\,\boxed{ei12}$	$ei2$ overlaps $ei12$

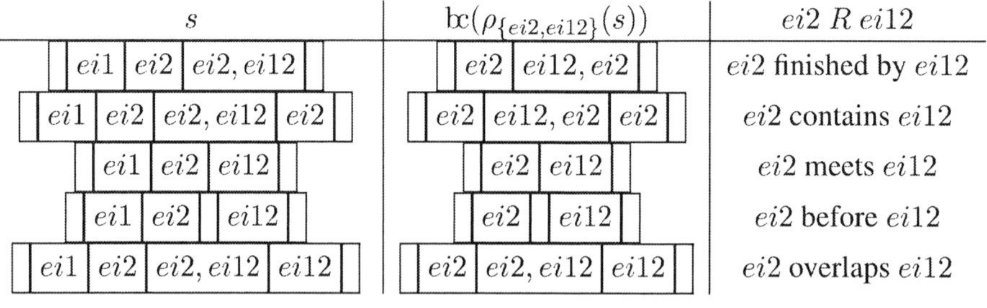

Table 3: Results of superposition $s \in \boxed{\;\boxed{ei1}\;\boxed{ei2}\;} \mathbin{\&_{vc}} \boxed{\;\boxed{ei1}\;}\;\boxed{\;\boxed{ei12}\;}$

It is impossible to determine which of the five is the correct relation for $ei2$ and $ei12$ given just the present data.

Given enough information, the exact relation between every fluent should be specifiable, achieving complete document closure and allowing the creation of a single string whose vocabulary is the set of the

---

[6]Document APW19980807.0261.tml

document's temporal propositions. The relation between any two entities e and e' would be determinable by applying the block compressed $\{e, e'\}$-reduct to the string, and seeing which Allen relation it projected to. However, in typical discourse (and the documents of TimeBank), this often cannot be done: two events may be presented ambiguously in their temporal ordering, either due to unclear wording, or due to the fact that the events were not put in any kind of relation to each other in the text. For example

$$\text{The girl stopped singing when the music on the radio ended.} \tag{27}$$

It is evident that the music and the girl's singing ended at the same time, but it's unclear as to which started first, or if they started at the same time: the information just isn't there. It might be surmised that there is a probable correspondence between the music and the singing, and they likely started together, but it is not possible to be certain. Perhaps she was singing to the song before as well, or perhaps she only sang the last verse of the song.

Freksa (1992) proposed the use of semi-interval relations based on conceptual neighbourhoods to allow for description and reasoning about this kind of uncertainty, as well as coarser-level reasoning. A potential method for extending the expressivity of the strings discussed in this paper so as to allow for these semi-intervals is described below.

First, an interval a will now be said to be bounded in a string s if that string projects to $\boxed{pre(a) \mid a \mid post(a)}$, where $pre(a)$ and $post(a)$ are negations of a conjoined with a formula specifying that a occurs immediately to the right (in the case of $pre(a)$) or to the left (in the case of $post(a)$). Allowing non-atomic formulas such as these inside the string components does pose a risk of trivialising the work done by superposition, and so further study is perhaps required here before making a decision on what exactly should be permitted. For now, in any case, these symbols are taken as being allowed.

The example in Table 3 is repeated here, with these new bordering symbols made visible (for the sake of conciseness, $ei2$ and $ei12$ are abbreviated to x and y, respectively):

$x \, R \, y$	$prepost(s)$
x finished by y	$\boxed{pre(x), pre(y) \mid x, pre(y) \mid x, y \mid post(x), post(y)}$
x contains y	$\boxed{pre(x), pre(y) \mid x, pre(y) \mid x, y \mid post(x), y \mid post(x), post(y)}$
x meets y	$\boxed{pre(x), pre(y) \mid x, pre(y) \mid post(x), y \mid post(x), post(y)}$
x before y	$\boxed{pre(x), pre(y) \mid x, pre(y) \mid post(x), pre(y) \mid post(x), y \mid post(x), post(y)}$
x overlaps y	$\boxed{pre(x), pre(y) \mid x, pre(y) \mid x, y \mid post(x), y \mid post(x), post(y)}$

Table 4: Applying pre and post to s

From Figure 7, p21 of Freksa (1992), it can be seen that the list of Allen relations here corresponds to the Freksa relation "older", which has the constraint that the beginning point of x should be before the beginning point of y. Table 5 shows what happens when a block compressed $\{pre(x), pre(y)\}$-reduct is performed on the strings of Table 4:

$x \, R \, y$	$\mathrm{bc}(\rho_{\{pre(x), pre(y)\}}(prepost(s)))$
x finished by y	$\boxed{pre(x), pre(y) \mid pre(y)}$
x contains y	$\boxed{pre(x), pre(y) \mid pre(y)}$
x meets y	$\boxed{pre(x), pre(y) \mid pre(y)}$
x before y	$\boxed{pre(x), pre(y) \mid pre(y)}$
x overlaps y	$\boxed{pre(x), pre(y) \mid pre(y)}$

Table 5: Performing a block compressed $\{pre(x), pre(y)\}$-reduct

It is clear from this that each of the Allen relations which make up the "older" Freksa relation project to $\boxed{pre(x), pre(y) \mid pre(y)}$. In fact, only these five Allen relations will project to that string, and as such we can use it to characterise that relation, similar to how the strings in Table 1 characterise the various

Allen relations. Below are the characteristic projections for some of the more "simple" Freksa relations (note that some relations have multiple projections which could be considered characteristic, but just one is shown for each):

$$s \models a \text{ ol "older" } b \iff s \text{ projects to } \boxed{pre(a), pre(b) \mid pre(b) \mid} \tag{28a}$$

$$s \models a \text{ yo "younger" } b \iff s \text{ projects to } \boxed{pre(a), pre(b) \mid pre(a) \mid} \tag{28b}$$

$$s \models a \text{ sb "survived by" } b \iff s \text{ projects to } \boxed{\mid post(a) \mid post(a), post(b)} \tag{28c}$$

$$s \models a \text{ sv "survives" } b \iff s \text{ projects to } \boxed{\mid post(b) \mid post(a), post(b)} \tag{28d}$$

$$s \models a \text{ hh "head to head with" } b \iff s \text{ projects to } \boxed{pre(a), pre(b) \mid \mid} \tag{28e}$$

$$s \models a \text{ tt "tail to tail with" } b \iff s \text{ projects to } \boxed{\mid post(a), post(b) \mid} \tag{28f}$$

$$s \models a \text{ bd "born before death of" } b \iff s \text{ projects to } \boxed{pre(a) \mid \mid post(b)} \tag{28g}$$

$$s \models a \text{ db "died after birth of" } b \iff s \text{ projects to } \boxed{pre(b) \mid \mid post(a)} \tag{28h}$$

These relations are dubbed simple here as they can all be projected to a single string with no further extensions to the framework, which would permit condensing a language of results from a superposition into a single string which is characteristic of that language. Conversely, the remaining Freksa relations all involve either a conjunction or disjunction of constraints, and thus require further mechanics in order to fit with this string representation.

For example, the relation "contemporary of" can be defined as

$$s \models a \text{ ct "contemporary of" } b \iff s \text{ projects to } \boxed{pre(a) \mid \mid post(b)}$$
$$\text{and } s \text{ projects to } \boxed{pre(b) \mid \mid post(a)} \tag{29}$$

and "precedes" can be

$$s \models a \text{ pr "precedes" } b \iff s \text{ does } \textbf{not} \text{ project to } \boxed{pre(b) \mid \mid post(a)} \tag{30}$$

where "precedes" is effectively the opposite of "died after birth of". This is obviously not ideal – while (29) is indeed a reduction from the nine Allen relations which correspond to "contemporary of", a conjunction of two strings cannot easily be used as an input to another superposition. (30) is a bit better in that there's only one string involved, but again, it's difficult to superpose a negated string.

An option here is to expand again the symbols which can be boxed: allowing any pair of fluents a and a' to be conjoined within a string component such that for any α_i in a string s

$$a \wedge a' \in \alpha_i \iff a \in \alpha_i \text{ and } a' \in \alpha_i \tag{31}$$

for example

$$\rho_{\{x \wedge y\}}\left(\boxed{\mid x \mid x, y \mid y \mid}\right) = \boxed{\mid \mid x, y \mid \mid} \tag{32}$$

This allows for further Freksa relations to be represented as single strings

$$s \models a \text{ ct "contemporary of" } b \iff s \text{ projects to } \boxed{\mid a \wedge b \mid} \tag{33a}$$

$$s \models a \text{ pr "precedes" } b \iff s \text{ projects to } \boxed{pre(b) \mid post(a) \wedge b \mid} \tag{33b}$$

$$s \models a \text{ sd "succeeds" } b \iff s \text{ projects to } \boxed{pre(a) \mid a \wedge post(b) \mid} \tag{33c}$$

While these methods do seem to have some potential, further work needs to be done in order to fully integrate the concept of semi-intervals into this framework. For example, consider

$$\boxed{\mid a \mid b \mid \mid d \mid} \&_x \boxed{\mid a \mid \mid c \mid} \tag{34}$$

which produces a language of 25 strings. The relation "b older than c" can be derived from this result without too much difficulty, but the relation between c and d is more problematic. There is not enough data to suggest any of Allen's or Freksa's relations with any kind of certainty, and this total lack of information cannot be represented as anything remotely concise using strings. The question then arises as to what to do with this result.

The number of times each Allen relation occurred in the 25 strings could potentially be examined, and a guess hazarded based on the most frequently occurring one, but this approach would require careful testing to determine whether there is real merit. For example, of the 25 strings in (34), five of them (20%) in the resulting language suggest the relation "c before d", three (12%) for each of "overlaps", "contains", "finished by", and "meets", with the remaining eight Allen relations featuring in just one (4%) string each. This means 68% of those strings project to one of the five relations corresponding to "c older than d" – but there is no way to say for sure what relation there truly is between c and d without additional data.

Though it should be proved by experiment, it may be more beneficial in scenarios like this to simply leave the strings separate, and to not superpose them. Seeing two separate strings is plausibly more useful to an annotator than 25 alternate possibilities. Generalising from this, one could imagine that, rather than aiming for a single string representing the entire document's temporal structure, a number of maximal substrings are given instead, each of which contain as much information as can be made certain – that is, all strings are superposed with each other only under the condition that the language generated by superposition contains exactly one string (or group of strings corresponding to a single Freksa relation). In this way, the document's structure would still be visualised, but in chunks rather than a single timeline.

As an example, taking one of the smaller documents from TimeBank,[7] translate all of the TLINKs to strings (35), then superpose until there are no more options for superposition which produce a single-string language. The resulting set of strings (36) are the maximal substrings for the document.

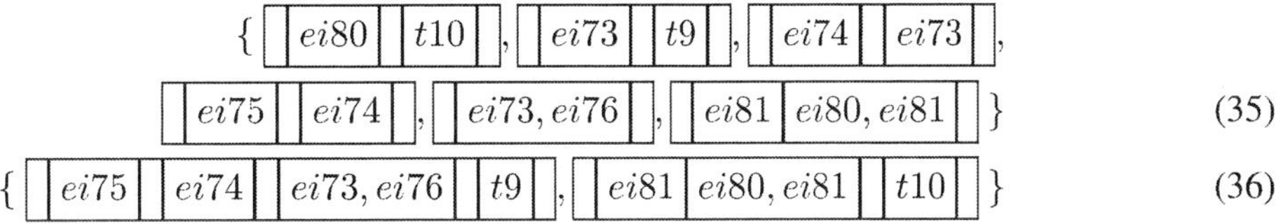

$$\{\ \boxed{\ \boxed{ei80}\ \boxed{t10}\ },\ \boxed{\ \boxed{ei73}\ \boxed{t9}\ },\ \boxed{\ \boxed{ei74}\ \boxed{ei73}\ },$$
$$\boxed{\ \boxed{ei75}\ \boxed{ei74}\ },\ \boxed{\ \boxed{ei73, ei76}\ },\ \boxed{\ \boxed{ei81}\ \boxed{ei80, ei81}\ }\ \} \tag{35}$$
$$\{\ \boxed{\ \boxed{ei75}\ \boxed{ei74}\ \boxed{ei73, ei76}\ \boxed{t9}\ },\ \boxed{\ \boxed{ei81}\ \boxed{ei80, ei81}\ \boxed{t10}\ }\ \} \tag{36}$$

5   Conclusion

An efficient refinement was given for the superposition operation using an approach which interleaves generation with testing of valid strings, and a method was described for increasing the expressiveness of temporal strings to allow for some level of partial information based on semi-intervals.

There is still further experimentation to be done on how exactly to best handle cases with incomplete data, especially in large documents. Derczynski (2016) notes that a careful balance is needed between being exact in distinguishing relations, and not letting the set of relations available become too large. The question of precisely what to do when the result of a superposition cannot be condensed to a single string needs to be answered, and whether to allow for branching timelines in cases of non-determinism. Tooling is also in development to demonstrate the uses of the strings, in particular as a visualisation aid which may complement existing tools for the annotation process.

Acknowledgements

This research is supported by Science Foundation Ireland (SFI) through the CNGL Programme (Grant 12/CE/I2267) in the ADAPT Centre (https://www.adaptcentre.ie) at Trinity College Dublin. The ADAPT Centre for Digital Content Technology is funded under the SFI Research Centres Programme (Grant 13/RC/2106) and is co-funded under the European Regional Development Fund.

---

[7]Document wsj_0006.tml

References

James F Allen. 1983. Maintaining Knowledge About Temporal Intervals. *Communications of the ACM*, 26(11):832–843.

Leon Derczynski. 2016. Representation and Learning of Temporal Relations. In *Proceedings of COLING 2016, the 26th International Conference on Computational Linguistics: Technical Papers*, pages 1937–1948.

Tim Fernando. 2015. The Semantics of Tense and Aspect: A Finite-State Perspective. In S Lappin and C Fox, editors, *The Handbook of Contemporary Semantic Theory*, number August, pages 203–236. John Wiley & Sons.

Tim Fernando. 2016. On Regular Languages Over Power Sets. *Journal of Language Modelling*, 4(1):29–56.

Christian Freksa. 1992. Temporal Reasoning Based on Semi-Intervals. *Artificial Intelligence*, 54:199–227.

Leonid Libkin. 2004. Monadic Second-Order Logic and Automata. In *Elements of Finite Model Theory*, pages 113–140. Springer Berlin Heidelberg, Berlin, Heidelberg.

James Pustejovsky, Inderjeet Mani, Luc Belanger, Linda van Guilder, Robert Knippen, Andrew See, Jon Schwarz, and Marc Verhagen. 2003. Tango final report. In *ARDA Summer Workshop on Graphical Annotation Toolkit for TimeML, MITRE Bedford and Brandeis University*.

James Pustejovsky, Marc Verhagen, Roser Sauri, Jessica Littman, Robert Gaizauskas, Graham Katz, Inderjeet Mani, Robert Knippen, and Andrea Setzer. 2006. TimeBank 1.2 LDC2006T08. Web Download: https://catalog.ldc.upenn.edu/LDC2006T08. Philadelphia: Linguistic Data Consortium.

James Pustejovsky, Kiyong Lee, Harry Bunt, and Laurent Romary. 2010. ISO-TimeML: An International Standard for Semantic Annotation. In *LREC*, volume 10, pages 394–397.

TimeML Working Group. 2005. TimeML 1.2.1. A Formal Specification Language for Events and Temporal Expressions. http://www.timeml.org/publications/timeMLdocs/timeml_1.2.1.html#tlink.

Marc Verhagen, Robert Knippen, Inderjeet Mani, and James Pustejovsky. 2006. Annotation of Temporal Relations with Tango. *Proceedings of the 5th Languange Resources and Evaluation Confernece (LREC 2006)*, (May 2014):2249–2252.

Marc Verhagen. 2005a. Drawing TimeML Relations with T-BOX. In Graham Katz, James Pustejovsky, and Frank Schilder, editors, *Annotating, Extracting and Reasoning about Time and Events*, number 05151 in Dagstuhl Seminar Proceedings, Dagstuhl, Germany. Internationales Begegnungs und Forschungszentrum für Informatik (IBFI), Schloss Dagstuhl, Germany.

Marc Verhagen. 2005b. Temporal closure in an annotation environment. *Language Resources and Evaluation*, 39(2-3):211–241.

David Woods, Tim Fernando, and Carl Vogel. 2017. Towards Efficient String Processing of Annotated Events. In *Proceedings of the 13th Joint ISO-ACL Workshop on Interoperable Semantic Annotation (ISA-13)*, pages 124–133.

Discourse Annotation in the PDTB: The Next Generation

Rashmi Prasad[1], **Bonnie Webber**[2], **Alan Lee**[3]

[1]Interactions LLC
rprasad@interactions.com
[2]School of Informatics, University of Edinburgh
bonnie@inf.ed.ac.uk
[3]University of Pennsylvania
alanlee@lexicontree.org

Abstract

We present highlights from our work on enriching the Penn Discourse Treebank (PDTB), to be released to the community in Fall 2018 as the PDTB-3. We have increased its coverage of discourse relations (from ~40K to ~53k), the majority in intra-sentential contexts. Our work on these new relations has led us to augment and/or modify aspects of the annotation guidelines, including the sense hierarchy, and all changes have been propagated through the rest of the corpus.

1 Introduction

The last decade has seen growing interest in enabling language technology and psycholinguistics to move beyond the sentence, to what can be derived from larger units of text. This has led to greater interest in the properties of discourse. One such property is the coherence between clauses and sentences arising from low-level discourse relations. This level of meaning has been made overt through manual annotation in the Penn Discourse TreeBank (PDTB), developed with NSF support.[1] Version 2.0. of the PDTB (Prasad et al., 2008), released in 2008, contains over 40K tokens of annotated relations, making it the largest such corpus available to date. Largely because the PDTB was based on the simple idea that discourse relations are grounded in an identifiable set of explicit words or phrases (discourse connectives) or simply in sentence adjacency, it has been taken up and used by many researchers in the NLP community and more recently, by researchers in psycholinguistics as well. It has also stimulated the development of similar resources in other languages (Chinese (Zhou and Xue, 2015), Czech (Poláková et al., 2013), Hindi (Oza et al., 2009), Modern Standard Arabic (Al-Saif and Markert, 2010), Turkish (Zeyrek and Webber, 2008) and French (Danlos et al., 2012)) and domains (biomedical texts (Prasad et al., 2011), conversational dialogues (Tonelli et al., 2010)), the organization of community-level shared tasks on *shallow discourse parsing* (Xue et al., 2015; Xue et al., 2016), and a cross-lingual discourse annotation of parallel texts, the TED-MDB corpus (Zeyrek et al., 2018), to support both linguistic understanding of coherence in different languages and improvements in machine translation of discourse connectives.

Given only three years in which to develop guidelines, and annotate and release the PDTB, we knew that it would be incomplete (Prasad et al., 2014). With additional support from the NSF, we have now addressed many of the gaps in the corpus, adding over 17K new discourse relations. Most of the new relations occur intra-sententially, but there are also ~300 inter-sentential implicit relations between adjacent sentences whose annotation is missing from the PDTB-2.[2] This paper focuses on the new intra-sentential relations annotated in the PDTB-3. We also discuss major modifications and extensions to the PDTB guidelines, including the sense hierarchy, which have resulted from our study of the new relations, and which have been propagated throughout the corpus. PDTB-3, which we plan to release to the community in Fall 2018, will contain over 53K tokens of discourse relations, and as with PDTB-2, will

---

[1]http://www.seas.upenn.edu/~pdtb

[2]Separate from the PDTB-3, Prasad et al. (2017) address the annotation of cross-paragraph implicit relations that are not annotated in either PDTB-2 or PDTB-3. These annotations are provided for 145 texts from Sections 01, 06, and 23 of the Wall Street Journal corpus, producing a full-text annotated sub-corpus merged with the PDTB-3 annotations for the same texts. However, because the annotation guidelines developed for the cross-paragraph annotation depart in some respects from the PDTB guidelines in ways not incorporated in PDTB-3, these annotations will be released to the community separately, via *github* (https://github.com/pdtb-upenn/full-text).

be distributed through the Linguistic Data Consortium (LDC), along with a detailed annotation manual (which will also be available from the PDTB website).

Section 2 describes the range of new constructions annotated in the corpus. Section 3 describes changes to the senses and relation types, and Section 4 describes some other modifications to the guidelines. We close with a discussion of mapping the new PDTB-3 senses to the ISO-DR-Core set of discourse relations (Section 5), and the conclusion (Section 6).

2 New Relations

While the PDTB-2 contains over 40K tokens of discourse relations, there are some syntactic and textual contexts where discourse relations were not annotated. In particular, PDTB-2 guidelines (PDTB-Group, 2008) limited annotation to (a) explicit relations lexicalized by discourse connectives, and (b) implicit relations between paragraph-internal adjacent sentences and between (semi-)colon separated clauses within sentences. Further, discourse connectives were drawn from the pre-defined syntactic classes of subordinating conjunctions, coordinating conjunctions, and discourse adverbials. And strict constraints were placed on the syntactic realization of relation arguments: with a few well-defined exceptions, arguments had to be realized as one or more clauses or sentences.

Defining the scope of the annotation in this way, however, precluded consideration of a wider set of discourse relations.

First, the general restriction to explicit connectives precluded subordinate clauses — in particular **free adjuncts** and **free TO-infinitives**, that can occur without lexical subordinators while bearing an implicit relation to their matrix clause. Ex. (1) shows a free adjunct related via an implicit REASON sense to its matrix clause, explaining why treasurys opened lower. The free TO-infinitive in Ex. (2) is related via CONDITION to its matrix clause, specifying the hypothetical purpose from which the competitive edge would have to follow.

(1) *Treasurys opened lower,* Implicit=as a result of **reacting negatively to news that the producer price index – a measure of inflation on the wholesale level – accelerated in September**. (CONTINGENCY.CAUSE.REASON)[wsj_2428]

(2) *Banks need a competitive edge* Implicit=if (they are) **to sell their products**. (CONTINGENCY.CONDITION.ARG2-AS-CONDITION)[wsj_0238]

Second, the restriction to explicit connectives from the limited set of syntactic classes precluded relations triggered by **prepositional subordinators** like *for, by, in, with, instead of,* etc., that can complementize for clauses, as in Exs. (3-6).

(3) *But* <u>with</u> **foreign companies snapping up U.S. movie studios**, *the networks are pressing their fight harder than ever.* (CONTINGENCY.CAUSE.REASON) [wsj_2451]

(4) Wall Street analysts have criticized Bethlehem *for not following its major competitors* <u>in</u> **linking with a foreign company to share costs and provide technology to modernize old facilities or build new ones**. (EXPANSION.MANNER.ARG2-AS-MANNER [wsj_0782]

(5) James Cleveland, a courier *who earned a Bravo Zulu* <u>for</u> **figuring out how to get a major customer's 1,100-parcel-a-week load to its doorstep by 8 a.m.**, considers himself far more than a courier. (CONTINGENCY.CAUSE.REASON) [WSJ_1394]

(6) But on reflection, Mr. Oka says, he concluded that Nissan is being prudent *in following its slow-startup strategy* <u>instead of</u> **simply copying Lexus**. (EXPANSION.SUBSTITUTION.ARG1-AS-SUBST) [WSJ_0286]

Third, the restriction on arguments to clauses (with a small set of specific exceptions) precluded relations between **conjoined verb phrases**. The PDTB-2 exceptions to clausal realization did allow verb phrases to be valid arguments, but not of the VP conjunction itself. Thus, in Ex. (7), while *because* was annotated, the VP conjunction *and* was not. Conjoined VPs have now been annotated in the PDTB-3 (Webber et al., 2016), as in Ex. (8) and Ex. (9).

(7) She became an abortionist accidentally, *and continued* <u>because</u> **it enabled her to buy jam, cocoa and other war-rationed goodies**. (CONTINGENCY.CAUSE.REASON) [wsj_0039]

(8) She *became an abortionist accidentally,* <u>and</u> **continued because it enabled her to buy jam, cocoa and other war-rationed goodies**. (EXPANSION.CONJUNCTION) [wsj_0039]

Intra-S Context	~Num
Free Adjuncts	~2200
Free TO-infinitives	~1500
Prep. Clausal Subordination	~1600
Conjoined VPs	~5800
S Conjunction Implicits	~1800
Total	**~13000**

Table 1: Approximate distribution of new intra-sentential relations in PDTB-3. Exact distributions will be announced with the release of the corpus.

(9) Stocks *closed higher in Hong Kong, Manila, Singapore, Sydney and Wellington,* <u>but</u> **were lower in Seoul**. (COMPARISON.CONTRAST) [wsj_0231]

As discussed in Webber et al. (2016), in order to maintain alignment with the shared subject of VP conjunctions, we excluded the shared subject from both the left and right conjunct arguments of the conjunction, as in Ex. (8-9). Webber et al. also discuss the fact that these arguments can also be linked by an additional implicit relation, as in Ex. (8), where an implicit temporal PRECEDENCE sense is inferred between the arguments in addition to the explicit CONJUNCTION. Rather than associating the additional sense inference with the conjunction itself, these implicit relations have been annotated as separate tokens, as in Ex. (10). However, the explicit and implicit relations are *linked* in the underlying representation, with a linking mechanism to indicate that two relations hold between the same two arguments.

(10) She *became an abortionist accidentally,* <u>Implicit=then</u> **and continued because it enabled her to buy jam, cocoa and other war-rationed goodies**. (TEMPORAL.ASYNCHRONOUS.PRECEDENCE) [wsj_0039]

The distribution of new intra-S relations is given in Table 1, showing VP conjunctions accounting for about half of the total. However, about 20% of these tokens are implicit relations inferred in addition to those associated with the explicit conjunction, as with the PRECEDENCE sense in Ex. (10). The "S Conjunction Implicits" category in the table is in fact a consequence of our finding that additional implicit inferences can be associated not just with VP conjunctions but with intra-sentential S conjunctions as well. In PDTB-2, these additional inferences were either not annotated, or associated with the explicit connective, alone or in addition to the default CONJUNCTION sense. For PDTB-3, therefore, all S conjunction relations in PDTB-2 were revisited and reconsidered for these additional inferences, with new implicit tokens added to the corpus where needed. The number of the additional implicit inferences shown in the table account for 32% of the discourse relations associated with S conjunctions in the corpus.

For the annotation task, the intra-sentential contexts discussed above were automatically identified using the Penn Treebank (Marcus et al., 1993) and Propbank (Palmer et al., 2005) annotations. As described in Prasad et al. (2015), subordinated clause contexts were identified by first searching for adjunct (ARGM) arguments of verbs in the Propbank, and then filtered to select clausal arguments, by aligning the Propbank ARGM arguments with the Penn Treebank (PTB). The resulting tokens were then divided into separate sets using further heuristics applied to the PTB clausal structures, thus creating distinct well-defined subtasks corresponding to free adjuncts, TO-infinitives, and preposition-subordinated clauses. Guidelines were then created separately for each of these subtasks after a study of a development sample within each subset. VP conjunction and S conjunction contexts were identified with heuristics applied solely to the PTB, and were also annotated as a separate subtask, with its own set of guidelines. Detailed guidelines for these different contexts will be included in the PDTB-3 manual accompanying the release of the corpus.

Temporal	Synchronous	--
	Asynchronous	Precedence
		Succession

Contingency	Cause $+/-\beta, +/-\zeta$	Reason
		Result
		Negative-result*
	Condition $+/-\zeta$	Arg1-as-cond
		Arg2-as-cond
	Negative condition $+/-\zeta$	Arg1-as-negcond
		Arg2-as-negcond
	Purpose	Arg1-as-goal
		Arg2-as-goal
		Arg2-as-negGoal

Comparison	Contrast	--
	Similarity	--
	Concession $+/-\zeta$	Arg1-as-denier*
		Arg2-as-denier

Expansion	Conjunction	--
	Disjunction	--
	Equivalence	--
	Instantiation	Arg1-as-instance
		Arg2-as-instance
	Level-of-detail	Arg1-as-detail
		Arg2-as-detail
	Substitution	Arg1-as-subst
		Arg2-as-subst
	Exception	Arg1-as-excpt
		Arg2-as-excpt
	Manner	Arg1-as-manner
		Arg2-as-manner

Figure 1: PDTB-3 Sense Hierarchy. Only asymmetric senses are specified further at Level-3, to capture the directionality of the arguments. Superscript symbols on Level-2 senses indicate features for implicit beliefs ($+/-\beta$) and speech-acts ($+/-\zeta$) that may or may not be associated with one of the defined arguments of the relation. Senses marked with the asterisk (*) are the subtypes that did not occur as belief and speech-act senses in the corpus. Features are shown on the sense only for clarity, but should not be seen as a property of the relation, rather of the arguments.

3 Changes to Senses and Relation Types

Figure 1 shows the most recent PDTB-3 sense hierarchy, which simplifies and extends the PDTB-2 sense hierarchy. Simplifications include (a) restricting Level-3 sense to differences in directionality, (b) eliminating rare and/or difficult-to-annotate senses, and (c) replacing separate senses with features that can be added to a given sense (Section 3.1). Extensions mainly involve senses needed for annotating some of the new intra-sentential relations (Section 3.2).

3.1 Simplifying the relation hierarchy

Although the hierarchy retains the same four Level-1 senses, senses at Level-3 now only encode *directionality* of the arguments, and so only appear with asymmetric Level-2 senses.[3] Those Level-3 senses in the PDTB-2 that did not convey directionality were either moved to Level-2 — SUBSTITUTION (renamed from the PDTB-2 CHOSEN ALTERNATIVE) and EQUIVALENCE — or eliminated due to their rarity or the difficulty they posed for annotators — in particular, those under the Level-2 senses of CONTRAST, CONDITION and ALTERNATIVE (now renamed DISJUNCTION).

With respect to directionality, annotating intra-sentential discourse relations revealed asymmetric Level-2 senses for which the relation's arguments occur in either order (rather than the single order assumed in the PDTB-2). In particular, the argument conveying the condition in CONDITION relations can be either **Arg2** (as was the case throughout the PDTB-2) or *Arg1* as in Ex. 11, while the argument conveying the "chosen alternative" (now called "substitute") in SUBSTITUTION relations can be either **Arg2** (as was the case throughout the PDTB-2) or *Arg1*, as in Ex. 12. In the case of the rare sense called EXCEPTION, it was not previously noticed that in some of the tokens so annotated, the exception appeared in **Arg2**, while in the rest, the exception appeared in *Arg1* (Ex. 13). Finally, while all cases of the INSTANTIATION sense in PDTB-2 were annotated with the assumption that it was always **Arg2** that provided the instance, we have now found (rare) evidence that the instance can be realized as *Arg1* as well (Ex. 14).

---

[3] A sense relation $\Re$ is *symmetric* iff $\Re(Arg1, \mathbf{Arg2})$ and $\Re(\mathbf{Arg2}, Arg1)$ are semantically equivalent. If a relation is not symmetric, it is *asymmetric*.

(11) ARG1-AS-COND: *Call Jim Wright's office in downtown Fort Worth, Texas, these days* and **the receptionist still answers the phone, "Speaker Wright's office.** [wsj_0909]

(12) ARG1-AS-SUBST: "The primary purpose of a railing is *to contain a vehicle* **and** not **to provide a scenic view,"** [wsj_0102]

(13) ARG1-AS-EXCPT: *Twenty-five years ago the poet Richard Wilbur modernized this 17th-century comedy merely by avoiding "the zounds sort of thing," as he wrote in his introduction.* Otherwise, **the scene remained Celimene's house in 1666.** [wsj_1936]

(14) ARG1-AS-INSTANCE: *In a country where a bribe is needed to get a phone, a job, and even into a school, the name Bofors has become a potent rallying cry against the government.* **That illustrates the kind of disappointment many Indians feel toward Mr. Gandhi, whom they zestfully elected and enthusiastically supported in his first two years in power.** [wsj_2041]

Level-2 pragmatic senses have been removed from the hierarchy and replaced with features that can be attached to a relation token to indicate an inference of *implicit* belief (epistemic knowledge) or of a *speech act* associated with arguments, rather than with the relation itself. Figure 1 shows the senses for which these features have so far been found to be warranted, based on the empirical evidence found during annotation. Ex. 15 shows an implicit CAUSE.RESULT relation but one where the result **Arg2** argument is the (speaker's/writer's) *belief* that the deadline could be extended. **Arg2** is therefore annotated with a +belief feature because the belief is implicit. Similarly, Ex. 16 shows a CONCESSION.ARG2-AS-DENIER relation, but what's being denied (or cancelled) is the speech act associated with **Arg2**, and this is annotated as a feature on **Arg2** because it is implicit.

(15) RESULT+BELIEF: That deadline *has been extended once* Implicit=so **and could be extended again.** [wsj_2032]

(16) ARG2-AS-DENIER+SPEECH-ACT: He spends his days *sketching passers-by,* or **trying to.** [wsj_0039]

Also simplifying the PDTB2 hierarchy is removal of the LIST sense, which turned out not to be distinguishable from CONJUNCTION. And the names of two asymmetric PDTB-2 senses have been changed to bring out commonalities. In particular, RESTATEMENT has been renamed LEVEL-OF-DETAIL, with its SPECIFICATION and GENERALIZATION subtypes in the PDTB-2 now just taken to be directional variants renamed ARG2-AS-DETAIL and ARG1-AS-DETAIL, respectively. Similarly, the sub-types of CONCESSION, opaquely called CONTRA-EXPECTATION and EXPECTATION, have been renamed to reflect simply a difference in directionality: ARG1-AS-DENIER and ARG2-AS-DENIER, respectively.

3.2 Augmenting the Sense Hierarchy

New senses have been introduced into the hierarchy on an "as needed" basis. These include the asymmetric Level-2 senses of MANNER under EXPANSION, and PURPOSE and NEGATIVE CONDITION under CONTINGENCY, along with their Level-3 directional variants. Parallel to the negative counterpart of CONDITION (NEGATIVE CONDITION), we also found evidence for negative counterparts of RESULT (NEGRESULT) and ARG2-AS-GOAL (ARG2-AS-NEGGOAL). The symmetric Level-2 sense SIMILARITY was added under COMPARISON because of its obvious omission from the PDTB-2 as the complement of the symmetric sense CONTRAST. The definitions and examples for these new senses are given in Table 2.

The entire PDTB2 has been updated to reflect the sense modifications. Most often, the mapping is simply 1:1 and has been done automatically. Where the mapping is 1:N or M:N, manual review has been required, with further adjudication to ensure both agreement and consistency.

3.3 Hypophora: A New Relation Type

Among the inter-sentential relations missing from PDTB-2, we found many pairs such as Exs. (17-18), where the first sentence (*Arg1*) expresses a question seeking some information, and the second (**Arg2**) provides a response to fulfil that need. As with the EntRel relations in the PDTB, these relations cannot be instantiated with connectives, explicitly or implicitly.

(17) *If not now, when?* **"When the fruit is ripe, it falls from the tree by itself," he says."** [wsj_0300]

(18) *Of all the ethnic tensions in America, which is the most troublesome right now?* **A good bet would be the tension between blacks and Jews in New York City.** [wsj_2369]

SIMILARITY: One or more similarities between *Arg1* and **Arg2** are highlighted with respect to what each argument predicates as a whole or to some entities it mentions. *..., the Straits Times index is up 24% this year*, so investors who bailed out generally did so profitably. <u>Similarly</u>, **Kuala Lumpur's composite index yesterday ended 27.5% above its 1988 close.** [wsj_2230]
CAUSE:NEGATIVE RESULT: *Arg1* gives the reason/explanation/justification for why **Arg2** does not result. *A search party soon found the unscathed aircraft in a forest clearing <u>much too</u> small* **<u>to</u> have allowed a conventional landing.**
NEGATIVE CONDITION: One argument describes a situation presented as unrealized (the antecedent or condition), which if it doesn't occur, would lead to the situation described by the other argument (the consequent). ARG1-AS-NEGCOND: In Singapore, a new law requires smokers to *put out their cigarettes before entering restaurants, department stores and sports centers* <u>or</u> **face a $250 fine.** [wsj_0037] ARG2-AS-NEGCOND: <u>Unless</u> **the Federal Reserve eases interest rates soon to stimulate the economy,** *profits could remain disappointing.* [wsj_0322]
PURPOSE: One argument presents an action that an agent undertakes with the purpose (intention) of achieving the goal conveyed by the other argument. ARG1-AS-GOAL: She ordered *the foyer done in a different plaid planting,* <u>Implicit=for that purpose</u> **and made the landscape architects study a book on tartans.** [wsj_0984] ARG2-AS-GOAL: *Skilled ringers use their wrists to advance or retard the next swing,* <u>so that</u> **one bell can swap places with another in the following change.** [wsj_0089] ARG2-AS-NEGGOAL: We can applaud Mr. Pryor's moment of epiphany, even as we understand *that he and his confreres need restraint* <u>lest</u> **they kill again.** [wsj_1698]
MANNER: The situation described by one argument presents *how* (i.e., the manner in which) the situation described by other argument has happened or is done. ARG1-AS-MANNER: He argued that program-trading by roughly 15 big institutions is *pushing around the markets* <u>Implicit=thereby</u> **and scaring individual investors.** [wsj_0987] ARG2-AS-MANNER: A native of the area, he is back now after riding the oil-field boom to the top, *then surviving the bust* <u>Implicit=by</u> **running an Oklahoma City convenience store.** [wsj_0725]

Table 2: New senses in PDTB-3

The response to the question can answer the information need explicitly, as in Exs. (17-18), or implicitly (Ex. 19). And the answer can also indicate that the information need cannot be fulfilled (Ex. 20).

(19) *So can a magazine survive by downright thumbing its nose at major advertisers?* **Garbage magazine, billed as "The Practical Journal for the Environment," is about to find out.** [wsj_0062]

(20) *With all this, can stock prices hold their own?* **"The question is unanswerable at this point"** she says. [wsj_0681]

Because these relations involve dialogue acts (Bunt et al., 2017), which we treat as distinct from discourse relations, and because they are uninstantiable as connectives, we have added a new coherence relation type for them — called HYPOPHORA.

Of course, not all questions in a discourse are dialogue acts. HYPOPHORA does not apply when the subsequent text relates to a question in other ways – for example, with rhetorical questions that are posed for dramatic effect or to make an assertion, rather than to elicit an answer, as in Ex. (21), or if the subsequent text provides an explanation for why the question has been asked, as in Ex. (22). In such cases, an implicit connective can be asserted and a discourse relation can be inferred to hold, as shown.

(21) *What's wrong with asking for more money?*
<u>Implicit=because</u> **Money is not everything, but it is necessary, and business is not volunteer work.** (CONTINGENCY.CAUSE.REASON+BELIEF) [wsj_0094]

(22) *"What sector is stepping forward to pick up the slack?"* he asked.
<u>Implicit=because</u> **"I draw a blank."** (CONTINGENCY.CAUSE.REASON+SPEECH-ACT) [wsj_0036]

4 Modifications to Other Guidelines

In this section, we present other major modifications to the PDTB guidelines.

4.1 Argument Labeling Convention

The first modification, described earlier in Webber et al. (2016), relates to the argument labeling two-part convention in PDTB-2, where

- For spans linked by an explicit discourse connective, **Arg2** was the argument to which the connective was attached syntactically, and the other was *Arg1*. This allowed the arguments to subordinating conjunctions to be labeled consistently, independent of the order in which the arguments appeared. The same was true for coordinating conjunctions, whose argument order is always the same, and for discourse adverbials, whose *Arg1* always precedes the adverbial, even when *Arg1* is embedded in **Arg2**.

- For implicit discourse relations, *Arg1* was always the first (lefthand) span and **Arg2**, the adjacent (righthand) span.

Blindly applying this convention in annotating *intra-sentential* discourse relations can produce inconsistent labeling because of (1) variability in where an explicit connectives can attach within a sentence; and (2) the ability of marked syntax to replace explicit connectives.

The first problem can be illustrated with paired connectives like *not only … but also*. Here, both members of the pair may be present (Ex. 23), or just one or the other (Ex. 24 and Ex. 25):

(23) Japan not only outstrips the U.S. in investment flows but also outranks it in trade with most Southeast Asian countries … [wsj_0043]

(24) The hacker was pawing over the Berkeley files but also using Berkeley and other easily accessible computers as stepping stones … [wsj_0257]

(25) Not only did Mr. Ortega's comments come in the midst of what was intended as a showcase for the region, it came as Nicaragua is under special international scrutiny … [wsj_0655]

A labeling convention that requires **Arg2** to be the argument to which the explicit connective attaches will choose a different argument for **Arg2** in Ex. (24) than in Ex. (25), and an arbitrary argument in the case of Ex (23), when semantically, the lefthand argument is playing the same role in all three cases, as is the righthand argument.

The second problem can be illustrated with preposed auxiliaries, which signal a CONDITION sense between the clause with the preposed auxiliary (as *antecedent*) and the other clause (as *consequent*). As with subordinating clauses, the two clauses can appear in either order:

(26) Had the contest gone a full seven games, ABC could have reaped an extra \$10 million in ad sales … [wsj_0443]

(27) … they probably would have gotten away with it, had they not felt compelled to add Ms. Collins's signature tune, "Amazing Grace," … [wsj_0207]

Since there is no explicit connective in either clause, if position is used to label *Arg1* and **Arg2**, the result can again be inconsistent.

To avoid inconsistency, while not requiring any change to existing labels in the PDTB-2, we have adopted the following new convention:

- The arguments to inter-sentential discourse relations remain labeled by *position*: *Arg1* is first (lefthand) argument and **Arg2**, the second (righthand) argument.

- With intra-sentential coordinating structures, the arguments are also labeled by *position*: *Arg1* is first argument and **Arg2**, the second one, independent of which argument(s) have attached coordinating conjunction(s).

- With intra-sentential subordinating structures, *Arg1* and **Arg2** are determined syntactically. The subordinate structure is always labeled **Arg2**, and the structure to which it is subordinate is labeled *Arg1*.

4.2 AltLex Identification and Annotation

The convention for identifying instances of *Alternative Lexicalizations* (or AltLex) in the PDTB-2 was that, in the absence of an explicit connective, if annotators inferred a relation between the sentences but felt that the insertion of a implicit connective would be redundant, they were encouraged to identify the non-connective expression in **Arg2** that they took as the source of the perceived redundancy as the AltLex,

Annotating intra-sentential discourse relations in the PDTB-3 has led to modifying the above convention in two ways — what is annotated as AltLex and where AltLex can be annotated.

With respect to what is annotated as AltLex, reliably identifiable AltLex expressions in the PDTB-2 included one part that conveyed the relation and one part that referred anaphorically or elliptically to *Arg1*, as in "after that" or "a likely reason for the disparity is" (Prasad et al., 2010). To allow for AltLex expressions in the context of intra-sentential discourse relations, we have allowed expressions of any form or syntactic class to be labeled as AltLex, including adjectives and adjective-modifiers such as *additional*, *next*, *further*, and *earlier*. While these expressions continue to suggest the relation, unlike AltLex expressions in PDTB-2, the reference to Arg1 may be implicit. That is, while *next* implies next to something, that something may be implicit.

One consequence of this new convention is that words such as *further* and *next*, that can appear as discourse adverbials, or as adverbials modifying verbs or adjectives, or as adjectives themselves, will be annotated as Explicit connectives when they are discourse adverbials, as in Exs. (28-29), and otherwise as AltLex phrases, as in Ex. (30), where *further* modifies *fractioning*.

(28) Stephen G. Jerritts, president and chief executive officer, said *customers weren't willing to commit to an expensive NBI hardware systems because of the company's financial troubles.* Further, he said, argii[the company doesn't have the capital needed to build the business over the next year or two]. (EXPANSION.CONJUNCTION) [wsj_0092]

(29) *Inspired by imports, Mr. Rosen now makes fur muffs, hats and flings. This year he produced a men's line and offers dyed furs in red, cherry red, violet, royal blue and forest green.... From Asia, he has mink jackets with floral patterns made by using different colored furs.* Next **he will be testing pictured embroidery (called kalega) made in the Far East.** (TEMPORAL.ASYNCHRONOUS.PRECEDENCE) [wsj_1586]

(30) *The show, despite a promising start, has slipped badly in the weekly ratings as compiled by A.C. Nielsen Co., finishing far below "Tonight" on NBC, a unit of General Electric Co., and "Nightline" on ABC-TV, a unit of Capital Cities/ABC Inc.* **Further fractioning the late-night audience is the addition of the "Arsenio Hall Show," syndicated by Paramount Communications Inc** (EXPANSION.CONJUNCTION) [wsj_2395]

With respect to where *AltLex* can be annotated, PDTB-3 annotators have been permitted to include material the AltLex expression from both Arg1 and Arg2. This is motivated by examples like Exs. (31-33), where the underlined segmented in *Arg1* and **Arg2** together signal the sense of the relation.

(31) *Marni Rice plays the maid with so much edge* **as to steal her two scenes.** (CONTINGENCY.CAUSE.RESULT) [wsj_1163]

(32) *some of the proposals are so close* **that non-financial issues such as timing may play a more important role.** (CONTINGENCY.CAUSE.RESULT) [wsj_0953]

(33) *Things have gone too far* **for the government to stop them now.** (CONTINGENCY.CAUSE.RESULT) [wsj_2454]

We have also allowed AltLex to span an entire argument, which would typically be **Arg2**, to adequately represent the expression of discourse relations with *syntactic constructions*. For example, in Ex. (34), it is the *syntactic inversion* of the predicate that signals the CONCESSION sense. And in Ex. (35), it is the AUX-inversion that signals the CONDITION sense. In both these cases, as in others like these, the entire **Arg2** is selected as the AltLex span, which is a unique indication that it is the syntactic construction that serves as the AltLex.

(34) **Crude as they were,** *these early PCs triggered explosive product development in desktop models for the home and office.* (COMPARISON.CONCESSION.ARG1-AS-DENIER) [wsj_0022]

(35) **Had the contest gone a full seven games,** *ABC could have reaped an extra $10 million in ad sales on the seventh game alone, compared with the ad take it would have received for regular prime-time shows.* (CONTINGENCY.CONDITION.ARG2-AS-CONDITION) [wsj_0443]

Since researchers may be interested in analyzing these constructional AltLex's further, we have assigned them the relation type ALTLEXC, to indicate that they are a sub-type of Altlex. Tokens of this type have all the same fields as an AltLex. They are just marked for easy identification and review.

5   Mapping to ISO-DR-Core

Existing annotation frameworks (which, apart from the PDTB, have led to the creation of several other corpora of coherence relations, including Afantenos et al. (2012), Carlson et al. (2003), Reese et al. (2007), Sanders and Scholman (2012), and Wolf and Gibson (2005)) exhibit some major differences in their underlying assumptions, but there are also strong compatibilities. ISO DR-Core (ISO 247617-8: 2016) forms part of an effort to develop an international standard for the annotation of discourse relations.[4] One of the outcomes of this effort (Bunt and Prasad, 2016) was to provide clear and mutually consistent definitions of a set of *core* discourse relations (senses) – ISO-DR-Core – many of which have similar definitions in different frameworks, and provide mappings from ISO-DR-Core relations to relations in different frameworks, including the PDTB.

With the extensions to the sense hierarchy in PDTB, it is therefore of interest to ask if the new senses in PDTB are mappable to the ISO-DR-Core relations. We find that while the new senses PURPOSE, NEGATIVE CONDITION, SIMILARITY and MANNER have a 1:1 mapping with the relations in ISO-DR-Core, ARG2-AS-NEGGOAL (under Level-2 PURPOSE) and NEGATIVE RESULT (under Level-2 CAUSE) do not. What this suggests is that like the negative counterpart of condition, ISO-DR-Core should be extended to include the negative counterpart for CAUSE, as NEGATIVE CAUSE, and for PURPOSE, as NEGATIVE PURPOSE. However, it remains an open question whether these relations should be defined in a way that captures both argument directionalities. In the PDTB, we have as yet found no evidence for the reverse directionality for either of these senses.

6   Conclusion

We have presented highlights from our work on enriching the PDTB with new relations, which has also led to modifications and extensions to the PDTB guidelines. Annotating a further ~13K discourse relations and reviewing existing PDTB-2 annotation to bring it in line with the new guidelines has highlighted the importance of assessing *consistency* across the corpus — that similar tokens are annotated in a similar way, no matter when they were annotated. Such *semantic consistency* (Hollenstein et al., 2016) is meant to facilitate improvement in all future applications of the PDTB-3. Consistency checks are described in the detailed annotation manual that will accompany the corpus in its LDC distribution, as well as being available at the PDTB website.

Acknowledgements

Missing from the list of authors is the name of our colleague and dear friend, Aravind K Joshi. Aravind conceived of the Penn Discourse TreeBank and was instrumental in its development from its beginnings in 2005 through the new PDTB-3. Aravind died peacefully on 31 December 2017, and we miss him more than we can say. An obituary will appear in *Computational Linguistics* 44(3), September 2018. We would also like to thank Robin Malamud, James Reid and Samuel Gibbon for their hard work and valuable contribution to annotating the PDTB-3. This work was supported by the National Science Foundation (NSF Grants 1422186 and 1421067).

References

Stergos Afantenos, Nicholas Asher, Farah Benamara, Myriam Bras, Cécile Fabre, Lydia-Mai Ho-Dac, Anne Le Draoulec, Philippe Muller, Marie-Paule Péry-Woodley, Laurent Prévot, et al. 2012. An empirical resource for discovering cognitive principles of discourse organisation: the annodis corpus. In *Proceedings of the Eight International Conference on Language Resources and Evaluation (LREC'12)*. European Language Resources Association (ELRA).

Amal Al-Saif and Katja Markert. 2010. The Leeds Arabic discourse treebank: Annotating discourse connectives for Arabic. In *Proceedings of the 7th International Conference on Language Resources and Evaluation (LREC-2010)*, Valletta, Malta.

---

[4] https://www.iso.org/standard/60780.html?browse=tc

Harry Bunt and Rashmi Prasad. 2016. ISO DR-Core (ISO 24617-8): Core concepts for the annotation of discourse relations. In *Proceedings 12th Joint ACL-ISO Workshop on Interoperable Semantic Annotation (ISA-12)*, pages 45–54.

Harry Bunt, Volha Petukhova, David Traum, and Jan Alexandersson. 2017. Dialogue act annotation with the iso 24617-2 standard. In *Multimodal Interaction with W3C Standards*, pages 109–135. Springer.

Lynn Carlson, Daniel Marcu, and Mary Ellen Okurowski. 2003. Building a discourse-tagged corpus in the framework of rhetorical structure theory. In *Current and new directions in discourse and dialogue*, pages 85–112. Springer.

Laurence Danlos, Diégo Antolinos-Basso, Chloé Braud, and Charlotte Roze. 2012. Vers le fdtb: French discourse tree bank. In *TALN 2012: 19ème conférence sur le Traitement Automatique des Langues Naturelles*, volume 2, pages 471–478. ATALA/AFCP.

Nora Hollenstein, Nathan Schneider, and Bonnie Webber. 2016. Inconsistency detection in semantic annotation. In *Proceedings of the 10th International Conference on Language Resources and Evaluation (LREC 2016)*.

Mitchell Marcus, Beatrice Santorini, and Mary Ann Marcinkiewicz. 1993. Building a large annotated corpus of English: The Penn TreeBank. *Computational Linguistics*, 19(2):313–330.

Umangi Oza, Rashmi Prasad, Sudheer Kolachina, Dipti Mishra Sharma, and Aravind Joshi. 2009. The Hindi Discourse Relation Bank. In *Proceedings of the ACL 2009 Linguistic Annotation Workshop III (LAW-III)*, Singapore.

Martha Palmer, Daniel Gildea, and Paul Kingsbury. 2005. The proposition bank: An annotated corpus of semantic roles. *Computational linguistics*, 31(1):71–106.

Lucie Poláková, Jiří Mírovský, Anna Nedoluzhko, Pavlína Jínová, Šárka Zikánová, and Eva Hajičová. 2013. Introducing the Prague discourse treebank 1.0. In *Proceedings of the Sixth International Joint Conference on Natural Language Processing (IJCNLP)*, pages 91–99.

Rashmi Prasad, Nikhil Dinesh, Alan Lee, Eleni Miltsakaki, Livio Robaldo, Aravind Joshi, and Bonnie Webber. 2008. The Penn Discourse TreeBank 2.0. In *Proceedings of the 6th International Conference on Language Resources and Evaluation*, pages 2961–2968, Marrakech, Morocco.

Rashmi Prasad, Aravind Joshi, and Bonnie Webber. 2010. Realization of discourse relations by other means: alternative lexicalizations. In *Proceedings of the 23rd International Conference on Computational Linguistics: Posters*, pages 1023–1031. Association for Computational Linguistics.

Rashmi Prasad, Susan McRoy, Nadya Frid, Aravind Joshi, and Hong Yu. 2011. The biomedical discourse relation bank. *BMC bioinformatics*, 12(1):188.

Rashmi Prasad, Bonnie Webber, and Aravind Joshi. 2014. Reflections on the Penn Discourse TreeBank, comparable corpora and complementary annotation. *Computational Linguistics*, 40(4):921–950.

Rashmi Prasad, Bonnie Webber, Alan Lee, Sameer Pradhan, and Aravind Joshi. 2015. Bridging sentential and discourse-level semantics through clausal adjuncts. In *Proceedings of the First Workshop on Linking Computational Models of Lexical, Sentential and Discourse-level Semantics*, pages 64–69.

Rashmi Prasad, Katherine Forbes-Riley, and Alan Lee. 2017. Towards full text shallow discourse relation annotation: Experiments with cross-paragraph implicit relations in the PDTB. In *Proceedings of the 18th Annual SIGdial Meeting on Discourse and Dialogue*, pages 7–16.

Brian Reese, Julie Hunter, Nicholas Asher, Pascal Denis, and Jason Baldridge, 2007. *Reference Manual for the Analysis and Annotation of Rhetorical Structure*. University of Texas at Austin.

Ted J. Sanders and Merel Scholman. 2012. Categories of coherence relations in discourse annotation. Presented at the International Workshop on Discourse Annotation. Utrecht Institute of Linguistics, Universiteit Utrecht.

PDTB-Group. 2008. The Penn Discourse TreeBank 2.0 Annotation Manual. Technical Report IRCS-08-01, Institute for Research in Cognitive Science, University of Pennsylvania.

Sara Tonelli, Giuseppe Riccardi, Rashmi Prasad, and Aravind Joshi. 2010. Annotation of discourse relations for conversational spoken dialogs. In *Proceedings of the Seventh International Conference on Language Resources and Evaluation (LREC 2010)*, Valletta, Malta.

Bonnie Webber, Rashmi Prasad, Alan Lee, and Aravind K. Joshi. 2016. A discourse-annotated corpus of conjoined VPs. In *Proceedings of the 10th Linguistic Annotation Workshop*, Berlin, Germany.

Florian Wolf and Edward Gibson. 2005. Representing discourse coherence: A corpus-based study. *Computational linguistics*, 31(2):249–287.

Nianwen Xue, Hwee Tou Ng, Sameer Pradhan, Rashmi Prasad, Christopher Bryant, and Attapol Rutherford. 2015. The CoNLL-2015 shared task on shallow discourse parsing. In *Proceedings of the CoNLL-15 shared task*, pages 1–16, Beijing, China.

Nianwen Xue, Hwee Tou Ng, Attapol Rutherford, Bonnie Webber, Chuan Wang, and Hongmin Wang. 2016. The CoNLL-2016 shared task on multilingual shallow discourse parsing. In *Proceedings of the CoNLL-16 shared task*, pages 1–19, Berlin, Germany.

Deniz Zeyrek and Bonnie Webber. 2008. A discourse resource for Turkish: Annotating discourse connectives in the METU corpus. In *Proceedings of the 6th Workshop on Asian Language Resources, The Third International Joint Conference on Natural Language Processing, (IJCNLP-2008)*, pages 65–71, Hyderabad, India.

Deniz Zeyrek, Amalia Mendes, and Murathan Kurfali. 2018. Multi-lingual extension of PDTB-style annotation: The case of TED multi-lingual discourse bank. In *Proceedings of the 11th International Conference on Language Resources and Evaluation, LREC-18*, Miyazaki, Japan.

Yuping Zhou and Nianwen Xue. 2015. The chinese discourse treebank: a chinese corpus annotated with discourse relations. In *Proceedings of Language Resources and Evaluation (LREC)*, pages 397–431.

Towards Understanding End-of-trip Instructions in a Taxi Ride Scenario

Deepthi Karkada[2*], **Ramesh Manuvinakurike**[1*], **Kallirroi Georgila**[1]
[1]Institute for Creative Technologies, University of Southern California
[2]Intel Corp
deepthi.karkada@intel.com, [manuvinakurike,kgeorgila]@ict.usc.edu

Abstract

We introduce a dataset containing human-authored descriptions of target locations in an "end-of-trip in a taxi ride" scenario. We describe our data collection method and a novel annotation scheme that supports understanding of such descriptions of target locations. Our dataset contains target location descriptions for both synthetic and real-world images as well as visual annotations (ground truth labels, dimensions of vehicles and objects, coordinates of the target location, distance and direction of the target location from vehicles and objects) that can be used in various visual and language tasks. We also perform a pilot experiment on how the corpus could be applied to visual reference resolution in this domain.

1 Introduction

The last few utterances in a typical taxi ride are the passengers directing the driver to stop their ride at the desired target location. "Stop right next to the white car", "behind the big tree should work", "drop me off in front of the second black pickup truck" are all examples of such utterances. Resolving these requests, while a simple task for the human drivers, assumes complex vision and language understanding capabilities. Some of the sub-tasks that the driver needs to perform to resolve these requests are: i) Visual reference resolution: Identifying the visual objects that the rider is referring to (called the referent(s)) among the visual distractors present in the scene (the big tree, the second black pickup truck, the white car, etc.); ii) Directional description understanding: Predicting the target location that the rider refers to with respect to the referent(s) present around (in front of, right behind, a little further from, etc.); and iii) Action identification: The action that the rider wants to take (stop, drop me off, etc.). The purpose of this work is to build a dataset that comprises of such utterances and build an annotation scheme supporting the understanding of such utterances.

We introduce a novel dataset which contains the human-authored natural language descriptions of the desired target location in an end-of-trip taxi ride scenario with synthetic images and real street images. We describe the annotation scheme for these descriptions which comprises of referents, directional descriptions, and actions, and show that the inter-annotator agreement is high. Our dataset contains the images with the ground-truth target location coordinates that are described by the users. The image annotations also contain object ground-truth labels, coordinates, dimensions along with the distance and direction of the target location with respect to the objects that are present in the image. We refer to the position of the target location as a function of 'r' and 'θ' where 'r' is the magnitude of the vector, and θ is the direction between the referent and the target location. This quantification provides the capability to predict the target location coordinates using natural language sentences given the visual context. Figure 1 shows an example where the combination of r and θ determines the target location with respect to the referent(s).

The contributions of this work are: 1) A novel corpus containing user descriptions of target locations for synthetic and real-world street images. 2) The natural language description annotations along with the visual annotations for the task of target location prediction. 3) A baseline model for the task of identification of referents from user descriptions.

---

* Equal contribution.

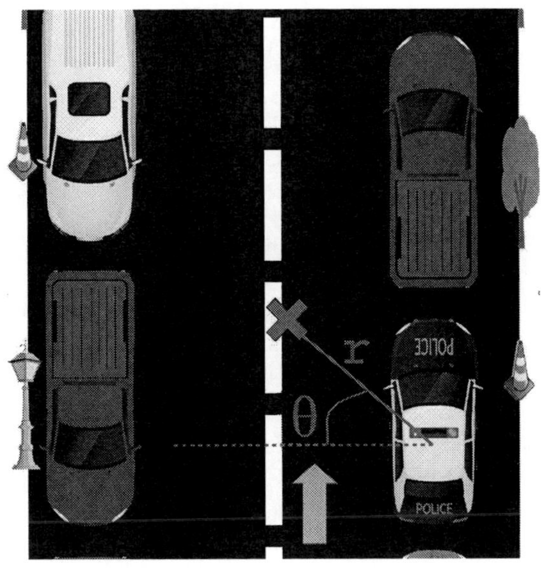

Figure 1: Example from the synthetic section of the dataset. The annotation labels of r and θ define the target location for an example utterance "drop me off in front of the cop car". The green arrow shows the direction of motion of the taxi.

2   Related Work

There is a strong relation between the language and vision modalities, and the information in the vision modality influences the associated spoken language (Tanenhaus et al., 1995). In recent times, automating various tasks involving vision and language has attracted much interest. The task of reference resolution is one such example. This task typically involves identification of one of the objects referred to in a set of similar distractors through dialogue (Clark and Wilkes-Gibbs, 1986; Kennington and Schlangen, 2015; Paetzel et al., 2015; de Vries et al., 2017; Manuvinakurike et al., 2017).

Other tasks that combine language and vision are: visual question answering which requires answering questions about an image (Antol et al., 2015), a related question generation task (Mostafazadeh et al., 2016), storytelling (Huang et al., 2016), and conversational image editing (Manuvinakurike et al., 2018a; Manuvinakurike et al., 2018b). Furthermore, other relevant approaches are automatic image captioning and retrieval by using neural networks to map the image into a dense vector, and then conditioning a neural language model on this vector to produce an output string (Mitchell et al., 2012; Kulkarni et al., 2013; Socher et al., 2014; Vinyals et al., 2015; Devlin et al., 2015).

Annotation of spatial information including objects and their spatial relations in real-world images has been studied in detail for developing the ISO-Space annotation scheme (Pustejovsky et al., 2011; Pustejovsky and Yocum, 2014). The semantics of spatial language have also been studied in detail; see for example Varzi (2007) and Bateman et al. (2010). The focus of our work is not on the study of spatial semantics but rather on the task of target location identification using simplistic annotations.

The goal of this work is to study user descriptions in an "end-of-taxi" ride scenario which involves studying language and vision in a situated environment. Related to our work, Lemon et al. (2006) built a dialogue system for an in-car domain and Eric et al. (2017) studied dialogues with regard to helping a driver navigate to a specific location. However, these works did not specifically study the interaction and combination of the vision and language modalities in a situated in-car environment. Our work contributes to the literature with a corpus combining the language and vision modalities in a situated environment. We extract the embedded representations of descriptions generated from the users and use them for the task of reference resolution by comparing them to similar embeddings extracted for the object ground truth labels. We also discuss $r\theta$ annotations that can be used to understand directional relations using the outputs of the reference resolution module, which is a particularly novel feature of our annotation scheme. Note that in prior work, reference resolution is performed using models that understand the meaning of words using classifiers trained with visual features (Kennington and Schlangen, 2015; Manuvinakurike et al., 2016).

3   Data Collection

We use the crowd-sourcing paradigm[1] to collect user descriptions instructing a taxi to stop at a given location (we will refer to this location as the "target location"). The Amazon Mechanical Turk users (called turkers) are shown an image (similar to Figure 2 or Figure 3) and are asked to imagine a scenario where they are in a taxi about to reach their destination. As they approach their destination they need to instruct the taxi driver in natural language to stop at the bright red cross. The turkers needed to provide at least three unique descriptions. Only native English speakers whose location was the US (United States) were chosen for the task.

The images shown to the turkers contain vehicles and other objects which are used as referents to describe the target location. These images were either i) Synthetic (programmatically generated) or ii) Street-view images (extracted from Google maps[2]) which we refer to as real-world images. The synthetic images are generated with a 2-dimensional top-view perspective containing vehicles that are typically observed on the streets in US parked on either side of the street. The street-view images are collected using a popular street navigation application (Google street-view[3]), which contains the images of real streets taken from a car-top mounted camera. Below we describe the methods followed in the construction of these images.

3.1   Synthetic Images Construction

The synthetic images were constructed programmatically by overlaying the vehicle and object templates on the street with a median in the middle. The synthetic images were constructed from bird's eye point of view which helps us overcome the problem of frame of reference. Templates of the different categories of vehicles such as cars (of different colors[4]) including taxi and police cars, pickup trucks[5], red truck, white van, and limousine were overlaid on either side of the street randomly. The vehicles were placed in a parked position on a two-way right-side-driving street[6]. Four objects (street lamp, fire pump, traffic cone, and tree) were placed on the sidewalk randomly. A maximum of up to 4 vehicles were placed on either side of the street. The distance between the vehicles was not uniform. Figure 2 shows a sample synthetic image: vehicles and objects along with three user-authored descriptions. A "red cross" was also randomly placed on the street part of the image which was to be used by the users as the target location for the taxi to stop. The synthetic images provide an environment devoid of complexities (e.g., visual segmentation, object identification, masking) otherwise present in real-world images which are not the focus of this work.

3.2   Real-World Images Construction

We extracted the real-world images from Google street-view imagery in the streets of a busy city. The images were captured manually using the Linux snapshot tool. Since, the street-view images are taken from the roof-mounted camera placed on a right-side-driving vehicle we do not face the issue of unknown frame of reference. A sample image is shown in Figure 3. The "red cross" was overlaid randomly on the street which was the designated target location for the users to describe in the image.

3.3   Structure of the Descriptions

Table 1 shows the statistics of the dataset collected. The descriptions mainly consist of three parts: i) Actions: the words used by the user instructing the driver to perform an operation (e.g., "stop", "keep

---

[1]https://www.mturk.com

[2]https://maps.google.com

[3]https://maps.google.com, official endorsement should not be inferred.

[4]The colors of the cars were chosen based on the most common car colors. We chose blue, brown, green, grey, yellow, orange, pink, red, and white. We did not choose black as it is difficult to spot against the background.

[5]Blue and white color.

[6]As the majority of countries are right-side-driving, we choose the right-side-driving orientation for generating the images.

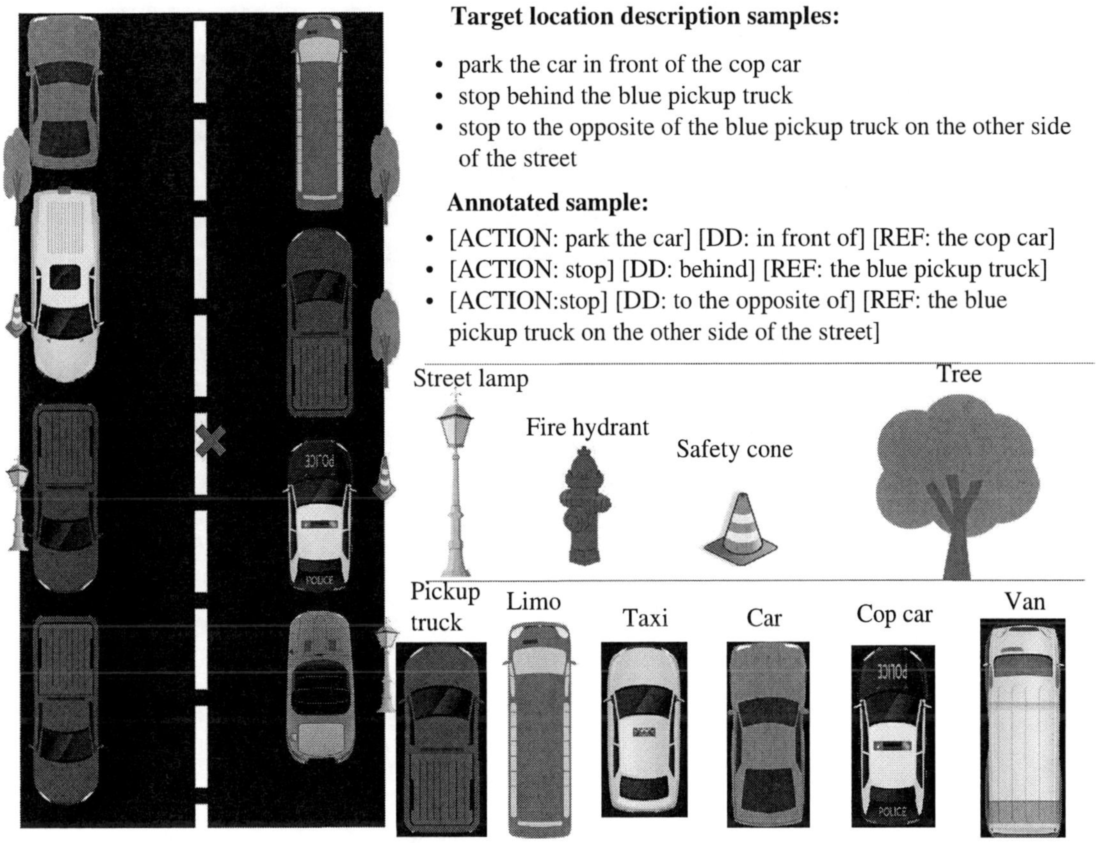

Figure 2: Sample data from the synthetic image set. The figure shows sample user instructions and the annotations performed. The ground truth labels of the vehicles and objects are also provided. The color information of the vehicles is also present in the dataset.

Synthetic			Real-world			Combined	
images	descriptions	tokens	images	descriptions	tokens	unique	common
324	1069	9708	68	212	1863	457	128

Table 1: Statistics of the dataset collected across the synthetic and the real-world images. The "combined" section contains the total unique tokens and common tokens shared across the descriptions in the synthetic and real-world. We observe that the difference in the language is mainly related to the referent descriptions.

going until"). Since we had directed the users to provide instructions for stopping, the actions for nearly all the actions specified were similar to the "stop" command. ii) Referent (REF): The words/phrases used to refer to the vehicles or the objects present in the image. The users typically refer to vehicles or objects close to the target location and these references are either simple or compound. In simple referent descriptions, the users refer to a single object in the scene, e.g., "the blue car", "the white van". In compound referent descriptions, the users refer to multiple objects such as "the two blue vans" in the phrase "please park in front of the two blue vans". They also use the position of the vehicles or objects such as "the third car on the right" in "stop next to the third car on the right". A few descriptions contained multiple referents, such as ''stop in between the taxi and the white SUV''. In this case, we mark each referent separately. iii) Directional description (DD): This is the part of the description indicating direction that is used to refer to the target location in relation to the referent (REF). Instances of directional descriptions include phrases such as "close to", "next to", "top of", "near", "between", etc.

Target location description samples:	Annotated sample:
Stop next to the first white car you see.	[ACTION: Stop] [DD: next to] [REF: the first white car you see]
Stop next to the car behind the blue car.	[ACTION: Stop] [DD: next to] [REF:the car behind the blue car]
Stop next to the white car.	[ACTION: Stop] [DD: next to] [REF:the white car]

Figure 3: Example data from the real-world 3d street images.

Synthetic			Real-world		
Actions	Ref	DD	Actions	Ref	DD
273	408	372	173	217	219
Synthetic unique			Real-world unique		
Actions	Ref	DD	Actions	Ref	DD
8	185	89	13	181	75

Table 2: Annotations statistics.

Figures 2 and 3 show sample annotations. Two expert annotators annotated the same 25 randomly chosen descriptions to calculate inter-rater reliability. The annotations at the word level were considered to be the same if both the labels and the boundaries were agreed upon by both annotators. The inter-rater reliability scores were measured using Cohen's kappa and was found to be 0.81 indicating high agreement. Most of the disagreements were limited to marking the beginning and the endpoints (typically articles and prepositions).

We annotated a section of the data collected (see Table 2). We observed that there are fewer actions than user descriptions as a few turkers chose only to provide the directional description and referent. The number of referents and directional descriptions is greater than the number of total phrases. This is because the users provide compound descriptions mentioning multiple descriptions for the same target location (e.g., "park to the left of the brown car, across the white van"). In such cases we label the referents and directional descriptions separately. There were also instances of images with multiple vehicles which looked similar. In such cases, the turkers supplemented the language used to identify the referent with descriptions of other objects. This can be observed in the description "park the car near the blue sedan next to the light post" where "the blue sedan" was not sufficient to identify the referent, hence it was supplemented with further descriptions of the objects surrounding the referent. There are a lot more unique referent descriptions per unit description for the real-data as the array of real-world objects used for referents were more diverse.

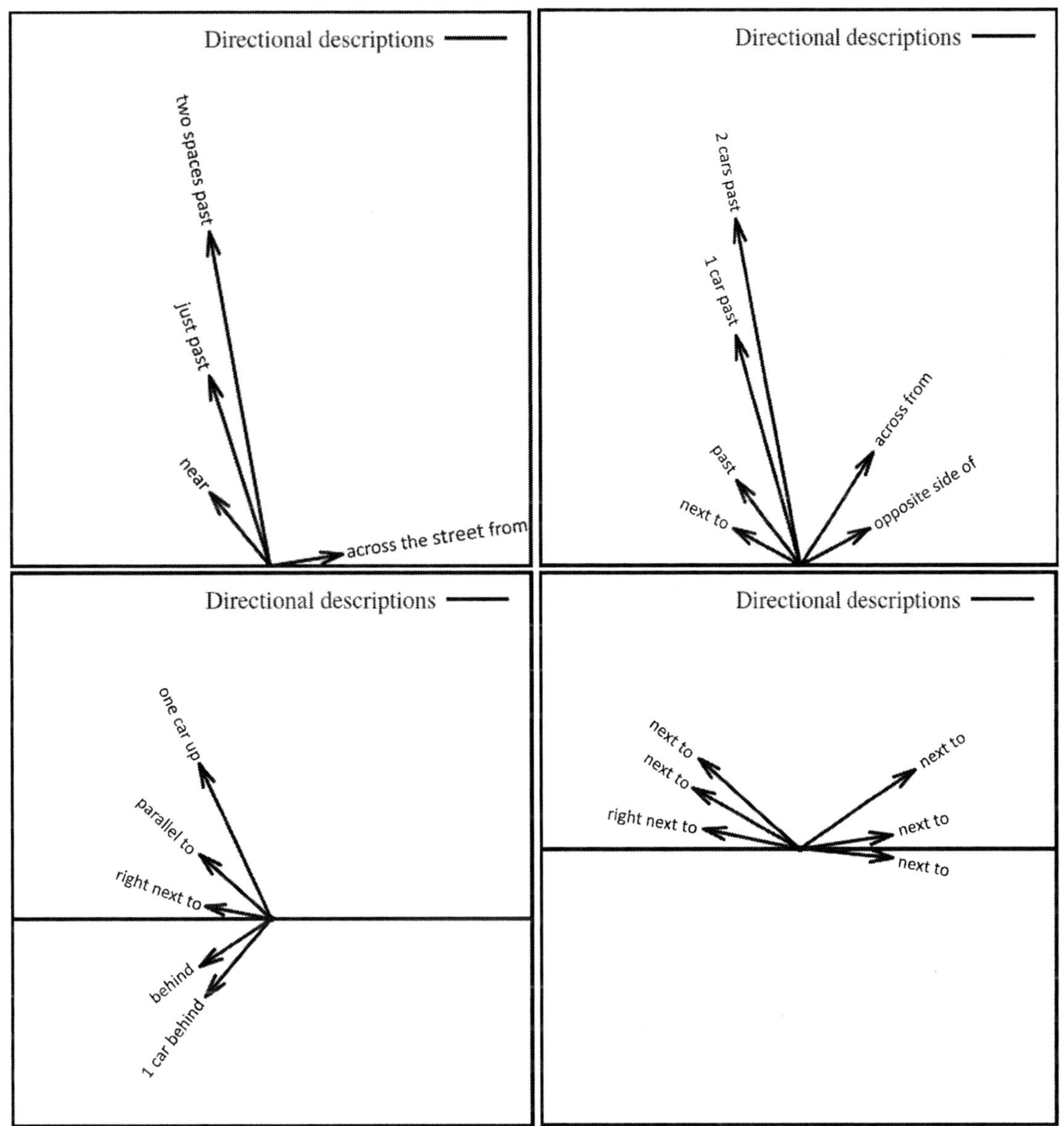

Figure 4: The graphs in the figure show the position of the target location (head of the arrow) with respect to the referent (nock of the arrow) for different images. The users describe the target location with respect to the referent.

3.4 The rθ Labels

In order to estimate the coordinates of the target location, the coordinates of the objects in the scene, the directional description, and the referent are required. The dataset contains the coordinates of all the objects present in the image along with the ground truth labels. Given the target location description, its position from the referent is available as an (r, θ) tuple. Figure 4 shows a few examples. In Figure 4, the position of the target location is shown with respect to the referent in different descriptions with the label of the directional description. The figure shows different directional descriptions from the referent to the target location. We can observe (top-left) that the directional description "next to" has a lower angle 'θ' and 'r' (top left) compared to "just past" (as in "stop just past the blue car") which in turn has lower values of 'θ' and 'r' compared to "two spaces past". We can also see (bottom-right) that "next to" is used to mean different positions with respect to the referent. "Behind" typically refers to a negative value of

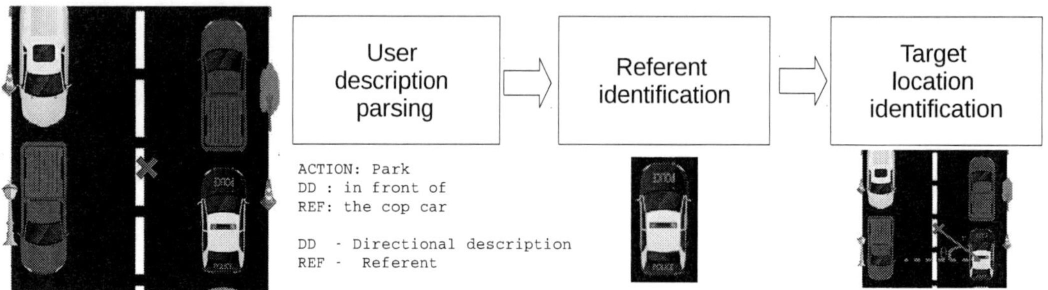

Figure 5: Task pipeline for identification of the target location using the user descriptions.

'θ' and "right next to" refers to a positive value (bottom-left). The synthetic and real-world data include 372 and 219 such directional descriptions respectively (see Table 2). The 'r' in the $r\theta$ model refers to the radial distance between the center of the referent vehicle or object and the target location, and the 'θ' refers to the angle measured from the horizontal direction.

4   Understanding User Descriptions

Given the user description, images, and the annotations (language annotations such as action, referent, directional description, and visual annotations such as ground truth object labels and $r\theta$ labels), we define three separate tasks (see Figure 5): i) Identification of the action, referent and directional relations descriptions in the user instructions: This step is also sometimes referred to as segmentation and intent labeling and is not the focus of this work. We assume oracle data, i.e., the complete and correct identification of the action, referent, and directional relations descriptions in the user instructions. ii) Referent(s) identification: The users refer to vehicles or objects in the images in their descriptions. The task of reference resolution refers to the identification of the correct vehicle or object based on the user description. In the cases where there are multiple referent descriptions, we identify all the referents in the dataset. iii) Target location identification: This task refers to combining the information from the referent identification and the directional relation description to identify the final target location.

In this work we focus on the second problem. We do not perform parsing on the user descriptions and assume the availability of referent descriptions. We will pursue the goal of automating the complete pipeline (see Figure 5) in future work. Below we describe the referent identification task.

4.1   Referent Identification

Given the referent description (REF) and the image, the task is to identify the object that is being referred to by the user. In this section, we describe the approach that we take to identify the referent based on the user description. We use the data for the synthetic images. We assume the availability of the referent (text with REF label). The ground truth descriptions of the vehicles (e.g., pink car, white van, blue pickup truck) and the objects (e.g., fire pump, tree, traffic cone) are available from the image annotations (see Figure 2).

The first approach is the "random baseline". Each image can have up to 16 vehicles and objects and randomly predicting one such object as the referent yields 6.25% accuracy and is noted to be a random weak baseline. For the second approach we use the "sub-string matching" method to identify the referent object. In this approach we compare the user provided referent string (text with REF label e.g., "the pink sedan") and the ground truth label (e.g., pink car, red car, white van) available from the images. We use the number of matching words to get the best match for a given image. In the case of a tie with multiple objects matching the same number of words, we randomly select one of the objects and check if the referent is correct. This method yields an accuracy of 47.5% which we use as a stronger logical baseline for comparison. This approach yields lower numbers because of the diverse set of vocabulary used to describe the referents. For instance, "police car" is referred to as "cop car" or "sheriff's car". To overcome this problem, we use the sentence embeddings approach (Mikolov et al., 2013).

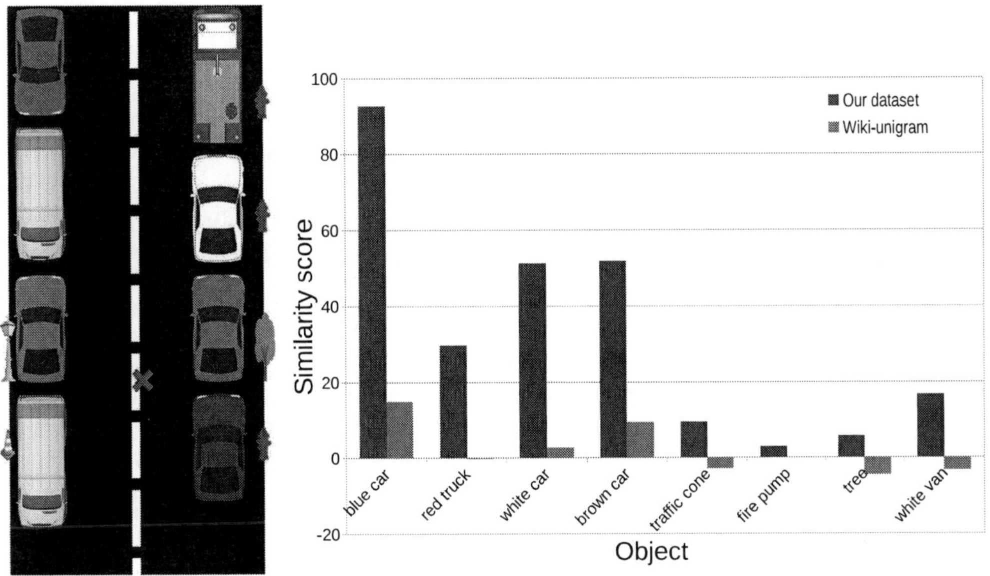

Figure 6: Street image as seen by the user. For the description of "drop me off in front of the blue car", the referent (the blue car) is extracted and then the similarity scores are calculated with the objects present in the image. We can see that the model identifies the correct referent using this method.

Random baseline	6.25%
Sub-string matching	47.5%
Embedding model (training set)	60%
Embedding model (Wiki-unigram)	70.2%

Table 3: Results of reference resolution performed using different methods (synthetic images). We can see that the sentence embedding models outperform the baseline and sub-string matching. The out-of-the-box embedding model performs significantly better than the model trained using the in-domain trained embeddings (p<.05).

We obtain a vector representation of the referent description ($\vec{r}$) and the objects present in the image ($\vec{o}$). These vectors are generated using sent2vec (Pagliardini et al., 2018) . We then get the best candidate for the referent description by choosing the object with the maximum value of the dot product between the objects present in the image and the description. Thus the best suited object for the referent description is chosen using $\arg\max_i \vec{o}.\vec{r_i}$. The dot product is a measure of cosine similarity between the referent description (REF) and the ground truth labels.

Embeddings To choose the best embeddings we ran experiments with two approaches: i) out-of-the-box (Wiki-unigram embeddings) and ii) embeddings trained on user descriptions from this domain (training set only). We split the data into 30% for the testing set and 70% for the training set. Figure 6 shows the comparison of the similarity score ($\vec{O}.\vec{R_i}$) using the embeddings trained on our corpus (in blue) and the pre-trained vector (in red). The embeddings trained on the training set gave a good representation of the similarity scores despite being sparse. A major drawback was the limited vocabulary of the training set. This means that words present in the test set but absent in the training set are problematic and thus the sentence embeddings for such descriptions are not produced satisfactorily. However, the Wiki-unigram embeddings had a much larger vocabulary (1.7 billion words). This larger vocabulary resulted in a better estimate of the vectors for the REF and ground truth object descriptions. Hence, to extract the sentence embeddings, we use the pre-trained Wiki-unigram embeddings (600 dim, trained on English Wikipedia). Table 3 shows the reference resolution accuracy of the model. This method yields the best performance at 70.2% accuracy in finding the referent.

5   Conclusion and Future Work

We introduced a novel dataset of users providing instructions about target locations in a taxi-ride scenario. We collected the dataset in two parts, with synthetic images and real-world images. We showed that the dataset can be used in many challenging tasks: i) visual reference resolution, ii) direction description understanding, and iii) action identification. We presented our novel annotation scheme for natural language and image-related information and performed referent identification experiments on the synthetic images data.

Our approach is still limited in its capability. Cases where multiple similar objects were present in the image were not well handled. In such cases, a single sentence/phrase description may not be sufficient to estimate the referent, and we believe that a conversation between the driver and the rider could clarify the referent. We will extend our work to include dialogue data between the driver and the rider in a similar simulated setting. Our model is currently not capable of performing the reference resolution of objects when multiple similar objects are present in the scene and the user description is sufficient to resolve the references, e.g., "the second blue truck on the right", "the last car on the left", etc. Another case where the model fails to perform well is with plural descriptions of the referents (e.g., "park in between the 2 blue cars"). In such cases we resolve the tie by randomly selecting one of the objects as the referent. We intend to address these issues in future work.

We also intend to validate and extend this work to real-world images. Note that the real-world images descriptions contain more elaborate referent descriptions with e.g., names of car brands, sticker on the car, which can further complicate the task.

Our annotation scheme has been developed to be task specific. Investigating whether the ISO-Space annotation framework (Pustejovsky et al., 2011; Pustejovsky and Yocum, 2014) can be applied to our domain is a fruitful direction for future work.

Acknowledgments

This work was partially supported by the U.S. Army; statements and opinions expressed do not necessarily reflect the position or policy of the U.S. Government, and no official endorsement should be inferred.

References

Stanislaw Antol, Aishwarya Agrawal, Jiasen Lu, Margaret Mitchell, Dhruv Batra, C. Lawrence Zitnick, and Devi Parikh. 2015. VQA: Visual Question Answering. In *Proceedings of ICCV*, pages 2425–2433, Santiago, Chile.

John A. Bateman, Joana Hois, Robert Ross, and Thora Tenbrink. 2010. A linguistic ontology of space for natural language processing. *Artificial Intelligence*, 174(14):1027–1071.

Herbert H. Clark and Deanna Wilkes-Gibbs. 1986. Referring as a collaborative process. *Cognition*, 22(1).

Harm de Vries, Florian Strub, Sarath Chandar, Olivier Pietquin, Hugo Larochelle, and Aaron Courville. 2017. GuessWhat?! visual object discovery through multi-modal dialogue. In *Proceedings of CVPR*, pages 5503–5512, Honolulu, Hawaii, USA.

Jacob Devlin, Hao Cheng, Hao Fang, Saurabh Gupta, Li Deng, Xiaodong He, Geoffrey Zweig, and Margaret Mitchell. 2015. Language models for image captioning: The quirks and what works. In *Proceedings of ACL-IJCNLP (Short Papers)*, pages 100–105, Beijing, China.

Mihail Eric, Lakshmi Krishnan, Francois Charette, and Christopher D. Manning. 2017. Key-value retrieval networks for task-oriented dialogue. In *Proceedings of SIGDIAL*, pages 37–49, Saarbrücken, Germany.

Ting-Hao (Kenneth) Huang, Francis Ferraro, Nasrin Mostafazadeh, Ishan Misra, Aishwarya Agrawal, Jacob Devlin, Ross Girshick, Xiaodong He, Pushmeet Kohli, Dhruv Batra, C. Lawrence Zitnick, Devi Parikh, Lucy Vanderwende, Michel Galley, and Margaret Mitchell. 2016. Visual storytelling. In *Proceedings of NAACL-HLT*, pages 1233–1239, San Diego, California, USA.

Casey Kennington and David Schlangen. 2015. Simple learning and compositional application of perceptually grounded word meanings for incremental reference resolution. In *Proceedings of ACL-IJCNLP*, pages 292–301, Beijing, China.

Girish Kulkarni, Visruth Premraj, Vicente Ordonez, Sagnik Dhar, Siming Li, Yejin Choi, Alexander C. Berg, and Tamara L. Berg. 2013. BabyTalk: Understanding and generating simple image descriptions. *IEEE Transactions on Pattern Analysis and Machine Intelligence*, 35(12):2891–2903.

Oliver Lemon, Kallirroi Georgila, James Henderson, and Matthew Stuttle. 2006. An ISU dialogue system exhibiting reinforcement learning of dialogue policies: Generic slot-filling in the TALK in-car system. In *Proceedings of EACL (Demonstrations)*, pages 119–122, Trento, Italy.

Ramesh Manuvinakurike, Casey Kennington, David DeVault, and David Schlangen. 2016. Real-time understanding of complex discriminative scene descriptions. In *Proceedings of SIGDIAL*, pages 232–241, Los Angeles, CA, USA.

Ramesh Manuvinakurike, David DeVault, and Kallirroi Georgila. 2017. Using reinforcement learning to model incrementality in a fast-paced dialogue game. In *Proceedings of SIGDIAL*, pages 331–341, Saarbrücken, Germany.

Ramesh Manuvinakurike, Jacqueline Brixey, Trung Bui, Walter Chang, Kim Doo Soon, Ron Artstein, and Kallirroi Georgila. 2018a. Edit me: A corpus and a framework for understanding natural language image editing. In *Proceedings of LREC*, pages 4322–4326, Miyazaki, Japan.

Ramesh Manuvinakurike, Trung Bui, Walter Chang, and Kallirroi Georgila. 2018b. Conversational image editing: Incremental intent identification in a new dialogue task. In *Proceedings of SIGDIAL*, pages 284–295, Melbourne, Australia.

Tomas Mikolov, Ilya Sutskever, Kai Chen, Greg S. Corrado, and Jeff Dean. 2013. Distributed representations of words and phrases and their compositionality. In *Proceedings of NIPS*, Lake Tahoe, USA.

Margaret Mitchell, Jesse Dodge, Amit Goyal, Kota Yamaguchi, Karl Stratos, Xufeng Han, Alyssa Mensch, Alex Berg, Tamara Berg, and Hal Daumé III. 2012. Midge: Generating image descriptions from computer vision detections. In *Proceedings of EACL*, pages 747–756, Avignon, France.

Nasrin Mostafazadeh, Ishan Misra, Jacob Devlin, Margaret Mitchell, Xiaodong He, and Lucy Vanderwende. 2016. Generating natural questions about an image. In *Proceedings of ACL*, pages 1802–1813, Berlin, Germany.

Maike Paetzel, Ramesh Manuvinakurike, and David DeVault. 2015. So, which one is it? The effect of alternative incremental architectures in a high-performance game-playing agent. In *Proceedings of SIGDIAL*, pages 77–86, Prague, Czech Republic.

Matteo Pagliardini, Prakhar Gupta, and Martin Jaggi. 2018. Unsupervised learning of sentence embeddings using compositional n-gram features. In *Proceedings of NAACL*, New Orleans, USA.

James Pustejovsky and Zachary Yocum. 2014. Image annotation with ISO-Space: Distinguishing content from structure. In *Proceedings of LREC*, pages 426–431, Reykjavik, Iceland.

James Pustejovsky, Jessica L. Moszkowicz, and Marc Verhagen. 2011. Using ISO-Space for annotating spatial information. In *Proceedings of the International Conference on Spatial Information Theory*.

Richard Socher, Andrej Karpathy, Quoc V. Le, Christopher D. Manning, and Andrew Y. Ng. 2014. Grounded compositional semantics for finding and describing images with sentences. *Transactions of the Association for Computational Linguistics*, 2(1).

Michael K. Tanenhaus, Michael J. Spivey-Knowlton, Kathleen M. Eberhard, and Julie C. Sedivy. 1995. Integration of visual and linguistic information in spoken language comprehension. *Science*, 268(5217).

Achille C. Varzi. 2007. Spatial reasoning and ontology: Parts, wholes, and locations. In *Handbook of Spatial Logics*, pages 945–1038. Springer.

Oriol Vinyals, Alexander Toshev, Samy Bengio, and Dumitru Erhan. 2015. Show and tell: A neural image caption generator. In *Proceedings of CVPR*, Boston, USA.